SAGE was founded in 1965 by Sara Miller McCune to support the dissemination of usable knowledge by publishing innovative and high-quality research and teaching content. Today, we publish over 900 journals, including those of more than 400 learned societies, more than 800 new books per year, and a growing range of library products including archives, data, case studies, reports, and video. SAGE remains majority-owned by our founder, and after Sara's lifetime will become owned by a charitable trust that secures our continued independence.

Los Angeles | London | New Delhi | Singapore | Washington DC | Melbourne

ADVANCE PRAISE

In his very well-researched book, Professor Shukla draws lessons from over 120 Indian social entrepreneurs and changemakers to present a compelling narrative on the power of entrepreneurial thinking to create transformative change for some of society's most pressing problems. His book is very timely because India (and the world) faces sizable challenges if we are to chart a future that is sustainable, equitable and just for all segments of society. Professor Shukla explains how complex societal challenges are also windows of opportunity for transformative solutions that can drive change that benefits society. Highly recommended for individuals, donors and policy makers seeking inspiration and ideas on how to build an ecosystem that promotes sustainable enterprises with purpose and soul.

M. Hari Menon, *India Country Director,*
Bill & Melinda Gates Foundation

Madhukar Shukla has created an architecture that defines and places the rise of social entrepreneurship in India as no one else has done supporting it with numerous real-life examples of entrepreneurs and models. It is a compulsive read for anyone interested and willing to invest in social entrepreneurship.

Mahesh Yagnaraman, *India Country Director, Acumen*

Madhukar Shukla's book is a comprehensive yet very readable treatment of the subject. He covers a vast ground, from the definition of social enterprise to the attributes of a social entrepreneur, going on to tackling the different stages of a social enterprise in each chapter, all the way till scaling up. In each chapter, he uses appropriate theoretical inputs by various scholars and peppers those with apt examples of real social enterprises. This inter-weaving of theory and practice makes the book useful for both students of the field as well as for practitioners. I think this book is a landmark addition to the understanding of this emerging trend in society, which many claim will be the unique institutional solution of the 21st century.

Vijay Mahajan, *CEO, Rajiv Gandhi Foundation;*
Founder, BASIX Social Enterprise Group

This book is the most comprehensive account of the social enterprise ecosystem in India. It also provides the most elaborate historical account of the evolution of social enterprises and the inspiration behind the first set of social enterprises including Amul, Grameen and SEWA. The book examines the crucial drivers and values which underpin the social enterprises. A very important and recommended text for students, researchers and practitioners alike. Based on hosting many social enterprises at XLRI, Professor Madhukar Shukla provides rich and empirical insight into the functioning and characteristics of these enterprises.

Parmesh Shah, *Global Lead, Rural Livelihoods and*
Agriculture, World Bank

Madhukar Shukla's *Social Entrepreneurship in India: Quarter Idealism and a Pound of Pragmatism* is a unique exploration of social entrepreneurship in India, both in theory and practice, fleshing out rich experiences from a repertoire of 120 social ventures and offering valuable insights. It is an absorbing tale of lessons from these real life social ventures which use and apply innovative approaches and models to the country's most pressing problems. The book is interesting, stimulating and informative, and sure to serve as an inspiration for anyone battling between profit and purpose.

Vipin Sharma, *Chief Executive Officer,*
ACCESS Development Services

Social enterprises do not succeed or scale easily, given the challenge they grapple with, while trying to fuse social causes with profitable business models. Passionate social entrepreneurs craft them with considerable artistry through a lot of idealism and some trial and error. Often, even with the benefit of hindsight, some of them cannot explain why they succeeded. Certainly not to the extent another entrepreneur can replicate the 'model'.

In this backdrop, Madhukar's book is a boon to this domain. He analyses how the 'markets of the poor' are different, where the 'opportunity structures' exist, describes the various 'entrepreneurial models' that enable the poor to access markets' and places the different 'archetypes of social entrepreneurship' in that context.

The book is a must-read for both the 'been there, done that' social entrepreneurs intending to scale, and the 'wannabe' entrepreneurs looking at social problems to engage with or, for that matter, even for the social impact funds trying to make sense of the proposals they receive all the time.

S. Sivakumar, Group Head, Agri and
IT Businesses, ITC Limited

Madhukar's academic interest in social entrepreneurship and his deep engagement with its practitioners over the past several years has culminated in the publication of this well researched and superbly articulated book on entrepreneurship. The book comprehensively reviews a wide spectrum of impact approaches, highlights how entrepreneurs have created new markets for products and services, and lays it out for the reader to appreciate the nuances of each model and approach. At a time when entrepreneurship appears to be the hope for addressing social, economic and environmental challenges facing India as well as the world, Madhukar has enriched existing entrepreneurship literature with a solid framework based on the actual work of several mission-driven people. I congratulate Madhukar for having authored a book that keeps the reader engaged all through, while cleverly navigating a complex web of market dynamics inter-mingled with issues of social impact and market failure.

Manoj Kumar, *Founder and Chair,*
Social Alpha (Tata Trusts)

Professor Madhukar Shukla is one of the first Indian academicians in the area of social entrepreneurship. This book *Social Entrepreneurship in India: Quarter Idealism and a Pound of Pragmatism* covers every fundamental aspect of social entrepreneurship which any reader would find easy to understand. Systematic presentation of history of social entrepreneurship, especially in India, has also been nicely presented in the book. This book is a true depiction of social entrepreneurs and social enterprises, and would be of immense value to the students, teachers, researchers and the social entrepreneurs.

Satyajit Majumdar, *Professor, Centre for*
Social Entrepreneurship, Tata Institute of
Social Sciences, Mumbai, India

The book by Professor Madhukar Shukla on social entrepreneurship is welcome addition to the fast-growing domain. The book fulfils the need of many teachers of courses in India who have been looking for a book with not just Indian examples but also Indian perspectives. The book examines the models, ideas and challenges of Indian social entrepreneurs with an intimate understanding of the domain, empathy for the journeys of social entrepreneurs and a critical lens that helps us navigate the diversity of experiences and insights. The chapters are well structured and explain concepts without too much of academic jargon and are easy to read and comprehend. The book is an extremely valuable addition which would inspire the next generation of social entrepreneurs as well as the researchers to build an Indian understanding of the field.

Research on social entrepreneurship from India has insufficiently reflected Indian perspectives and nuances that Professor Shukla brings out admirably in this book. For those looking for ways to combine purpose and profit here is a valuable resource for inspired pragmatism.

C. Shambu Prasad, *Professor of Strategy and Policy, IRMA (Indian Institute of Rural Management, Anand)*

Social entrepreneurship is a much-cluttered term, without a clear definition and many enterprises claiming to be 'social' in nature. In this context, this new book picks up diverse examples of social enterprises and examines them to see what makes them tick, why are they indeed social and what is the nature of entrepreneurship.

What is fascinating about Professor Shukla's book is the sheer diversity of examples that he picks up from across the sectors and puts them through an analytical frame to make us unclutter the space and provide clarity. The book at one level is an encyclopaedia on the Indian social enterprise sector in terms of information, and at another, a treatise that adds much to clarity, classification and codification of the sector.

Professor Shukla's annual conferences on social entrepreneurship in Jamshedpur have been legendary, and this was a much-awaited culmination of several years of such deep scholarly engagement.

M. S. Sriram, *Distinguished Fellow at the Institute for Development of Research in Banking Technology (Reserve Bank of India) and Professor of Public Policy, IIM, Bangalore*

SOCIAL ENTREPRENEURSHIP in INDIA

SOCIAL ENTREPRENEURSHIP IN INDIA

QUARTER IDEALISM AND A POUND OF PRAGMATISM

MADHUKAR SHUKLA

Los Angeles | London | New Delhi
Singapore | Washington DC | Melbourne

First published in 2020 by

SAGE Publications India Pvt Ltd
B1/I-1 Mohan Cooperative Industrial Area
Mathura Road, New Delhi 110 044, India
www.sagepub.in

SAGE Publications Inc
2455 Teller Road
Thousand Oaks, California 91320, USA

SAGE Publications Ltd
1 Oliver's Yard, 55 City Road
London EC1Y 1SP, United Kingdom

SAGE Publications Asia-Pacific Pte Ltd
18 Cross Street #10-10/11/12
China Square Central
Singapore 048423

Published by Vivek Mehra for SAGE Publications India Pvt Ltd. Typeset in 11.5/14.5pt Adobe Garamond Pro by Fidus Design Pvt Ltd, Chandigarh.

Library of Congress Cataloging-in-Publication Data Available

ISBN: 978-93-5388-237-2 (PB)

SAGE Team: Namarita Khatait, Neena Ganjoo and Anupama Krishnan

To my daughter,
Manasi Saxena,
and my wife,
the late Geeta Saxena

Thank you for choosing a SAGE product!
If you have any comment, observation or feedback,
I would like to personally hear from you.

Please write to me at **contactceo@sagepub.in**

Vivek Mehra, Managing Director and CEO, SAGE India.

CONTENTS

Foreword by Professor Muhammad Yunus   ix

Preface   xi

Acknowledgements   xv

1. A Term in Search of a Definition   1
2. The 'Entrepreneur' in Social Entrepreneurship   31
3. Entrepreneurial Thinking: A Method to the Madness   53
4. Social and Commercial Entrepreneurship   77
5. Quarter Idealism and a Pound of Pragmatism   97
6. Strategies for Scaling the Impact   115
7. Five Archetypes of Social Entrepreneurship   137
8. Unequal Access: 'Markets of the Poor'   169
9. Entrepreneurial Models for Providing Access   191

Epilogue   229

References   231

About the Author   247

Index   249

FOREWORD

Indian social activists did not wait for new concepts like social entrepreneurship or social business to emerge to get their actions started. For them, action preceded the theory. They were impatient to address the problems they saw in front of them. They saw business as a good way to address them. Amul, Aravind Eye Care, Lijjat, Sulabh Shauchalaya, etc., are excellent examples of such initiatives in India. These and many others like them drew admiration widely for their innovative ways of addressing social problems.

Over time, these examples inspired many others. During the last three decades, the sector has not only evolved and acquired its own identity in the mainstream but also inspired many entrepreneurial solutions to address the issues of poverty and lack of justice. These solutions helped to create hope for a better society by providing affordable access to education, health care, credit, clean energy, water, linkages to markets, etc.

Anybody can read from these examples a significant departure from the traditional passive role of citizens to an activist role in bringing changes in the society. Citizens are frustrated with the fact that solutions through conventional methods are not forthcoming and old problems are becoming more acute. Promises of more private investment to create jobs and more plans from governments to address social issues such as health care, water, nutrition, housing and education no longer generate hopes in people's mind. Some citizens thought that they should abandon the role of passive observers and instead jump in and address these issues in small bites. Through their experiences, citizens started discovering their own ability and creativity to play a decisive role in changing the world.

In this context, this book is a welcome and timely contribution to the understanding of social activism and entrepreneurship. It draws lessons from real-life examples and provides a panoramic view of the diversity of approaches and solutions which characterize the practice of social entrepreneurship in India. The examples the author presents are both inspiring and insightful. Given the wide range of geographical, socio-economic and cultural diversity that he covered, problems created by absurd wealth concentration in the hands of a few and poverty among the masses in India show up sharply in varied ways in different contexts.

At first look, it may appear that diversity of problems must need diversity of approaches. But in the end, it turns out that the small local solution is the germ of the global solution. Global problem is nothing but a sum of local problems. A problem may appear differently in different countries and societies but in its DNA it is the same problem, only wearing different native dresses. It needs a bit of creativity to get to the inner code of the DNA and reveal how a common solution applies to them.

Instead of mixing personal profit and social impact in social enterprises, in our work, we took a different path; we went to its extreme end by totally discarding the intention of making any personal profit and devoting the business solely to achieving social goal. We call these businesses social businesses. Both social enterprise and social businesses are departure from personal-profit-maximizing businesses. Understanding of both will be enormously helpful to any entrepreneur in deciding which entrepreneurship he/she will choose given his/her purpose of business.

I thank Madhukar for writing this excellent book to make it clear to readers, particularly young readers, what social entrepreneurship is all about, to help them make their choices of type of business when they are ready to choose a type.

Professor Muhammad Yunus
Nobel Peace Laureate 2006
Founder, Grameen Bank

PREFACE

This book is about a personal learning journey on which I had embarked about a decade and a half back. It started with a happenstance when, in 2005, a small team from Ashoka: Innovators for the Public visited XLRI as a part of their roadshow across campuses to promote teaching of social entrepreneurship. It was a coincidence that at that time, after 25 years of professional engagements with the corporate sector as a consultant, trainer and academic, I was feeling saturated and was looking for some other exciting field to explore. That interaction opened up an entirely new vista for me. The very idea that ordinary individuals can solve critical social problems through entrepreneurial means—and are actually doing so—seemed exciting and lured me into a voyage of discovery.

The curiosity about the sector led me to many interesting detours in my career. These included compiling a list of social entrepreneurship courses in India for Ashoka, a couple of consultancy projects for social ventures, starting a course on social entrepreneurship for my students, an online discussion group on social entrepreneurship, becoming part of the assessment team for India NGO Awards, undertaking some sector-level studies, etc.

To understand the sector better, in 2007 (and then again for next two years) I decided to attend the Skoll World Forum on Social Entrepreneurship at Saïd Business School, University of Oxford. The forum brings together more than 600 social entrepreneurs from 40–50 countries across the world to share their experiences, learn from each other and form partnerships. It is a stimulating three-day event packed with theme-based sessions, interactive workshops, keynotes by global leaders, felicitation of

Skoll Social Entrepreneurs of the Year, etc. Besides the obvious intellectual takeaway from the forum, what I discovered was that there were so many Indian social entrepreneurs who were globally renowned and featured among the speakers, awardees and resource persons.

During those forums, some of us also discussed the need for a similar platform in India to strengthen the Indian social entrepreneurship ecosystem. When I proposed that we host such a conference at our institute, the then director, Fr E. Abraham, SJ, readily agreed—and so in 2009 we started organizing the annual National Conference on Social Entrepreneurship at XLRI, Jamshedpur (I coordinated the conference till 2017, and now the students' team, SIGMA, has taken over the baton).

Organizing these conferences turned out to be an adventure. Every conference hosted about 25 social entrepreneurs who shared their stories, the innovations and model they used, their successes and failures and so on. Over the years, I had the benefit of knowing, listening to and learning from more than 200 such social change-makers. I could also visit many of their ventures to get a first-hand understanding of their work and impact. Many also became good friends, and many of those stories have also enriched this book.

All these learning experiences gave me a sort of ringside view of the sector as it kept on evolving. My own understanding of the social entrepreneurship also became more nuanced around three themes which also became the underlying theme of this book.

First one was dealing with a very unique breed of people who combined two seemingly contradictory predispositions. On the one hand, these were individuals who were passionate about an idea or a cause, were emotionally committed to solve a social problem and were idealistic about their vision of human society. On the other hand, they had their feet solidly on the ground, and were practical and pragmatic in the manner they addressed and solved the problem. This 'inspired pragmatism' perhaps was also the source of their exciting innovative approaches.

Second, given the diversity of social problems in India, and the numerous barriers to solve them, there is no single way to address them. The variety of approaches of the Indian social entrepreneurs, and multiple forms of their ventures to achieve their mission, defies pigeonholing them into a single neat definition. Writing this book was my way to appreciate and celebrate this diversity to understand Indian social entrepreneurship.

And finally, the Indian social entrepreneurship is a bubbling hotbed of social innovations. One of my most valuable takeaways in this journey was to learn and appreciate the variety of models which could address and solve the same social problem. I have tried to share my understanding of these different models and approaches in the book.

Writing this book itself was a sort of stocktaking of my learning during this journey. As I wrote this book and made sense of my experiences, I enjoyed the thrills of discovery and insights about this evolving terrain. I hope the readers will find this book as exciting and enjoyable to read as I did in keying it in.

PREFACE

ACKNOWLEDGEMENTS

A book of this nature cannot be the work of a single person. There were numerous people who contributed in different ways to make it happen. I am indebted to their inputs, ideas, support and encouragement in writing this book.

During my explorations in this field, I was lucky to get the opportunity to interact with, and learn from, many creative and passionate individuals, the social entrepreneurs, whose stories provided both the inspiration and content for this book. This book could not have been possible without them and the stories of their journey which they shared. The list is too long to mention, but most of them are mentioned in the book. I owe them the debt of being my teachers and helping me to develop and refine my understanding about this field.

Many of my professional colleagues, both academics and practitioners, made themselves regularly available as the sounding board for my evolving ideas, even though they may not be aware of their contribution to my learning. They also recommended people I should meet, ventures to visit, books and reports to read and so on. Among the many academics, I would specifically like to thank Professor Shambu Prasad (IRMA), Professor Satyajit Majumdar (TISS), Professor Gerard Farias (Fairleigh Dickinson University, USA), Dinesh Awasthi (ex-EDI) and my former colleague, Professor Prabal Sen, for sharing their insights and experience about the sector.

My journey into the field of social entrepreneurship (which finally culminated in this book) was also greatly facilitated by many guides and mentors. These social/development sector professionals and practitioners with their vast experience provided me with direction, forums and platforms to learn more about the sector and its constituents. They are too many to mention all of them, but some who I would especially like to acknowledge are Pritha Sen, Sohini Bhattacharya, Tinnie Mukherjee, Kalpana Kaul, earlier with Ashoka: Innovators for the Public, for giving me the initial push to start the journey; Rati Misra and Rajshri Sen, earlier with Resource Alliance, for providing multiple opportunities for field visits to social ventures; Payal Randhawa, earlier with Khemka Foundation, and Manisha Gupta of Start Up! for the opportunities to meet some of the most remarkable social entrepreneurs; M. V. Ashok, earlier with NABARD, for supporting the conferences which I organized which gave me the chance to meet and know more than 200 social entrepreneurs; Ajit Kanitkar, earlier with Ford Foundation, who facilitated many interactions and visits in the field; Vipin Sharma of ACCESS Development Services, for introducing me to the larger ecosystem of the sector. The list can go on, and is, obviously, not exhaustive.

I often jocularly say that I live a retired life in my present job, which meets my financial needs, provides me with supportive friends and colleagues, and gives me ample freedom to pursue what excites me. I would like to thank my colleagues for their help and interest. This book particularly owes a lot to the successive directors of the XLRI—Fr N. Casimir Raj, SJ, Fr E. Abraham, SJ, and Fr P. Christie, SJ,—who not only supported but also encouraged me to explore and develop some competence in an area which is not the mainstream discipline in a business school.

Authors are universally known to be biased about their manuscript, and therefore make bad editors. The burden of cleaning and polishing the text into an easily readable form is borne by the editors. But for the extremely supportive team from SAGE, Aarti David, Manisha Mathews and Namarita Kathait, this book would not have reached its final form. I would particularly like to thank Namarita, who was understanding and patient with my constraints, super helpful and efficient in editing the text to make it a smooth reading, and firm with the deadlines—all at the same time.

Last but not least, thanks are also due to two people for their indirect support. During all these years, my daughter, Manasi Saxena, showed sufficient curiosity and tolerance about what I was doing to make me feel that whatever I was doing must be worth it. The other person, who remains invisible in her presence, is my household help/housekeeper, Raheela Begum—or Raheela 'Chachi' as she is to most who know her. In her own way, she contributed to this book by keeping away the daily pressures of living from impinging on my time and gave me the freedom to explore, reflect and key in my learning.

A TERM IN SEARCH OF A DEFINITION

Interestingly, some social entrepreneurs do not even know they are 'social entrepreneurs' until they receive an award or are recognized by organizations such as Ashoka or the Schwab Foundation.

—*Christian Seelos and Johanna Mair (2005)*

The Tipping Point

In October 2006, Professor Muhammad Yunus and Grameen Bank, the institution which he had founded, were conferred the Nobel Peace Prize for their pioneering work in using microcredit 'to create economic and social development from below'. In awarding the prize, The Norwegian Nobel Committee had also acknowledged that 'lasting peace cannot be achieved unless large population groups find ways in which to break out of poverty.... Development from below also serves to advance democracy and human rights.' In linking peace and social justice to development and poverty alleviation, the Committee had also made a significant departure from looking at them through the conventional lenses of rights-based approaches.

Professor Yunus, an erstwhile economics professor, had started his journey in 1976 by giving personal loans worth $27 to 43 poor women in a small village Jobra in Chittagong, Bangladesh, to help them get out of the clutches of the money-lenders. He had gone on to establish Grameen Bank, a bank entirely for and of the poor, in 1983; 94 per cent of the bank's total equity was owned by the borrowers (the rest was owned by the government). In establishing the bank, he had tried to address a problem which he had encountered earlier while trying to help the poor access credit from the commercial banks, namely, the traditional banking system does not treat the poor people, who actually need the loans most, as bankable. Professor Yunus, on the other hand, worked on the assumption that, given suitable support and conditions, even the poorest of the poor can manage their own financial affairs and move out of the cycles of poverty.

Grameen Bank was established to provide small long-term loans to the poor on easy terms and without any collateral or legal instrument. By 2006, Grameen Bank had scaled up its operations to over 70,000 villages in Bangladesh and had disbursed loans worth $5.72 billion to its 6.61 million poor 'customers', of which 97 per cent were women. Despite having reasonably high interest rates of 20 per cent (on declining basis) for income-generating loans, it had quite a high loan recovery rate of 98.85 per cent. In addition, Grameen Bank also gave other loans at lower interests to meet the other needs of the poor, for example, housing loans, education loans for students and interest-free loans to destitute and beggars.

The major achievement of Professor Yunus, however, was not just the scale and operating efficiency of the Bank. More significantly, Grameen Bank had demonstrated a viable and sustainable model to provide access to credit as a means of poverty alleviation. Half of Grameen's borrowers had moved out of poverty, and in all but 3 years of its operations, the bank had remained profitable. The success of Grameen Bank had also spurred the replication of the 'Grameen Model', spawning thousands of similar microfinance institutions (MFIs) across the world.

This was also the first time that the Nobel Prize was given to a person who was globally recognized as a 'social entrepreneur' for his work. Since 2001, Professor Yunus has been one of the founding members of the Global Academy for Social Entrepreneurship.

The Academy was established by Ashoka: Innovators for the Public[1] to bring together a group of social leaders who had demonstrated (and who could provide guidance about) how social entrepreneurial solutions can address global problems on a global scale.

Due to India's large and growing microfinance sector, Professor Yunus and Grameen Bank were well known in the developmental sector (India had the largest Grameen replicants of MFIs outside Bangladesh [Ghate 2006]). In the coming months, Professor Yunus was widely covered in the media and was felicitated by various Indian organizations (*Economic Times* 2006; Gopalan 2007; Rediff.com 2006). The Grameen Bank model also demonstrated that it is possible to run a financially viable venture with the mission of delivering social good. Around this time, Professor Yunus had also started advocating that the 'social business entrepreneurs/enterprises' (Yunus 2006) are necessary to effectively address and solve critical social problems. According to Yunus, these are the 'non-loss, non-dividend' businesses 'which are created to do good to people, not paying any attention to making

[1] Ashoka: Innovators for the Public is the largest network of social entrepreneurs worldwide, with nearly 3,000 Ashoka Fellows in 70 countries. Founded in India by Bill Drayton in 1980, Ashoka launched the field of social entrepreneurship by recognizing, supporting and providing a platform for people dedicated to solve critical social problems. It provides start-up financing, professional support services and connections to a global network to social entrepreneurs.

Ashoka Global Academy of Social Entrepreneurs was launched in 2001 to guide and putting system changing ideas into practice on a global scale. Besides Professor Yunus, other members of the Academy consisted of social entrepreneurs such as Fazle Abed (founder of BRAC), Peter Eigen (founder of Transparency International), Alice Tepper Marlin (founder of Social Accountability International and The Council on Economic Priorities), Ela Bhatt (founder of SEWA), Oded Grajew (founder of The Ethos Institute for Business Social Responsibility and World Social Forum), Bill Drayton (founder of Ashoka: Innovators for the Public), etc.

personal gains.' While delivering the 2nd Rajiv Gandhi Oration at University of Mumbai, he had said:

> People need help in areas such as health, education, safe drinking water.... While doing social business, we want to reach out to people.... Profit maximisation need not be the only aim. (*The Hindu* 2007)

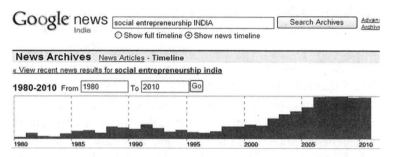

Figure 1.1 Showing Sudden Increase in Awareness about Social Entrepreneurship in India during 2005–2006

The Nobel Prize to Professor Yunus, and the subsequent wide coverage and publicity, also seemed to coincide with (and perhaps also contributed to) a quantum increase in activities and initiatives related to social entrepreneurship in India. For reasons which one can only conjecture about, 2005–2006 also appeared to be a turning point for the sector (see Figure 1.1); 'social entrepreneurship' had entered the popular lexicon of searched terms. In their study of the landscape of social enterprises in India, Allen et al. (2012) also noted,

> Nearly half of the enterprises in our survey have been operational for less than three years, and nearly 80% launched operations in 2007 or later. The take-off appears to have occurred in 2005–2006. (p. 12)

Emergence of a Sector

Interestingly, even before the term 'social entrepreneurship' was coined,[2] in practice, India has had a rich history of initiatives which can be (and are) now described as social entrepreneurial ventures. As Shukla (2010) noted, the sociocultural milieu and historical context of India provide a fertile ground for proactive social engagement to make an impact. Culturally, the orientation of 'giving' and the need to fulfil one's duty towards the society and collective well-being is deep-rooted in Indian social values and identity (Chakraborty 1987; McClelland 1985). These values were further reinforced during the Indian Independence Movement during the first half of 20th century, led by leaders like Mahatma Gandhi. The notion of freedom promoted by the forefathers of the country was not just the political independence but also to develop an empowered grassroots society (Gandhi's concept of *gram swaraj*) with a strong focus on developing social leaders who can facilitate economic and social equality. This idea of developing an empowered society was carried forward by many of Gandhi's followers (such as Vinoba Bhave, Baba Amte and Jai Prakash Narain), and became a guiding principle of many large social ventures in the early days of independent India (see Box 1.1 for some examples).

[2] The term 'social entrepreneur' is normally attributed to Bill Drayton, the founder of Ashoka: Innovators for the Public, who coined and popularized it in the 1980s. However, it was used first time by Joseph Ambrose Banks (1972) in his book to describe the Welsh social reformer, Robert Owen, who 'saw the possibility of using managerial skills directly for socially constructive purposes.'

BOX 1.1   SOME OLD SOCIAL ENTREPRENEURIAL VENTURES IN INDIA

Amul (or Gujarat Cooperative Milk Marketing Federation Ltd) started in 1946, when some milk-producers formed a cooperative in Kaira district of Gujarat to escape the exploitation by the middlemen, and to have control over the procurement, processing and marketing of their produce. Guided by Tribhuvandas Patel and Dr Verghese Kurien, this small collective, producing just 247 litres of milk then, now has a turnover of ₹230 billion, and procures 14.85 million litre milk every day, ensuring livelihood of its 3.37 million members, forming 18,536 village milk cooperatives across 31 districts. Its cooperative model has been replicated across about 150,000 cooperatives in 184 districts, which sell milk and milk products through 22 State Marketing Federations.

Lijjat (or Shri Mahila Griha Udyog Lijjat Papad) started in 1959, when Jaswantiben Jamnadas Popat and six other semi-literate women got together on the terrace of their building in Girgaum, Mumbai to roll and sell *papad*. As the group enlarged (within a year, the group had grown to about 100 women, with a turnover of about ₹6,200), it adopted the Gandhian principles of self-help and trusteeship, and became a symbol of women's economic enfranchisement. From that small beginning, Lijjat is now an organization with 43,000 women members/owners, spread across and 81 Branches and 27 Divisions in different states of India, with a turnover of ₹6.5 billion.

Sulabh International Social Service Organization was founded by Dr Bindeshwari Pathak in 1970. Its mission was the emancipation of scavengers, who carry human excreta manually, and are ostracized as untouchables. Dr Pathak innovated two-pit, pour-flush compost toilet, which does not require scavengers to clean the pit, and also pioneered the 'pay-per-use' model for community toilets. Sulabh rehabilitates the scavengers by providing them with education and vocational training. Over the years, Sulabh has constructed 1.3 million household toilets, and operates more than 8,500 community toilets across India, which are connected to biogas plants. About 54 million government toilets are also constructed based on Sulabh design.

SEWA (Self Employed Women's Association) was founded in 1971 by Ela Bhatt with a mission to empower and provide 'full employment' (i.e., employment with work security, income security, food security and social security) to the women in unorganized sector. To make the sister-members self-reliant, SEWA has created a network of decentralized and self-supporting services, such as SEWA Bank to provide savings and credit facilities, legal aid, insurance, affordable housing, capacity building, trade facilitation centres, childcare, etc. Starting with a membership of about 1,000 women members, SEWA is now the largest registered central trade union with close to 2 million members across India.

However, till the end of the last century, as a concept and as a defined field of endeavour, social entrepreneurship had largely remained confined to the sector practitioners, mainly the Ashoka Fellows. During the first decade of the 21st century, social entrepreneurship had gradually started emerging as a more widespread phenomenon. For any sector to grow, a supporting ecosystem is an essential prerequisite. Around that time, a rudimentary supporting ecosystem for the practice had just started emerging. Between 2001 and 2005, a few pioneering initiatives such as incubators for entrepreneurs addressing social problems (e.g., Dasra and Villgro), social venture funds (e.g., Aavishkaar and Lok Capital), courses on social entrepreneurship, recognition of social entrepreneurs in public forums, etc. had started appearing on the scene. The second half of the decade, however, saw a sudden surge of activities in the social entrepreneurship space (see Box 1.2 for some key developments in the ecosystem during the decade). By the end of the decade, the broad contours of an ecosystem of social entrepreneurship had started emerging in India.

BOX 1.2   GROWTH OF SOCIAL ENTREPRENEURSHIP ECOSYSTEM IN INDIA 2001–2010: SOME KEY MILESTONES

2001:

Aavishkaar India Micro Venture Fund was launched to support early stage ventures serving the under-served markets.

Rural Innovation Network (now Villgro) was founded to identify and disseminate promising rural innovations by helping them to develop into social enterprises.

Acumen Fund made an entry by making its first impact investment in Aravind Eye Hospital.

Centre for Social Initiative and Management (CSIM) was launched in Chennai and offered India's first practice-oriented course on social entrepreneurship.

Outlook, a mainstream magazine, started a regular column 'Make a Difference' documenting the initiatives of ordinary individuals which made an impact on society.

2002:

For the first time, in the *World Economic Forum's India Economic Summit 2002*, President A. P. J. Abdul Kalam felicitated 10 outstanding social entrepreneurs from India and Bangladesh. Their achievements were highlighted in a special plenary session, 'Recognizing Outstanding Social Entrepreneurs.'

Lok Capital, a venture capital firm was launched to support and make long-term equity investments in 'social enterprises that are commercially viable and can deliver basic services and livelihood solutions to low income households and underserved segment.'

Dasra was launched with the aim to incubate, build skills and capacity of social ventures, and connect them with donors and investors.

2003:
Marico Ltd launched *Marico Innovation Foundation* with the aim to mentor and support 'direct impact' innovations in the areas of renewable energy, waste management, employability & livelihoods and healthcare.

2004:
IIT-Madras and Rural Innovations Network (Villgro) jointly launched the *Lemelson Recognition and Mentoring Programme (L-RAMP)* for social entrepreneurs, supported by The Lemelson Foundation USA.

IIM Bangalore launched the first academic course on social entrepreneurship.

2005:
The first *Social Entrepreneur of the Year Award*, supported by Nand & Jeet Khemka Foundation, was given to Dr Devi Shetty, the founder of Narayana Hrudayalaya.

Ashoka: Innovators for the Public went on a roadshow across college and institutes to stimulate interest in social entrepreneurship among students and faculty.

2006:

The first *International Conference on Social Entrepreneurship* was organized by Tata Institute of Social and UnLtd Foundation at TISS, with support from Skoll Centre, Oxford University.

Rural Technology Business Incubator (RTBI) was launched at IIT-Madras.

Four major institutes (Indian Institute of Forest Management-Bhopal, Institute of Rural management-Anand, Xavier Institute of Management-Bhubaneswar and XLRI-Jamshedpur) started offering *courses on social entrepreneurship* as a part of their programmes.

ISB-Hyderabad became the partner in the Global Social Venture Competition, a global competition partnered by different educational institutions, and organized the first major competition for students and budding social entrepreneurs.

Acumen Fund opened its office in India with a focus on investing in social ventures in agriculture, education, energy, health, housing and water.

Pravah and *Ashoka's Youth Venture* jointly launched the Change Looms programme to recognize, encourage and support the exceptional achievements of young people who are actively promoting social change in society.

2007:

UnLtd India was launched as an incubator for early stage social entrepreneurs to help them scale up and accelerate their impact.

IIM-Ahmedabad launched the *Centre for Innovation Incubation and Entrepreneurship (CIIE)* to incubate, mentor and fund innovative start-ups, which can bring about societal change in areas like energy, environment, agriculture, healthcare and affordable technology (CIIE was founded in 2002, but till now focused primarily on academic research).

Tata Institute of Social Sciences started a *2-year full-time programme on social entrepreneurship.*

IIM-Ahmedabad launched a course on social entrepreneurship as a part of the regular programme.

Deshpande Foundation was established in Hubli-Dharward to nurture social leaders and nurture and promote social enterprises-based innovation relevant to local needs.

Piramal Foundation launched *Gandhi Fellowship*, a 2-year programme 'to develop a cadre of leaders exposed to the complexities of bringing change in social and public systems'.

Central Himalayan Rural Action Group (CHIRAG) launched the, *Swadesh Ki Khoj* Fellowship, providing youth an opportunity to work with a rural development agency in India for a year.

2008:

The first *Development Dialogue* was organized by the Deshpande Foundation, which is an annual event which brings together social entrepreneurs and other stakeholder who are involved in creating ecosystems to nurture social innovation and entrepreneurship.

The first *Jagriti Yatra*, a 15-day long train journey across India with more than 300 youth was organized with an aim to sensitize, inspire and build entrepreneurial skills to address social problems through enterprises.

Elevar Equity was founded to invest in early stage ventures providing market-based solutions to deliver essential services to underserved communities.

Ennovent Fund was launched to invest in social innovations which improve the lives of low-income people communities.

Three online portals were launched, which covered the gamut of entrepreneurship, changemakers and social enterprises: *Think Change-India*, an online bog-website covered the news and developments in the social enterprise space;

Your Story was founded with the aim of championing the untold stories of entrepreneurship in India; *Better India* was founded with the aim to share the stories of unsung heroes and little-known innovations making a social impact.

TiE Entrepreneurship Summit 2008 was organized on the theme of Inclusive Entrepreneurship with a key-note session on social entrepreneurship.

2009:

Four national level conferences on social entrepreneurship were organized (*National Conference on Social Entrepreneurship* by XLRI, Jamshedpur; *Sankalp Forum* by Intellecap; *Khemka Forum for Social Entrepreneurship* by Khemka Foundation and *Unconvention* by Villgro), which provided a platform for social entrepreneurs and other stakeholders to connect, share and learn from each other.

ICICI Fellowship programme was launched, which aimed to nurture young social leaders by 15-month long experiential learning through working on grassroots development projects, management inputs and personal mentoring.

ISB-Hyderabad and IIT-Madras organized the first national-level social venture competitions, *iDiya* and *Genesis*. Besides the prizes, these competitions also provided mentoring and training support, and connecting the winners with funders/investors.

As a first *collaboration between an academic institution and a social venture*, Villgro and IIT-Madras co-designed and offered a course on social entrepreneurship for the engineering students.

Monitor Group, a global consultancy firm, published the first empirical report based largely on business models of the social enterprises, 'Emerging Markets, Emerging Models: Market-Based Solutions to the Challenges of Global Poverty'.

Outlook Business magazine brought out a full special issue featuring 50 social entrepreneurs.

Beyond Profit, a magazine entirely devoted to social entrepreneurs and enterprises was launched. Social enterprise magazine presents the stories, people and ideas behind these innovating social ventures.

2010:
IIT-Madras founded The *Centre for Social Innovation and Entrepreneurship (CSIE)* with a focus on teaching and research related to social enterprise in India.

Piramal Foundation launched 2-year *Piramal Fellowship for Sustainable Business* programme which aimed to develop social leaders by hands-on learning in taking up roles in social enterprises.

Etc.

As often happens with the initial efforts, though many of these early initiatives did not survive after a few years, they did add momentum to the developments which were shaping the field. Some of the key trends which had started becoming discernible by the end of this period were:

- **Pipeline of talent:** There were an increasing number of initiatives focusing on creating a pipeline of socially sensitive youth. Many educational institutes had started offering courses on social entrepreneurship, which would make the students aware about the field as well as equip them with some basic skills to participate in the emerging sector. In addition, many innovative and impactful initiatives, such as designed and planned field-exposures (e.g., Jagriti Yatra and Swadesh Ki Khoj), competitions (e.g., Genesis, iDiya and GSVC), fellowships (e.g., ICICI Fellowship and Gandhi

Fellowship), etc. had emerged, which aimed to sensitize, encourage and prepare the youth and students to understand and try to solve social issues.

- **Incubation support:** Incubation initiatives in India had largely focused on technology start-ups under initiatives of Department of Science and Technology, Government of India. During the decade, the first few incubators and accelerators (e.g., Villgro, UnLtd and CIIE), which were entirely dedicated to social ventures, had started emerging.

- **Funding and investment:** Though the venture capital/angel investment community was still in its nascent stage in India, social ventures/enterprises were increasingly seen as a high-growth sector. Correspondingly, during this period, the first few social impact investment funds (e.g., Aavishkaar, Elevar Equity and Lok Capital) were launched. Besides funding, these organizations also provided technical support to the investees.

- **Conferences, awards and recognitions**: By the end of the decade, there were at least four large annual conferences (National Conference on Social Entrepreneurship, Sankalp Forum, Social Entrepreneurship Summit and Unconvention), which brought together the social entrepreneurs and other stakeholders on a common platform. These forums not only showcased and felicitated their stories and innovations, but also helped connecting them with each other and in creating partnerships.

- **Media coverage:** Media plays an important role in popularizing the sector as well as in dissemination of ideas and examples. During the decade, some dedicated media platforms had started appearing, which would collect and share information and stories about events. Some popular web portals (e.g., Better India and Think-Change India) had created their own audience, and one mainstream magazine, *Outlook Business*, had also started publishing an annual issue featuring the stories of social entrepreneurs.

Why Social Entrepreneurship Needs to Be Defined

Despite the increasing currency of the term in India and abroad, there is still a lack of unanimity among both the practitioners and the academics about a precise definition of a social entrepreneur, or what constitutes social entrepreneurship. As Brodbar (2009) observed:

> Social entrepreneurship is allergic to definitions. Like Associate Justice Potter Stewart's take on obscenity, many of us can't describe social entrepreneurship, but we know it when we see it. (p. 30)

Broadly, it is agreed that social entrepreneurs are individuals who solve social problems, and thus create social change by impacting the lives of people and communities they serve. But beyond this, there is little consensus. Such a broad understanding, however, raises many more questions than it answers. For instance:

- Many NGOs also implement innovative solution and impact the lives of people they serve; so how are social entrepreneurial ventures different than the NGOs?
- Even a commercial entrepreneur impacts the lives of people by putting up an industry and providing employment; would not that also make them a social entrepreneur?
- Can social movements and social activism be considered acts of social entrepreneurship, since they too aim to solve social problems?
- Many large corporates design and offer products and services to people who do not have access to them (e.g., mobile phone services); would that be considered social entrepreneurship? and so on.

As Dees (1998) observed in his seminal paper on social entrepreneurship:

> Though the concept of 'social entrepreneurship' is gaining popularity, it means different things to different people. This can be confusing. Many associate social entrepreneurship exclusively with not-for-profit organizations starting for-profit or earned-income ventures. Others use it to describe anyone who starts a not-for-profit organization. Still others use it to refer to business owners who integrate social responsibility into their operations. (p. 1)

In many ways, such a lack of clarity about the definition is also understandable. There are a number of reasons why it is not easy (and perhaps not possible) to arrive at a precise, all-encompassing and universally accepted definition of social entrepreneurship:

1. **The definitional challenge:** First, there is a definitional issue with the term 'entrepreneurship' itself. As Martin and Osberg (2007) pointed out, 'entrepreneurship' is a phenomenon which can be only be recognized ex post facto, that is, a venture can be described as entrepreneurial only after it is successful and its impact becomes visible. Even if a person shows all the characteristics normally associated with an entrepreneur (e.g., opportunity identification, innovation, risk-taking and perseverance) but fails in his/her endeavour, he/she will still be recognized only as a failure, not as an entrepreneur.

   Adding the prefix 'social' to entrepreneurship further complicates the definitional focus. For the commercial entrepreneur, at least the evidence of success is clearly defined and measurable in terms of profits, turnover or market share. Measuring 'social impact', on the other hand, is not so easy since often the goals are qualitative in nature, and expressed in terms of immediate consequences of the venture's activities/efforts (e.g., providing affordable and quality education to marginalized children, providing access to energy to off-grid population and improving rural household income by creating market access). Even when it is possible to quantify the ultimate outcomes (e.g., increasing rural artisans' income twofold by connecting them to market and training and placing x-number of rural youths in jobs), it is often difficult to define them within a timeframe.

2. **Diversity of social entrepreneurial efforts:** By its very nature social entrepreneurship is a complex and multifaceted phenomenon. Unlike other social agents (e.g., doctors, lawyers, government officials or even commercial entrepreneurs), social entrepreneurs widely differ in their approaches to achieve their social goals. Consider, for instance, the profiles and work of three well-known social entrepreneurs (see Box 1.3): Anshu Gupta (founder of Goonj), Arbind Singh (founder of Nidan) and Harish Hande (founder of SELCO). All three have found innovative solution to make large-scale social impact and have been felicitated for their work with Social Entrepreneur of the Year Award; Anshu Gupta and Harish Hande are also Ramon Magsaysay Award winners, while Arbind Singh received the Skoll Award for his work. On all other counts, however, there is not much similarity among them. They come with different set of professional expertise: Anshu Gupta is a postgraduate in mass communication; Arbind Singh did masters in sociology; and Harish Hande is a PhD in energy engineering. The foci of their efforts are also very different: Goonj's goal is to reposition the urban discard as a development resource for villages; Nidan's mission is to empower the unorganized workforce through creating collective institutions; and SELCO aims to the enhance quality of life of the poor through sustainable energy solutions and services. SELCO is a for-profit organization; Goonj is a not-for-profit venture, while Nidan is also a not-for-profit but promotes for-profit entities and so on.

A TERM IN SEARCH OF A DEFINITION

BOX 1.3 PROFILES OF THREE SOCIAL ENTREPRENEUR

Anshu Gupta: Anshu Gupta founded *Goonj*, a not-for-profit volunteer-based organization, which recycles clothes and other items which are discarded as urban 'waste' into 'resources' for the marginalized rural and urban communities and for calamity-hit areas. The clothes and other materials are collected, sorted and processed in centres run by *Goonj* across the country. Every year, Goonj transports and distributes about 1,000 tonnes of materials to the ultra-poor communities in 21 states through a network of about 250 grassroots NGOs, 200 engaged business houses, 100 schools and 500+ volunteers (2015 figures). Its cumulative cost of operations is 97 paise per kg of material.

Under its 'Cloth of Work' programme, the village and slum communities organize local development and infrastructure building programmes (e.g., building schools, concrete roads, bridges, wells, irrigation canals and toilets) in return for clothes, which also free up their meagre resources for other expenditures. About 500 such infrastructure projects in 1,500 villages are undertaken every year, inculcating self-respect and belief in one's own capacity to catalyze change among the communities. In addition, *Goonj* has been carrying out large-scale relief and rehabilitation operations during calamities, such as floods, earthquakes and droughts etc. Using the remnants of waste cloth, Goonj has also made and distributed more than 2 million sanitary napkins to the first-time rural women users.

Arbind Singh: Arbind Singh founded *Nidan* with a mission to empower unorganized workers by collectivizing them, and thus increasing their bargaining power and giving them economies of scale. Founded in 1996 in Bihar, *Nidan* works to empower the informal sector workers such as waste workers, rag pickers, vegetable vendors, construction labourers, domestic helpers, farmers and street vendors across many states to become financially and socially self-dependent. It provides its members the access to financial services (savings, loans, insurance, pension, etc.), legal services and education for members' children, etc.

Though *Nidan* is a grant-based not-for-profit organization, it has nurtured more than 20 self-sustaining and profitable entities which are owned and managed by workers. These businesses incubated by *Nidan* have brought together 500,000 informal sector workers and positioned them as legitimate competitors in markets.

Harish Hande: Harish Hande pioneered solar energy solutions in India when he established *SELCO Solar Pvt. Ltd* in 1995. SELCO's mission is to provide sustainable energy solutions and services to under-served households and businesses. To provide energy access to families living below poverty line, SELCO pioneered many innovations. To make the solar systems affordable, it provides consumer finance through grameen banks, cooperative societies, commercial banks and microfinance institutions to end users, which can be repaid through a customized schedule based on their cash flow and energy expenditure; instead of selling standard products, SELCO customizes the energy systems based on the needs of different users; and for installation and after-sales service the venture has created dedicated 45 regional energy centres for prompt maintenance and service. SELCO also made many other innovations, such as the 'SELCO entrepreneurs', who lease solar-powered lights to street vendors in the evening. Over the years, SELCO has been able to directly provide solar lightning systems to more than 200,000 marginalized households in Karnataka, Gujarat, Maharashtra, Bihar and Tamil Nadu.

As one can see, these social entrepreneurs have addressed different social problems, have different approaches to solve them and have created organizations which are unlike the other. Putting them in a single definition is not only difficult, but would perhaps also deprive the diversity of the phenomenon they represent.

3. **Contextual embeddedness of the practice:** By their very nature, social entrepreneurial initiatives are embedded in the local context of the community and society. They address the social needs and problems of that context, develop solutions using the local available resources, and are shaped by the support ecosystems which are available (or not available) in the community/society. Since these contexts differ across societies, they both create and restrict the choices for the social ventures due to the variations in critical social problems that need to be addressed, government policies, sources of revenue, funding and investments, availability of markets and skills, etc. As Mair (2010) noted:

> If the opportunity space for social entrepreneurship is defined by the local social, economic and political arrangements, then it is not surprising that the social entrepreneurship phenomenon manifests itself differently in different contexts. As a result the researchers, policy makers or businesses have to situate the phenomenon (or the social entrepreneurial actor) in a specific context to understand it fully. (p. 5)

For instance, in more developed economies and segments of society, which have well-developed and mature markets, it is possible to develop market-based models to provide various goods and services (and thus, create a for-profit entity to deliver these). However, if the critical social problems in a society/community revolve around segments which essentially exist outside the 'markets' (e.g., ultra-poor, destitute, abandoned children, landless peasants and marginal subsistence farmer), the venture would need to support and develop them till they can become a part of the mainstream; this, however, can largely be done only through grants, subsidies, donations, etc.

Similarly, some countries provide for a separate legal form for social ventures, which allow them greater flexibility in use of their resources and assets, government support for their mission and/or easy access to philanthropic investors. In USA, for instance, regulatory framework allows for a separate legal form, L3C (Low-Profit Limited Liability Company), which erases the not-for-profit versus for-profit dichotomy, and facilitates investments in socially beneficial, for-profit ventures by simplifying the rules. Likewise, in UK, the legal form CIC (Community Interest Company) is specifically designed for social enterprises that want to use their profits and assets for the public good. In comparison, in India, such legal forms do not exist; traditionally most old social ventures are registered under either the Societies Registration Act or the Indian Charitable Trusts Act, which disallow them from seeking investments or making profits (though, in recent years, many social ventures are registering as Private Ltd Companies, Section 8/25 or as Limited Legal Liability companies, or are creating a 'hybrid' structure with both a for-profit and a not-for-profit entity).

While such differences across societies and communities give a distinct regional 'flavour' to the social ventures in terms of the viable business models, structure and strategies, they also create a challenge in finding an all-encompassing common thread which can describe and define these diverse efforts.

4. **Infancy and diversity of the discipline:** Studying social entrepreneurship as an academic subject is relatively new; it does not have a set of academics and scholar who can claim it to be their basic area of expertise. Rather, academician and researchers studying social entrepreneurship come from diverse academic disciplines, ranging from economics, livelihoods, public administration, agriculture, finance and accounting to social development. Understandably, their focus and perspective in understanding and defining the field are guided by the lenses of their discipline. As one would see from Table 1.1, even on just three dimensions—that is, (a) whether innovation is an essential element of social entrepreneurship or not, (b) whether the focus of impact is solving local social problems or making large-scale systemic changes and (c) whether the appropriate organizational form is a for-profit or a not-for-profit entity— there is not much consensus.

The Pre-paradigmatic Churn

From the previous discussion and Table 1.1, it is clear that, at least at this stage, the task of arriving at a single definition is not easy. From an academic point of view, the field of social entrepreneurship is still in its nascent stages, with many competing definitions and approaches to understand the phenomenon. In many ways, the academic discipline of social entrepreneurship is at, what Thomas Kuhn (1962) described as, a 'pre-paradigmatic stage' which dominates the scene, prior to the emergence of a new scientific paradigm in his book *The Structure of Scientific Revolutions*.

According to Kuhn, at any point in time, the 'normal science' is characterized by a 'paradigm' (i.e., a set of assumptions, terminologies and definitions, etc.) which researchers agree on, and which can adequately explain the known facts. These conceptual boundaries and world view promoted by the existing paradigm also guide the academic research and policy discourse within that discipline. A new science or discipline, however, does not emerge gradually from the existing paradigm nor is it built on the foundations of the

TABLE 1.1: Showing Comparison of Definitions of Social Entrepreneurship on Dimensions of Innovation, Nature of Social Impact and Organizational Form

	INNO-VATION	SOCIAL IMPACT	ORG. FORM
Ashoka: Innovators for the Public[a] Social entrepreneurs are individuals with innovative solutions to society's most pressing social problems. They are ambitious and persistent, tackling major social issues and offering new ideas for wide-scale change. Rather than leaving societal needs to the government or business sectors, social entrepreneurs find what is not working and solve the problem by changing the system, spreading the solution and persuading entire societies to move in different directions.	Yes	Large scale systemic	Either
Barendsen and Gardner (2004) Social entrepreneurs are individuals who approach a social problem with entrepreneurial spirit and business acumen.	Not mentioned	Problem solution	Either
Boschee and McClurg (2003) A social entrepreneur is any person, in any sector, who uses earned income strategies to pursue a social objective.	Not mentioned	Problem solution	For profit

(continued)

(continued)

	INNO-VATION	SOCIAL IMPACT	ORG. FORM
Dacanay (2006) Social entrepreneurship involves the promotion and building of enterprises or organizations that create wealth, with the intention of benefiting not just a person or family, but a defined constituency, sector or community, usually involving the public at large or the marginalized sectors of society.	Not mentioned	Large scale	For profit
Dees (1998) Social entrepreneurs play the role of change agents in the social sector, by (a) adopting a mission to create and sustain social value (not just private value), (b) recognizing and relentlessly pursuing new opportunities to serve that mission, (c) engaging in a process of continuous innovation, adaptation and learning, (d) acting boldly without being limited by resources currently in hand, and (e) exhibiting a heightened sense of accountability to the constituencies served and for the outcomes created.	Yes	Large scale	Either

Fuqua School of Business, Duke University[b] Social entrepreneurship is the process of recognizing and resourcefully pursuing opportunities to create social value. Social entrepreneurs are innovative, resourceful and results oriented. They draw upon the best thinking in both the business and nonprofit worlds to develop strategies that maximize their social impact. These entrepreneurial leaders operate in all kinds of organizations: large and small; new and old; religious and secular; nonprofit, for-profit and hybrid.	Yes	Social value	Either
Hartingan and Billimoria (2005) A social entrepreneur identifies practical solutions to social problems by combining innovation, resourcefulness and opportunity…is a mover and a shaker, the motor of social transformation…. They cannot be lumped easily into the non-profit or for-profit worlds that we cling to….	Yes	Large scale systemic	Either
Leadbeater (1997) Social entrepreneurs are most usually found in what is called the voluntary sector…. Social entrepreneurs are: (a) Entrepreneurial: they take under-utilized, discarded resources and spot ways of using them to satisfy unmet needs; (b) Innovative: they create new services and products, new ways of dealing with problems, often by bringing together approaches that	Yes	Local	Not-for-profit

(continued)

	INNO-VATION	SOCIAL IMPACT	ORG. FORM
have traditionally been kept separate (c) Transformatory: they transform the institutions they are in charge of, taking moribund organizations and turning them into dynamic creative ones. Most importantly, they can transform the neighbourhoods and communities they serve.			
Mair and Marti (2006) ...a process of creating value by combining resources in new ways... intended primarily to explore and exploit opportunities to create social value by stimulating social change or meeting social needs...social entrepreneurship can take place equally well on a not-for-profit basis or on a for-profit basis.	Yes	Local and large scale	Either
Martin and Osberg (2007) Social entrepreneurship is the: (a) identification a stable yet unjust equilibrium which excludes, marginalizes or causes suffering to a group which lacks the means to transform the equilibrium, (b) identification of an opportunity and developing a new social value proposition to challenge the equilibrium, and (c) forging a new, stable equilibrium to alleviate the suffering of the targeted group through imitation and creation of a stable ecosystem around the new equilibrium to ensure a better future for the group and society.	Yes	Large scale systemic	Not mentioned

Schwab Foundation for Social Entrepreneurship[c] Social entrepreneurs drive social innovation and transformation in various fields including education, health, environment and enterprise development. They pursue poverty alleviation goals with entrepreneurial zeal, business methods and the courage to innovate and overcome traditional practices. A social entrepreneur, similar to a business entrepreneur, builds strong and sustainable organizations, which are either set up as not-for-profits or companies.	Yes	Large scale	Either
Skoll Foundation[d] The social entrepreneur aims for value in the form of transformational change that will benefit disadvantaged communities and ultimately society at large…social entrepreneurs act as the change agents for society, seizing opportunities others miss by improving systems, inventing new approaches and creating sustainable solutions to change society for the better.	Yes	Large scale	Not mentioned

Notes: [a]Ashoka: Innovators for the Public. 'Social entrepreneurship: Building the field'. Accessed October 1, 2019, https://www.ashoka.org/en-IN/focus/social-entrepreneurship

[b]Fuqua School of Business, Duke University. The Center for the Advancement of Social Entrepreneurship. 'What is social entrepreneurship'. Accessed October 1, 2019. https://centers.fuqua.duke.edu/case/about/what-is-social-entrepreneurship/

[c]Schwab Foundation for Social Entrepreneurship. 'What is social entrepreneurship?' What is Social Entrepreneur? Accessed October 22, 2019. https://widgets.weforum.org/social-entrepreneurs-2015/

[d]Skoll Foundation. 'What is social entrepreneur?' Accessed June 10, 2014. http://www.skollfoundation.org/aboutsocialentrepreneurship/whatis.asp

existing one (e.g., Einstein's Relativity Theory was not built on the tenets of Newtonian physics). Rather, the advancements in science are marked by 'revolutions', that is, by the emergence of an entirely new paradigm, which replaces the existing one.

The phase prior to the emergence of the new paradigm starts when new facts and findings start emerging, which cannot be adequately explained by the existing set of theoretical and conceptual tools. Initially they are explained away as 'exceptions' or a 'special case'. But as these exceptions become more widespread, they force and invite a more rigorous enquiry to make sense out of them. This 'pre-paradigmatic' period is conceptually rather messy: researchers look at the same phenomenon but interpret them in different ways, there are multiple and competing schools of thought highlighting different aspects of the phenomenon, and disagreements abound. Over time, some consensus emerges as one set of interpretations are able to explain the new facts more adequately, and a new paradigm becomes the dominant principle.

The conceptual foundations of social entrepreneurship appear to be passing through the same pre-paradigmatic stage. There are different understandings of its nature and impact, competing definitions about what it means (or should mean), differing interpretations of its intended impact, etc.; for example, is it just about solving social problems, or about transforming the society? Should it be a for-profit or not-for-profit entity—or either? Is social activism or volunteerism also a part of social entrepreneurship? Can the impact be only local or should it address the larger society?

To add to the complication, even the field of practice is evolving with discovery of new problems of significance to be addressed (e.g., impact of climate change on marginal farmers) and innovations of models and strategies by the practitioners to achieve their goals. This kind of churn makes a precise and all-encompassing definition neither possible nor perhaps desirable at this stage, since it would deprive the richness of the phenomenon.

At a broad level, as Mair (2010) observed, the definition and understanding of social entrepreneurship are 'caught in between seemingly conflicting demands for relevance and rigor.' For emerging new fields, Hirsch and Levin (1999, p. 200) described this as a struggle as between the 'umbrella advocates' (i.e., 'those who argue that broad perspectives are necessary to keep the field relevant and in touch with the larger, albeit messier, world... [otherwise, the] field risks becoming disconnected and irrelevant.') and the 'validity police' (i.e., the 'more methodologically oriented researchers who call for narrower perspectives that conform to more rigorous standards of validity and reliability.').

For any field to develop, both the 'umbrella advocates' and the 'validity police' are equally important. However, as a field which is evolving and still being discovered, it would be premature to narrow the field down to a definition. It would enrich one's understanding more if one takes an 'umbrella' stance, and develop a broad-based understanding of the phenomenon, that is, what all constitutes social entrepreneurship, what do social entrepreneurs do to accomplish their mission, what are the different ways in which they address the social issues and make an impact, etc.

An 'Umbrella' Definition of Social Entrepreneurship

So what is the 'umbrella' perspective to define social entrepreneurship?

Across the diverse approaches and literature discussed earlier, at least three common points characterize the understanding of the phenomenon. These three common themes provide a working definition of social entrepreneurship, and which we will be using to explore the field in this book:

1. **Social mission:** The primary motive to solve an existing social problem is what distinguishes the social entrepreneurs from the commercial entrepreneurs, and even from the socially responsible businesses (Dees, 1998). The social entrepreneurs start their initiatives to address an existing social problem or problems.

2. **Innovative and sustainable solutions:** Social entrepreneurs seem to operate from the premise that the social problems exist because the existing solutions are not efficient and long-lasting enough to eradicate them. They approach the problems differently, interpret them in newer ways and devise solutions which are more insightful and effective.

3. **Entrepreneurial strategies:** Finally, as the term suggests, social entrepreneurs are first and foremost entrepreneurs, albeit of a special kind; they use entrepreneurial strategies to develop and implement solutions to social problems. According to Bill Drayton, the founder of Ashoka: Innovators for the Public:

> Entrepreneurial quality—is by far the toughest (criterion for a social entrepreneur). For every one thousand people who are creative and altruistic and energetic, there's probably only one who fits this criterion, or maybe even less than that. By this criterion...we do not mean someone who can get things done. There are millions of people who can get things done. (Bornstein 2004, p. 121)

In the discussions on social entrepreneurship, however, this entrepreneurial quality is often either ignored, or is considered in a very narrow and misleading sense (e.g., someone who starts a small business). Any attempt to understand social entrepreneurship needs to start by appreciating what entrepreneurship means, how the entrepreneurial mindset shapes the thoughts and actions of the person, how do entrepreneurs approach and solve a problem, etc. As Dees (1998) observed:

> What does 'social entrepreneurship' really mean? What does it take to be a social entrepreneur? To answer these questions, we should start by looking into the roots of the term 'entrepreneur'. (p. 1)

In Chapters 2 and 3, we will discuss the meaning of entrepreneurship and what being entrepreneurial means.

THE 'ENTREPRENEUR' IN SOCIAL ENTREPRENEURSHIP

2

Entrepreneurship rests on a theory of economy and society. The theory sees change as normal and indeed as healthy. And it sees the major task in society…as doing something different rather than doing better what is already being done…(the theory) is a declaration of dissent.

—*Peter Drucker (1986)*

The Aura of Entrepreneurial Personality

In the popular imagination and media, entrepreneur is the new contemporary idol. The term evokes image of a modern-day business hero who takes bold risks, goes through trials and tribulations, overcome hurdles and finally 'arrives' by creating a large business empire. Kets de Vries (1977) described this narrative as

> …the gospel of enterprise and business leadership. Not surprisingly these themes of individual success and failures are highly popular; they catch the reader's imagination and are empathy-provoking since they awaken the rebellious spirit present in each of us. We see that Prometheus and Odysseus have been replaced by that folk hero, the entrepreneur. He has become the last lone ranger, a bold individualist fighting the odds of environment. (p. 34)

This aura of awe and wonder around the entrepreneurs also makes them seem to be qualitatively different than an ordinary person on the street. In fact, there are also many studies which do indicate that the successful entrepreneurs are endowed with specific personality characteristics. Studies on 'entrepreneurial personality', for instance, have found that compared to others (specifically, managers), entrepreneurs have higher need for achievement (Atkinson and Birch 1979; McClelland 1961), are more extraverted and conscientious (Brandstätter 2011; Rauch and Frese 2007), have internal locus of control (Borland 1974; Hansemark 2003; Mueller and Thomas 2000), a propensity for risk-taking (Brockhaus 1982; Kilby 1971; McClelland 1961; Palmer 1971), high tolerance of ambiguity (Begley and Boyd 1986; Sexton and Bowman 1984) and so on.

However, while such studies give us insights into entrepreneurial personality, they provide only a limited and incomplete understanding of entrepreneurship phenomenon for two reasons. First, in selecting their sample subjects, most of these studies have used a colloquial (even though widely prevalent) definition of an entrepreneur, that is, any person who starts and owns a business is an entrepreneur. This is also not surprising, since this is a popular understanding of entrepreneurship which is used not just in media but also in government policies and academic programmes on entrepreneurship. However, such a broad definition blurs the conceptual distinction between a person who sets up any business to offer products or services (e.g., a street vendor, a shop merchant and an industrialist putting up a plant) which are already available in the market, and a person who innovates a new product, service or business model which transforms how the market operates. While it is true that most entrepreneurs (though not all, as we will see later) start a business, all small business owners are not necessarily entrepreneurs. As Drucker (1986) observed:

...all new small business have many factors in common. But to be entrepreneurial, an enterprise has to have special characteristics over and above being new and small. Indeed, entrepreneurs are a minority among new businesses. They create something new, something different; they change or transmute values. (p. 36)

Second, trying to understand entrepreneurship only through the personality lenses has another limitation: the same personality characteristics which describe that the entrepreneur also predispose others to different professions. For instance, Need for Achievement has also been found to be related to success in competitive sports (Weinberg and Gould 1999, 25–46); similarly, high risk-taking behaviour is also seen among gamblers and stockbrokers. Therefore, to understand the field of entrepreneurship, it is important to not only focus on the personality (the traits, motivations, styles, etc.) but also on the actions which make people entrepreneurs. A comprehensive understanding of entrepreneurship must incorporate 'the study of sources of opportunities; the processes of discovery, evaluation, and exploitation of opportunities and the set of individuals who discover, evaluate, and exploit them' (Shane and Venkataraman 2000, p. 218).

Entrepreneurship Decoded

Clearly, to understand entrepreneurship one needs to go beyond 'what entrepreneurs are' (the personality) to 'what entrepreneurs do' (their behaviour). The term 'entrepreneur' is credited to the 19th-century French businessman and economist Jean-Baptiste Say (Dees 1998). Say was impressed by the success of the English Industrial Revolution and wanted to bring it to France. He noticed that the transformations in England were driven by individuals who created new kind of economic activities by using the same resources which were available in the society. Often, for instance, these individuals would buy the raw material (e.g., farm produce), process them to create new products and resell these to create a new market. In doing so, they would innovate, change the nature of the market and take risks since they had to discover the undefined price for these new products. Say saw these people as change agents and called them entrepreneurs—individuals who take up a project and create an enterprise.

It was, however, Joseph Schumpeter who, in early 20th century, elaborated Say's idea of entrepreneurship and brought it into the mainstream theory of economic development. Economic development, according to Schumpeter, was not a smooth linear process of change but was punctuated by disruptions which changed the very structure of economy. In fact, he contended that the causes of these changes were triggered by factors outside the economy:

> ...economic development is not a phenomenon to be explained economically, but that the economy...is dragged along by the changes in the surrounding world, that the causes and hence the explanation of the development must be sought outside the group of facts which are described by economic theory. (Schumpeter 1934)

He viewed these discontinuities, which bring structural changes in the economy and society, as the core of economic development. Such qualitative changes happen due to entrepreneurial innovations (or 'new combinations' as he described them) which destroy and replace the existing products, services and business models. For instance, the advent of locomotives and railways was not just an 'improved' means of transport over the horse carriages; they made the horse carriages obsolete and replaced them. Similarly, in recent times, computers with word-processing software made the type-writers redundant, or the innovations in electronic communication (e.g., initially telex and fax, and then emails) almost wiped out the traditional postal letters as a means of communication. Schumpeter called these disruptive transformations in the economy the 'perennial gale of creative destruction', which are brought about by the entrepreneurs:

> The function of entrepreneurs is to reform or revolutionize the pattern of production by exploiting an invention, or more

generally, an untried technological possibility for producing a new commodity or producing an old one in a new way, by opening up a new source of supply of material or a new outlet for products, by reorganizing an industry and so on. ...To undertake such new things is difficult and constitutes a distinct economic function, first because they lie outside of the routine tasks which everybody understand, and secondly, because the environment resists in many ways. (Schumpeter 1942, 132)

According to Schumpeter, these acts of entrepreneurial innovation mostly do not come from the existing players but from individuals and firms which are 'outsiders' to the existing industry structure ('it is not the owner of stage-coaches who builds railways'). They are the acts of individuals who do not fit into the mould of the Economic Man, and are not the result of rational decision-making; rather, the process of innovation is characterized by uncertainty, imagination and personal initiatives:

Schumpeter was the first economist to develop an integrated theory of innovation and entrepreneurship. His influence in the field of entrepreneurship extended not only to the other academic theorists, but also beyond the academic domain to policy making (Giersch 1984; Hosper 2005).

Themes and Functions of Entrepreneurship

Later theorists in the field of entrepreneurship added other nuances to the understanding of the entrepreneurship phenomenon. For instance, Drucker (1986) elaborated on the role of innovations in entrepreneurship. He contended that opportunities for entrepreneurial innovations arise when there are unexpected and qualitative changes in the environment. Entrepreneurs identify and seize these opportunities through a 'purposeful and organized search for changes.' Similarly, Venkataraman (1997) and Shane and Venkataraman (2000) highlighted the need to focus on how entrepreneurs discover, evaluate and exploit the opportunities to create future goods and services. Stevenson (1983) pointed out 'resourcefulness', that is, the ability of the individual to mobilize resources, as a critical dimension of entrepreneurship. In fact, in this writing, he defined entrepreneurship as 'a process by which individuals—either on their own or inside organizations—*pursue opportunities without regard to the resources they currently control* (Stevenson and Jarillo 1990, 23, italics added).'

Across such academic contributions and studies of the field of entrepreneurship, three themes emerge as common:

1. **Entrepreneurs create social and economic value by bringing transformative changes in the economy and society**

   Successful entrepreneurs, as we discussed above, innovate new products or services, create new industries and discover/create new markets. The implication of entrepreneurial success, however, is not limited only to the entrepreneur. It also spills over and creates other ripples in the society. A successful model of a venture attracts others to copy or improve upon it. In fact, sometimes even if the entrepreneur fails, the possibilities of his innovation attract other similar individuals.

   The story of the growth of American automobile industry provides an illustration of this process of transformation:

   The modern-day gasoline automobile was originally designed and perfected in the 19th century in France and Germany by people such as Nicolaus Otto, Gottlieb Daimler and Carl Benz. However, the first American automobile was designed by two bicycle mechanics, J. Frank and Charles E. Duryea, who got the inspiration to design a vehicle when they saw a gasoline engine displayed in a fair in 1886. By 1891 they had designed a single-cylinder, four-horsepower vehicle. In 1896, their company, The Duryea Motor Wagon Company, constructed 13 identical automobiles, making them the first American company that moved from making a single car to making multiple copies for sale. While the company failed, by 1899, there were 30 American manufacturers who had produced 2,500 motor vehicles. In the next decade, close to 500 new automobile manufacturing firms were launched. In fact, during the first two decades of the 20th century about 2,000 automobile companies were launched, though very few survived (by 1920 the number of firms had decreased to about 100 and by 1929 to 44, out of which three—Ford, General Motors and Chrysler—accounted for about 80 per cent of industry's output).

In those early years, automobiles were still seen as a rich man's means of transport. But one young entrepreneur, Henry Ford, who had started **Ford Motor Company** in 1903, saw an opportunity for a mass market for cars. People living in the American countryside had limited mobility, and therefore limited opportunities to buy and sell their produce; they relied on either horse-carriages, which had a reach of 15–20 miles, or trains for long route travel which were cumbersome. To address this need, Ford launched the legendary Model-T in 1908 with the aim to make cars affordable to middle-class Americans. Even though at that time Model-T was priced equivalent to the annual salary of a worker, it was still one-fifth the cost of the existing automobiles, was easy to drive and maintain by the owner and was far more fuel efficient. Ford also innovated the production technology to create world's first assembly line, which brought down the costs and improved the efficiency. The Model-T became a popular car with increasing demand. By 1914, Ford was producing half a million Model-Ts per year, which was more than the rest of the US auto industry combined; by 1927, Ford had sold more than 15 million cars.

Ford's impact on industry and society was widespread. For instance, to compete, rival General Motors also introduced a stripped-down low-cost version of its Chevrolet model, as did many other automobile manufacturers. The proliferation of automobiles also created new businesses such as gasoline stations, motel, car-repair services and so on. Over time, assembly-line technology was not only adopted by other car manufacturers, but also became the generic prototype for all kinds of mass manufacturing. Greater demand for the cars also stimulated the instalment buying and the advent of consumer credit which spread to other consumer items as well. Owning the car also freed people from being tied to locations, such as being near the place of employment, train stations or urban centres. The increased mobility allowed people to travel as and when they would like and this new lifestyle spurred the growth of suburban living, motels, drive-ins, convenience stores, etc.

While all entrepreneurial innovation may not have the spectacular impact like the Ford's Model-T, by its very nature, any entrepreneurial venture changes the existing patterns in the segment it serves. For instance, in India in the 1950s, when T. T. Narasimhan and H. D. Vasudeva launched their respective brands of pressure cookers, Prestige and Hawkins, they were targeting to fulfil the need for reduced cooking fuel cost to the family. However, the reduction in cooking time and ease in cooking also had an impact on the lifestyle of the housewives, working women and bachelors by freeing them up for other pursuits.

It is important to note that wealth creation through entrepreneurship is much more than just the financial gains for the entrepreneur (e.g., higher profits, increased income, material possessions and property). Entrepreneurship impacts the society in diverse ways, for example, by increasing employment, enhancing standards of living, improving efficiency and productivity of people and creating efficient market linkages. In fact, Schumpeter clearly differentiated 'entrepreneurial profits' which accrue to the entrepreneur from the wealth which they create for the society. In his views,

> ...entrepreneurship would redirect and allow future income streams to flow to individuals through their work efforts. Also, incomes would flow to the general public as more materials, more efficiency and more employment became available. The resulting wealth would be spread to the whole society. (McDaniel 2011, 23)

Just like the commercial entrepreneurs, the social entrepreneurs too cause changes in the social dynamics by opening up new options for society to function. Even when their immediate impact is local or regional, they create a replicable prototype to cause a larger transformation. For instance, the major impact of Professor Muhammad Yunus was not that he established the Grameen Bank for the poor. In fact, Accion had started micro-lending in Latin America during the late 1960s, and SEWA Bank in India has been providing microloans to poor since 1974–1976 years prior to Grameen Bank. His major contribution, rather, was that he created a prototype of microcredit which was easy to replicate, and through the Grameen Bank Replicator Program (GBRP) provided financial and technical assistance to organizations in more than 40 countries to replicate the Grameen Model. In addition, through advocacy he was also able to persuade multilateral organizations (e.g., World Bank and Asian Development Bank) to provide assistance to countries and organizations to promote microcredit. These efforts led to the acceptance of microcredit as a legitimate financial sector, when United Nations declared 1996 as the 'Year of Micro-Credit' (Hulme, 2008).

Given the nature of problems the social entrepreneurs aim to solve, often large-scale social changes also require changes in policy and regulations. In fact, many policy changes in India and elsewhere have happened due to the efforts of individuals who were aiming to address a social issue (we will discuss such 'social transformers' in detail in Chapter 7). For instance, in the 1970s, Gloria de Souza, a schoolteacher in Mumbai, was troubled by the passive rote learning through which education was imparted. Realizing that this was raising a generation of passive learners rather than active problem solvers, she devised her own experiential methodology which allowed the children to learn by asking questions and discovery. She knew that she would succeed only if her approach, which she called 'Environmental Studies' (EVS), was adopted by all the schools across the country. Since this was possible only if it was incorporated and recommended by the government, she worked towards its acceptance by demonstrating the impact of EVS, convinced the Mumbai municipal school board to start using it and gradually was able to get it integrated in the national syllabus (see Box 2.1 for details).

BOX 2.1   GLORIA DE SOUZA— TRANSFORMING THE EDUCATION SYSTEM

As an elementary school teacher in Mumbai, Gloria de Souza was always perturbed by what and how her pupils learn. The syllabus was filled with stories, rhymes and examples which did not reflect local realities, and so the children would only learn by rote without any understanding. In 1971, she attended a workshop on experiential and environmental learning, and realized that there were more exciting and engaging teaching methodologies which she could use.

She set aside the books and started taking children outside on excursions. She would show them local birds, plants, monuments, etc., and discuss questions about weather, environment, history, civics, etc. Initially, her colleagues and the school administration did not approve her method. However, the students' response was very positive and with much persistence over next few years, she was able to convince the school to adopt her method.

Her goal, however, was much larger. She had seen that her method had helped the children to learn to think, ask questions and solve problem, rather than merely to memorize and repeat. If she could make it part of the school curriculum across the country, she visualized, it would create an entire generation of active and creative learners. This, however, would have required her to work full time on the idea, and in 1982, she decided to quit her job to realize her vision.

Around that time, the newly founded *Ashoka: Innovators for the Public* was also looking for passionate social entrepreneurs to support, and she was selected as the first Ashoka Fellow. Using the fellowship money and her own savings, she founded an organization *Parisar Asha* (Hope for the Environment) and started research and documentation on her approach to teaching, which she called 'Environmental Studies (EVS)'.

In the following years, she was able to empirically demonstrate that her approach significantly improved students' performance. In 1985, she was able to persuade Mumbai municipal school board to run a pilot using EVS methodology in its 1,700 schools. The success of this programme got EVS featured in the National Policy of Education document in 1986, and the end of 1980s, NCERT (National Council for Education Research and Training) had integrated EVS in the national curriculum for grades I–III as an official methodology (Bornstein, 2004).

2. **Entrepreneurs create economic/social value or wealth by shifting resources from areas of low yield or productivity to areas of high yield or productivity**

In 1958, a young American, John Bissell, was sponsored by the Ford Foundation to help and advise the Central Cottage Industries Corporation of India about how to design and export the handwoven textiles made by the rural artisans. Bissell had earlier worked with Macy's, the American departmental store as a buyer, and had some knowledge of the handwoven fabrics. During the 2 years of his assignment, Bissell travelled across the small towns and small villages, interacting with the rural weavers, embroiderers and craftsmen. He was struck by two observations: first, despite their remarkable traditional skills and products, these artisans remained poor since they were cut off from the markets and second, their handwoven and handprinted fabrics would have a great demand in the American market.

After the assignment got over, Bissell decided to stay back in India to build an export business which would connect these rural producers with the markets abroad. Using the legacy of $20,000 left to him by his grandmother as the start-up capital, he registered his company, **Fabindia Inc.**, in Canton, CT, USA, and started his venture in two small rooms in his flat in Golf Links, New Delhi.

Initially, Bissell focused on home furnishings and tied up with local carpet manufacturers and foreign home furnishing sellers. In the early 1970s, a line of clothing (handmade kurtas and kaftans) was introduced. Khadi kurtas were introduced in 1977. During the 1970s also, due to new rules restricting foreign equity to 40 per cent, Fabindia restructured its equity and became an Indian company. It also opened its first showroom in India in New Delhi. Over the years, Fabindia continued to grow and created a niche for itself as a brand which was identified with good quality, ethically made, handwoven products.

After the death of John Bissell in 1996, the mantle passed on to his son, William Bissell, who steered the company to diversify into a new line of products made by rural producers (e.g., garments, accessories, furniture, home décor, personal products and organic products), and to become a chain of retail outlets. By 2015, Fabindia had become a global brand with a turnover of more than ₹11 billion. It was providing sustained livelihoods to about 55,000 rural artisans by selling their products through its 220 retail stores across more than 80 Indian cities and eight overseas stores. More importantly, Fabindia had created and demonstrated a sustainable business model of leveraging the skills of rural producers, which became the benchmark for many similar enterprises to emulate and customize later on (Ramachandran et al. 2012; Sethi 2010; Wee 2015).

Like John Bissell, entrepreneurs identify unused or underused societal resources and put them to more productive purposes. This 'shifting of resources' can be as large as in the case of Fabindia, or as small as an entrepreneur who uses fly ash to make and sell bricks. In either case, in doing so, they create or unlock the value/wealth for the society and economy.

This larger socio-economic role of entrepreneurship is significant since in any society, many resources remain unutilized or underutilized due to systemic inefficiencies. Consider some examples:

- Farmers are unable to realize the full value of their produce because they are not directly connected to the markets. Correspondingly, due to low income, they are unable to invest in technologies which can improve their productivity.
- Most self-employed urban artisans and labour (e.g., carpenter, mason and plumber) spend a large part of their working day idle since they do not know where their services are required.

- In many large cities, people spend a large amount of time unproductively while commuting for work.
- A significant proportion of youth in India are college dropouts, unemployed and lack relevant skills for gainful employment.
- Many educated housewives and senior citizens are unable to find opportunities where they can use their education and expertise.

In all such instances, the natural or human capital or resource available in the society is blocked from accessing platforms and opportunities where it can be used productively. This happens due to the failure or inadequacies of the existing structural arrangements in the society, such as the market barriers, government policies, infrastructural gaps, societal values and norms, etc. Until it gets utilized this resource is considered to be a waste. By bringing about changes in the social and economic structures, entrepreneurs free up this waste to be used as a resource (Drucker 1986).

For instance, it is estimated that on average, urban Indian households produce about 500 g of organic waste as a by-product of cooking. It is thrown away as waste and ends up in landfills causing pollution, even though it can be converted into compost. To tackle this problem, Kiran Bir Kasturi set up **Daily Dump** to promote recycling of this waste into compost by the households themselves in 2006. A designer by profession, she redesigned the waste bins used in the households into aesthetically appealing terracotta pots, known as 'Khambas', which would fit into small apartments. To match the size of the family and the volume of kitchen waste, these pots came in different sizes. She also designed large composters for apartment complexes for community composting. Easy to maintain and with no foul smell, these pots convert the organic waste into compost over 2 months.

Starting with a modest investment of ₹200,000, Daily Dump broke even within 3 years, and has been doubling the turnover every year. Its products help save almost 33 tonnes of organic waste every day, and convert it into compost. More importantly, Kiran also kept the design 'open' and encouraged others to copy, improve and replicate the product, which catalysed a network of more than 70 urban compost entrepreneurs across 17 cities.

3. **Entrepreneurs bring about changes by identifying gaps or unmet needs in the society/markets, and then innovating new products/services to address these needs**

   As discussed earlier, opportunity identification and innovation are the key components of entrepreneurial behaviour. Successful innovations fulfil the needs of a segment which were either not being met or were addressed in an inefficient manner. According to Drucker (1986):

   > Innovation is the specific tool for entrepreneurs, the means by which they exploit change as an opportunity for a different business or a different service (p. 33).... Successful entrepreneurs...are not content simply to improve on what already exists, or to modify it. They try to create new and different values and new and different satisfactions, to convert a 'material' into a 'resource', or to combine existing resources in a new and more productive configuration. (p. 49)

   Similarly, Sahlman and Stevenson (1991) observed:

   > ...entrepreneurship is a way of managing that involves pursuing opportunity without regard to the resources currently controlled. Entrepreneurs identify opportunities, assemble required resources, implement a practical action plan, and harvest the reward in a timely, flexible way. (p. 1)

THE 'ENTREPRENEUR' IN SOCIAL ENTREPRENEURSHIP

Innovations, in fact, are the distinguishing feature of entrepreneurial activity. Successful entrepreneurs are able to innovate new solutions, because they are more conscious and persistent in looking for opportunities for innovations in their environment. While the gaps and needs of a user segment are often visible to many people, the entrepreneurs differ in that they are able to perceive an opportunity in these gaps, find innovative solutions to address those needs, build a sustainable model and mobilize resources to implement those solutions. Drucker (1986) contended that entrepreneurs are sensitive to changes which are occurring within a sector (e.g., an unexpected success or failure, incongruities between expected and actual outcomes, new process innovations and changes in the industry or market structure) and in the society (e.g., demographic changes and new discoveries in science and technology). For them, innovation is often a focused activity which '…consists in purposeful and organized search for changes, and in systematic analysis of the opportunities such changes might offer for economic and social innovations' (Drucker 1986, p. 49).

For instance, it is a well-known fact that a significant proportion of population in India does not have access to clean drinking water. This lack of safe water results in a variety of health-related diseases such as viral hepatitis, typhoid, cholera and dysentery. Seeing this as an opportunity, and to address this problem, Sudesh Menon founded **Waterlife Pvt. Ltd** in 2008, which offers a range of cost-effective water treatment technologies for a combination of water contamination issues. Waterlife installs community water systems that can serve populations from 2,000 to 25,000 at a price of ₹4–7 for 20 litres. It partners with local governments, NGOs, Panchayats, SHG, commercial institutions and local entrepreneurs/ franchisees by selling the capital equipment, and undertaking long-term operation and maintenance contracts for each system. By 2017, Waterlife had installed about 45,000 water systems in 15 states in India.

It is important to note that often the meaning of 'innovations' is limited to the innovations of new products or services. Entrepreneurial ventures, however, can cover a wide array of innovations which contribute to the success of the enterprise. Entrepreneurs are often not the inventors; rather mostly they use the existing inventions to leverage new opportunities to create wealth. Schumpeter (1934) had identified five different kinds of innovations, one or more of which can characterize an entrepreneurial venture:

a. A new product or service with which the user is not yet familiar: New products or services cater to latent needs of the users, and results in better utilization of societal resources. For instance, the household composters of Daily Dump (described earlier) leveraged on the gap in disposal of household organic waste, thus creating a resource out of what was considered a waste earlier. Similarly, Biplab Ketan Paul, the co-founder and director of Ahmedabad-based Naireeta Services, observed that in many regions due to erratic weather (long dry-spells followed by unseasonal heavy rains), the farmers suffer from the double whammy of parched fields or waterlogging. To address this problem, he innovated a water harvesting technique, **Bhungroo** (which means 'straw' in Gujarati), which injects and stores the excess rainwater underground. This water can then be pumped and used for irrigation during dry seasons. Over the years, Naireeta Services has developed 17 variants of Bhungroo for different agro-climatic zones, and offers them to farmers through local partners, NGOs, cooperatives, CSR wings of the companies, etc. (Singh 2016; Ubhaykar 2014).

b. A new method of production: Innovations in production methods improve efficiency, bring down the costs and make the product affordable to a larger segment of the population. As we saw earlier, Henry Ford was not the inventor of the automobile; rather, he identified an opportunity in the American middle class, and innovated a production method which could produce automobiles for the mass market at affordable cost. Likewise, when Suhani Mohan and Kartik Mehta established **Saral Designs** to provide high-quality sanitary pads to women from low-income backgrounds, they wanted to keep the prices as low as ₹4–7. Besides working on the product design, they decentralized manufacturing so that the product could be made near the markets. These micro-manufacturing units, which could be put up at a cost of ₹1 million, not only brought down the costs by cutting down the intermediaries in the distribution chain, but also made it easy to scale up across different geographies (*Business Standard* 2016; Rao 2016).

c. A new market which was not serviced earlier or did not exist: In some ways all entrepreneurial ventures create or service a market segment which was not being addressed earlier. However, many ventures discover or create an entirely new market which did not exist earlier. For instance, as we saw Grameen Bank identified and created a model for poor and ultra-poor who were considered as un-bankable earlier. Similarly, in 1999, the husband–wife duo Shanti Raghavan and Dipesh Sutariya started **EnAble India** with a belief that people with disabilities (PwDs) have the potential to get employed through their own abilities (not through reservations), and live a life of economic independence and dignity. They developed training modules for 11 disabilities (e.g., visually or hearing impaired, deaf blind, cerebral palsy, autism, intellectual disability and mental illness) to provide skills for different kinds of jobs ranging from high-skilled (e.g., MIS executives, medical transcriptionist, HR executive and accountant) to low-skilled jobs (e.g., petrol pump attendant, restaurant waiter/waitress and driver). Over the years, the EnAble India has trained and placed more than 130,000 PwDs across more than 270 job roles in 35 functions in 27 sectors in around 600 companies (EnAble India 2017).

d. A new supply of raw material or input resources: New sources of input supply change the configuration of the market by including new resources and players. By identifying and leveraging new input material and sources, entrepreneurs create new societal wealth by increasing the value of these inputs and resources. For instance, when the entrepreneurial trio, Gyanesh Pandey, Manoj Sinha and Ratnesh Yadav, were exploring off-grid electricity alternatives for rural Bihar, they identified rice husk, a waste from rice mills, which had high caloric value and could be used as biomass to generate power. Using gasifier, they developed technology to run mini-power plants and founded the **Husk Power Systems** in 2007. Each power plant can provide continuous electricity at a nominal charge to about 300–500 households in a radius of 2–3 km. By 2017, Husk Power Systems was operating 75 such power plants in India and Tanzania (Bornstein 2011; Mallya 2018).

e. A new form of organization: Entrepreneurs mostly pursue new goals such as tapping unexplored markets, novel offerings, innovative methods for producing and delivering products or services, building fresh supply chains, etc. To achieve these objectives, they often need to innovate new organizational structures, processes and systems. For instance, when Tribhuvandas Patel and Dr Verghese Kurien created **Amul** to protect the milk farmers' interest, they also innovated the Amul Model, a member-based, member-owned organization (see Box 1.1). Similarly, when Isaac Singer invented the **Singer Sewing Machine**, he could not raise funds to expand the manufacturing facility and sell more machines. To overcome this problem, he sold licences to others to sell his machines in defined territories for an upfront payment, and used the funds to expand manufacturing. The licensees were also trained to demonstrate how to use the machines to the customers. In the process, he also created a new model of distribution which later came to be known as the 'Franchising' strategy (Bannister 2012).

So what is the significance of the concept of entrepreneurship to the understanding and practice of social entrepreneurship? How does the entrepreneurial behaviour of the social entrepreneurs shape their actions and ventures? From the preceding discussions, one can derive the following three broad conclusions:

1. **Entrepreneurship as a concept is sector agnostic**
   Though the term emerged from the study of economic activities, entrepreneurship is not confined to only economic and commercial pursuits. As we saw in the preceding discussion and examples, entrepreneurship is a cross-sectoral behaviour, which applies to a wide spectrum of human endeavours. In their analysis of literature on entrepreneurship and its significance to social entrepreneurship, Shockley and Frank (2011) observed that one of the 'fundamental insights of the classical conception of entrepreneurship is the ubiquity of entrepreneurship in all human endeavours.' (p. 14)

Therefore, the basic functions of entrepreneurs remain the same, irrespective of whether their aim is to exploit a commercial opportunity or to solve a social problem. In fact, in his later writings, Schumpeter even wrote about 'political entrepreneurs' who cause changes in the social institutions. Similarly, Drucker (1986) observed that entrepreneurship applies to 'all activities of human beings':

> ...there is little difference between entrepreneurship whatever the sphere. The entrepreneur in education and the entrepreneur in healthcare...do very much the same things, use the same tools, and encounter very much the same problems as the entrepreneur in a business or a labour union. (p. 42)

2. **Opportunity identification is a key determinant of entrepreneurial behaviour**

Entrepreneurship, as we discussed, is rooted in the opportunities which the entrepreneurs identify in the failures of the market or government to service a segment/community. However, entrepreneurs differ in the opportunities they perceive in the similar market failures. For instance, depending on their orientation and intent, the problem of lack of affordable quality education in rural government schools can be seen by different entrepreneurs differently, for example, as an opportunity to open private schools, to train and build capacities of teachers in existing schools or to develop more engaging curriculum and teaching-learning material.

These differences in perception of the opportunities not only determine the mission and objectives of the entrepreneurs, but also their strategies to address them, the nature of resources they mobilize, the parameters of success against which they would assess their success, etc. (Austin et al. 2006). Social entrepreneurs perceive failures of markets and government to solve critical social problems as opportunities to develop entrepreneurial solutions.

3. **Entrepreneurship impacts the society/community or segment by creating new wealth or value**

In innovating new solutions to address the gaps and problems more efficiently, the entrepreneurs also change the existing social configurations which were in use: they reconfigure the value chains, bring in new stakeholders and players, create new markets, tap and utilize new resources and so on. If the new solutions are more efficient and impactful, they succeed in unlocking the value or socio-economic wealth which was un/underutilized till then in the community/segment served by the entrepreneur.

Though such wealth creation is common to all forms of entrepreneurship, the social entrepreneurs are distinct by their *conscious intent* to create public wealth. Since this is the core purpose of their efforts, they are more conscious of the value which they create for their served community, and focus their strategies, innovations, resource deployment, performance measures, etc. towards this goal.

ENTREPRENEURIAL THINKING: A METHOD TO THE MADNESS

3

> *The entrepreneur…bears no resemblance to that mythical creature of economic theory, the economic man. On the contrary, we are dealing with an individual often inconsistent and confused about his motives, desires and wishes, a person under a lot of stress who often upsets us by his seemingly 'irrational', impulsive activities.*
>
> —*Manfried Kets de Vries (1977)*

Effectual Reasoning: The Nature of Entrepreneurial 'Thinking'

What makes entrepreneurs different than other economic actors of the society such as a manager, a trader or a social worker? As we saw in the previous chapter, entrepreneurs identify and exploit new opportunities, devise innovative solutions to address problems of the community and market, and mobilize resources to create their ventures and so on. These definitions and descriptions, however, do not explain what makes it easier for them to do so as compared to others. For instance, how are entrepreneurs able to spot an opportunity which others in the same situation fail to notice, or what kind of thinking equips them to develop innovative solutions, manage risks or convert an idea into a sustainable venture. Is there an entrepreneurial method of approaching situations which is distinctive and unique to entrepreneurs?

Surprisingly, there is a dearth of research on how minds of entrepreneurs work, how they make or create their choices, or how they arrive at innovative solutions, etc. One of the few such isolated, but insightful, studies was conducted by Sarasvathy, a professor at University of Virginia, who studied the problem-solving process of 30 entrepreneurs (Sarasvathy 2001, 2008a). Her subjects were all successful entrepreneurs with businesses varying from US$200 million to US$6.5 billion in sectors varying from steel to teddy bears. The study asked them to solve the same 10 decision problems to build a business venture from exactly the same product idea, and share the rationale and steps of their reasoning as they took these decisions. While each came up with different kind of business ventures, their reasoning process showed remarkable similarity in the way they went about solving the problem and taking decisions. Sarasvathy called this 'effectual reasoning', which she differentiated from 'causal reasoning' which managers would typically use in problem-solving.

According to Sarasvathy, causal reasoning involves finding the optimal solution to achieve a predetermined goal with a given set of means. The focus is on arriving at a solution which is the most efficient, cheapest or fastest, etc. It is a useful way of approaching a problem when the situation is relatively predictable and the means and ends are more or less clearly defined (see Figure 3.1). Sarasvathy (2008a) likened causal reasoning to the act of solving a jigsaw problem. Solving a jigsaw puzzle assumes that the perfect picture already exists, and one only needs to find and put the right pieces together in the correct configuration. This is also the kind of linear and methodical rationality which is largely taught in the management education, and which is useful for a manager to address problems such as: Which market segment would give the best returns for a new product? Should one get the job done in-house or outsource it? How to deploy the budget across different projects? How to assign responsibilities to the team members for a project?

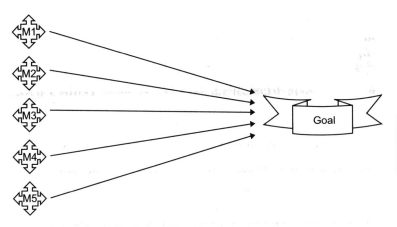

Figure 3.1 Managerial Thinking—Causal Reasoning

Source: Based on Saras Sarasvathy (2001, 2008a).

In fact, a causal reasoning approach is also quite prevalent in the academic and popular literature (as well as in teaching courses) on entrepreneurship. Such a view of entrepreneurial problem-solving presupposes that markets and opportunities exist, and the task of the entrepreneur is to discover and exploit them by efficiently bringing the required financial and technical resources.

In contrast, however, Sarasvathy found that an entrepreneur's reality is not very precisely defined; it is based on assumptions and imagination. At least when they start, entrepreneurs behave 'more like an accomplished quilter making a patchwork quilt' than solvers of jigsaw puzzles. A patchwork quilter, she noted, starts with a basket of random patches, which she/he matches and juxtaposes to create a pattern which looks meaningful to him/her; to enlarge the quilt, the expert quilter also works with other quilters who bring their own baskets of patches, and their own style and preferences. Likewise, entrepreneurs start with limited means and some vaguely defined vision of future(s) which they hope they will be able to create. In her studies, she found that more often than not, expert entrepreneurs started with an idea which they thought was worth pursuing and doable; they:

> ...tended to start small, without elaborate market analyses. The entrepreneurs then continually added on to their original projects, pushing them outward, reshaping them to work with new stakeholders, stretching themselves—just a bit at a time, to reach higher and thrust farther—until eventually they had transformed both their means and ends into unimagined new possibilities. (Sarasvathy 2008b, 7–8)

For instance, in his autobiographical book, Bill Gates (1996) described how **Microsoft** was founded based on a hunch in 1975. At that time, personal computers, as we know them now, were not even created; the only personal computer, Altair 8080, did not even have a screen, and the concept of stand-alone software was completely alien. Nevertheless, Gates and Paul Allen went ahead to form the company, because, as he wrote:

> We thought we saw what lay beyond that Intel 8080 chip and then acted on it. We asked, 'what if computing was nearly free?' We believed that there would be computers everywhere because computing power would be cheap.... We set up shop betting on cheap computer power and producing software when nobody was. (pp. 19–20)

Similarly, in her book, Ela Bhatt (2006) narrated how in the beginning the idea of forming a union of unorganized women workers was just a vague imprecise thought. In the late 1960s, two of Ahmedabad's large textile mills had closed down, rendering thousands of workers jobless. While the workers were busy agitating, the task of earning the money and feeding the family had fallen on women. To keep the household running, these women would take up jobs as manual labour, sell vegetables on streets, work on piece-rate jobs from homes, collect and sell recyclable material in the city, etc. As a legal staff of the Textile Labour Association, Ela Bhatt was asked to help them. She noted that these informal jobs:

> ...operated outside of any labour laws or regulations. They were jobs without definition. I learned for the first time what it meant to be self-employed...my legal training was of no use in their case.... I wanted to organize the women workers in a union so that they could enjoy the same benefits that organized labour received...*I am not sure (if I)...realized the scope or significance of such a trade union, and women's trade union in particular.* (pp. 9–10; Italics added)

This idea led her to start collectivizing these women to demand fair wages and justice, documenting their lives and problems, creating awareness about them by writing in papers, and so on. In 1972, the union, **Self Employed Women's Association (SEWA)** was registered and is now India's single largest trade union of unorganized sector women consisting of more than 100 trade-/craft-based cooperatives and with a membership of around 2 million.

According to Sarasvathy's studies, while many people also stumble upon such nebulous ideas and insights, entrepreneurs seem to have a talent for developing them into full-fledged ventures. She called the process through which they achieve this effectual reasoning or effectuation. Unlike causal reasoning, effectual reasoning does not start with precise objectives; rather, it starts with broad possibilities of yet-to-be-made future, and with the means and resources available to the entrepreneur. Entrepreneurs use these to make small experimental beginning, learn from the successes and failures of these steps, identify and co-opt partners, mobilize support and resources in the process, and tweak and modify their goals as they go along (see Figure 3.2). Consider, for instance, the story of Boond:

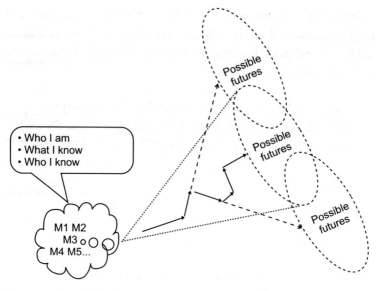

Figure 3.2 Entrepreneurial Thinking—Effectual Reasoning

Source: Based on Saras Sarasvathy (2001, 2008a).

Boond, a social enterprise which provides solar solutions to rural communities across 11 Indian states, was founded in 2010 by Rustam Sengupta. The idea of the venture started as a venture plan, Singlepoint, which Rustam had developed in 2008 for a B-plan competition while studying at INSEAD, France. Single-point was conceptualized as a platform to provide access to different services such as travel and transportation, healthcare, domestic services, etc. from a single point to urban customers in India. After working for a couple of years in UK, Rustam returned to India to work on implementing his plan.

During his travels across India, he realized that a larger opportunity was in rural areas, where many useful items which would improve the lives of villagers were not available. He renamed his organization Boond, and developed the 'Boond Development Kit', which contained three essential items—a solar light, water filter and a mosquito net. He reasoned that by bundling the three items together, he would be able to provide a complete package of products, and it would also reduce the cost of distribution. The Kit was sold through local level micro-entrepreneurs who earned a small commission on sales. If the villagers could not pay upfront, Boond would connect them with a financier so that they could take a loan to buy and then pay back in instalments.

Soon, however, he realized that there was a wide disparity in demand for the three items—often the villagers would buy the kit but would re-sell the items they did not want. He also discovered that the demand for solar lamps was high, and decided to focus only on solar products. Over a period of time, Boond kept discovering more opportunities and demands, and diversified into new regions and other solar products such as home lighting systems, solar heaters and water pumps, solar micro-grids, etc.

In different degrees, all entrepreneurs go through similar iterations of experimenting, learning, and discovering and refining their goals. This kind of reasoning, Sarasvathy (2001, 2) wrote, 'allows goals to emerge contingently over time from the varied imagination and diverse aspirations of the founders and the people they interact with.' Effectual reasoning is akin to what Mintzberg and Waters (1985) described as formulation of an 'emergent strategy'. They noted that entrepreneurial ventures are characterized by such a strategy formulation, and identified two of its key aspects:

> First,…vision provides only a general sense of direction. Within it, there is room for adaptation: the details of the vision can emerge *en route*. Secondly, because the leader's vision is personal, it can also be changed completely. To put this another way, since here the formulator is the implementer, step by step, that person can react quickly to feedback on past actions or to new opportunities or threats in the environment. He or she can thus reformulate vision…. (p. 261)

Causal versus Effectual Reasoning

The difference between the causal and effectual reasoning can be understood as two different ways of planning and undertaking a vacation trip. A person using the causal reasoning would consider the time and money available with him or her, go through the brochures of different destinations and select one which suits his or her budget and time, book the tickets and make reservations for the stay in advance, plan out the outings and activities for each day, and come back having enjoyed the vacation in the most efficient manner.

In contrast, the effectual reasoning may start with the person having a desire to visit a somewhat vaguely defined destination (e.g., the North-East regions of the country). She/he would consult a few brochures and websites, talk to a few people who have been there and then take a train or a flight to reach the nearest or most interesting place in the region. On the way, or on reaching the place, the person may consult a few local people, share his plans and revise them based on the new information. If she/he is lucky, some local person may even offer to be a guide or offer a homestay. This procedure would repeat as the person moves from one location to another, and in the end she/he would return having had experiences one had never anticipated, having tasted local exotic but lesser-known cuisines and having discovered and visited places one was not even aware of.

Both causal and effectual reasoning are relevant and useful in their own context, and require domain-specific skills (see Table 3.1 for the comparison). However, they differ significantly in that while the focus of causal reasoning is on efficiency, prediction and control, effectual reasoning relies on imagination, spontaneity and discovery. Causal reasoning is a valuable skill for managing a venture efficiently when the venture has matured and one is dealing with known and foreseeable situations. Once the venture grows and stabilizes, even the entrepreneur would need to hone this skill in order to manage and sustain it. However, *Effectuation* is a key process in opportunity identification and new venture creation

TABLE 3.1: Comparison of Causal and Effectual Reasoning

CAUSAL REASONING	EFFECTUAL REASONING
• Focuses on optimal utilization of resources to achieve predetermined goals and targets	• Focuses on leveraging available means and resources to shape and realize possible future goals.
• Relies on rationality, methods and control.	• Relies on imagination, initiatives and spontaneity.
• Aims at maximizing returns or chances of success	• Aims at containing losses and failures to affordable levels
• Analyses competitive landscape to take decisions	• Focuses on collaboration and partnerships to build the venture
• Aims to reduce contingencies through prediction and planning	• Leverages contingencies by converting them into opportunities
• Managerial Method: Useful for managing mature venture in known and defined environment, and needs efficiency of operations to grow and sustain	• Entrepreneurial Method: Useful for opportunity identification from ill-defined possibilities, and in new venture creation

when one is dealing with situations which are complex, unknown and unpredictable. As Chandler et al. (2011) observed in their validation study of the framework:

> In new venture creation, entrepreneurs following an effectuation approach might begin the new venture process with general aspirations to create a new venture, but as they make

decisions and observe the results of those decisions, they utilize this new information to change course. Because the future is unpredictable, entrepreneurs using an effectuation approach may try different approaches in the marketplace before settling on a business model. In addition, they are likely to put mechanisms into place that allow them to have some control over the outcome. (p. 277)

How Effectual Reasoning Works

Though it may seem counter-intuitive, innumerable entrepreneurial ventures started with 'small beginnings' without a clear long-term plan, but with an idea to which the entrepreneur was passionately committed. As we saw earlier, **Grameen** Bank started with a few personal loans to poor in a nearby village by Professor Yunus, or the beginnings of **SEWA** can be traced back to Ela Bhatt coming in contact with unorganized women workers. Similarly, many well-known commercial and social ventures had their inception in small acts and vaguely defined goals, for instance:

- Phil Knight, himself a running enthusiast, started **Nike** in early 1960s (initially called the Blue Ribbon Sports) by selling cheap imported athletic shoes out of the trunk of his car at the school track meets;
- **CRY (Child Rights and You)** started when 25-year-old Rippan Kapur and six of his friends created a small fund by pooling ₹50 each in 1979 to 'do something for the underprivileged Indian child';
- **Facebook** started as college prank website, Facemash, developed by Mark Zuckerberg in 2003, which allowed visitors to compare faces of two female students;
- **Goonj** (see Box 1.3) started when Anshu Gupta and his wife, Meenakshi, found that, just 3 years after their marriage, they had 67 surplus unutilized clothes which could be donated;

- **Sulabh Shauchalay** (see Box 1.1) started when Dr Bindeshwari Pathak received a grant of ₹500 from the municipal commissioner of Ara (Bihar) to construct six toilets and so on.

How did these nondescript beginnings grow into large impactful ventures? How did the entrepreneur give shape to what seemed like tentative, and sometimes even frivolous, first steps? How did they mobilize resources and created a market? What factors and circumstances contributed to their success?

To understand this dynamics of venture creation, and how effectual reasoning works in practice, let us look at one example in some detail—the founding of the e-commerce site, eBay:

> **eBay** was started by Pierre Omidyar, not as a full-fledged business idea, but as a hobby. Omidyar was working as software developer at General Magic, and was fascinated with the technical challenges in creating an online platform for person-to-person auctioning of collectible items. The first simple prototype of eBay, called AuctionWeb, was launched on his personal website on the Labour Day in September 1995. To test the portal, he listed a broken laser pointer which he had bought for $30, because 'it would be a good way to test out AuctionWeb, he figured, and it would cost him nothing' (Cohen 2003). He was surprised when after a week of being listed, the bidding started and this first item got sold for $14.85—since the buyer was collecting broken laser pointers! Soon word spread about the website, and people started registering a variety of items on the site. Instead of just collectibles, the users also started putting other items such as furniture, electronic items, cars, etc. for auction.
>
> AuctionWeb had started out as a free service, and Omidyar had no plans to make it into a business. However, soon as the volume of traffic grew, his internet provider forced him to move from a personal account to a business account, increasing his monthly charges from $30 to $250. To manage the

increased cost of hosting, Omidyar decided to charge a nominal fee of 10 cents for listing an item and a small percentage of final sale price. He was surprised when in the first month itself, he received $1,000 as fee. He changed the name of the site to eBay (his computer consulting firm was called Echo Bay Technologies), and used the fee to expand the site to include new features, such as a Feedback Forum on the website which allowed the users to rate the honesty and reliability of others.

When the revenue from the fee started exceeding his salary at General Magic, Omidyar left the job to devote himself fulltime to what was now becoming a business. In 1996, AuctionWeb hosted 250,000 auctions. The increased load of keeping a count of the checks coming in as user fee also resulted in hiring eBay's first employee, Chris Agarpao, and its first president, Jeffrey Skoll in 1996. The portfolio of AuctionWeb also expanded from customer-to-customer service to corporate-to-customer service when Omidyar signed a licensing deal to offer airline tickets online. In 1997, when the name of AuctionWeb was formally changed and incorporated as eBay, it was hosting 800,000 auctions every day.

Some years later, reflecting on his journey, Omidyar (2002) summed up his learning:

> So I guess what I'm trying to tell you is: Whatever future you're building.... Don't try to program everything.... Build a platform—prepare for the unexpected.... And you'll know you're successful when the platform you've built serves you in unexpected ways. That's certainly true of the lessons I've learned in the process of building eBay.

One can see that eBay, like many other entrepreneurial ventures, started and grew not from a well thought-out and detailed plan, but from a series of small actions and decisions taken by the entrepreneur. These actions and decisions were triggered by the successive opportunities and hurdles encountered by the initiative, and were based on the resources and constraints which the entrepreneur had at that time. In her studies too, Sarasvathy found that there was a certain design in the way the entrepreneur went about taking steps to build the venture. She identified five frequent patterns or principles which characterized these decisions by the entrepreneurs.

Principles of Effectual Reasoning/Effectuation

Despite seemingly random and arbitrary, effectual reasoning actually involves a set of decision-making principles. Sarasvathy's study identified certain recurring patterns of decision-making which the entrepreneurs used in dealing with uncertain situations. Based on her study, she identified five principles of effectual reasoning/effectuation.

1. **The bird-in-hand principle.** Entrepreneurs do not keep waiting for all the resources to be ready before launching their venture. They start with the means and resources they have, and leverage them to identify opportunities for new products and services, to create or enter new markets, to mobilize support and resources, etc.

   For instance, **Association for India's Development (AID)**, which supports grassroots organizations to promote sustainable and holistic development, was started in 1991 when Ravi Kuchimanchi, a physics graduate student at University of Maryland, mobilized his friends to make a small donation to support one school in any Indian village. Ravi had been attending many India-related meetings and rallies, but was frustrated that despite well-meaning discussions on issues like poverty, development, social justice, etc., they never led to any actionable agenda. Many years later he recounted (Kuchimanchi 2000):

   > I decided that I should have the strength to trust others, for the important thing is that almost everyone, the person

who discusses or the person who quietly wonders, has good intentions and is well-meaning.... On Independence day of 1991, I sent a mail 'Village Education Project'. If we contribute $10 a month each we could take a village in India where there was no school, and find someone who would be willing to teach there if we paid a small stipend. The challenge was to identify a village and a motivated teacher, make an appropriate syllabus and talk to the village children and inspire them to come to classes. Would anyone be interested?

Some of his friends responded with commitment to donate, helping in identifying such a village and garnering support of local community, keeping the accounts, etc. Soon the group started meeting regularly to discuss their plans. These discussions also refined and enlarged the scope of their work from only the school project and they

decided that it was a good idea to tackle all the problems, as they are all connected to each other, and over-all development of an individual or society has so much more meaning. Besides the challenge of addressing pressing problems requires us to work in all fields....

Soon more volunteers started joining the group; some who moved to other cities opened AID chapters there. Over time, AID has grown into a network of about 800 volunteers, with chapters across USA, India, UK and Australia, and supports close to 100 grassroots projects in India both financially as well as technical support.

Like Ravi Kuchimanchi, Sarasvathy (2008b) found that expert entrepreneurs start

...with a given set of means, rather than a predetermined goal or an opportunity to which they were strongly committed. That was the case even when they were provided with strong market research data supporting a clearly defined opportunity. In fact, starting with exactly the same 'opportunity,' the 27 expert entrepreneurs ended up building a variety of different ventures in 18 completely different industries! (p. 7)

Sarasvathy identified three categories of means which entrepreneurs have (in fact, everyone has these means but entrepreneurs seem to be more aware of them as resources to use and leverage):

a. **Who am I?** Compared to most others, entrepreneurs are much more aware about themselves. They have a realistic and clear understanding of their strengths and weaknesses, their goals and preferences, their traits and blind spots, the source of their motivation, etc. They know what they are good at doing, and what they cannot do; what excites them and what does not; what experiences made an impact on them, and what learning they derived from those which still remain with them; what is important and essential in their lives and what is not and so on.

b. **What do I know?** The second set of resources and means which the entrepreneurs consciously leverage is their expertise and experience. These do not only include the formal training and education which they may have received; they also consist of the skills and knowledge which they picked up or developed through their life experiences. In fact, often entrepreneurs leverage the skills which they acquired as a 'hobby' to start their ventures. An awareness of these resources not only helps them to leverage these, but also in identifying the knowledge and skill which they lack, and which they need to acquire either through their own efforts or through partnerships.

c. **Who do I know?** Lastly, entrepreneurs capitalize on their network or social capital. They make the most out of people they know (their family, friends, colleagues in job, old or current teachers and batchmates, etc.), whom they look as potential resources they can approach for help. In fact, many entrepreneurs do mobilize their initial seed capital from these connections. But more importantly, besides the financial help, they also use these contacts to bounce off and refine their ideas, reach out to other sources (e.g., experts in the field or a professional mentor), provide technical advice (e.g., how to register the firm), provide voluntary help (e.g., designing the logo or website for the business), etc.

Being aware and mindful of these three means they have is an important part of entrepreneurial approach; not only this awareness guides the budding entrepreneurs about what they can and should do, but also what they cannot and should not do (e.g., pursue unrealistic opportunities). The budding entrepreneurs leverage these assets to take the first nascent steps to build their ventures. These initial step-by-step forays also bring in new insights, and sometimes even open up new opportunities.

2. **The affordable loss principle.** This principle is a key element in how entrepreneurs manage risks. The causal reasoning approach relies on taking decisions which will maximize the returns or chances of success; effectual reasoning, in contrast, focuses on how much one can afford to lose at each step of building the venture, and how to minimize those losses. The typical thought process behind this principle works in the following ways:

• I will give myself 2 years to try to create a business out of this idea. If it does not work out, I can still go back to my job; all I will lose is some savings and 2 years.

- Instead of doing a full-fledged market research survey, I just gifted a few pieces of my products to people I knew. Some actually bought them; others also gave me suggestions for improvement and ideas about other possible buyers. I also got some leads for potential bulk buyers.
- In the beginning I did not invest in a production facility. Instead I tied up with a local industrial shed, and when I would get orders, they made my pieces on order.
- It made more sense to operate from my home or share an office space till we started making money. For formal meetings, we always invited our clients and investors to some up-market restaurant or café.
- I started my business by putting up a stall in our apartment building and inviting everyone to visit. I made some sale, and also got many references and contacts.

As these examples show, instead of relying on detailed plans whose success would depend on external factors (e.g., sanction of loan from the bank, market forces and a large order from a potential buyer), their actions rely on factors which are in their control. In this way, entrepreneurs also manage their risks by factoring in how much they can afford to lose in their plans. More importantly, these initial actions also provide them with new insights and contacts. In an interview (Mitra 2007), Harish Hande, the founder of **SELCO**, described how he started the solar lighting company:

> I used what little money I had left from my scholarship, something like 15,000 rupees (~$300), which was enough to buy one solar home lighting system. I bought the system, and then I went and sold it and installed it. Then I purchased additional systems, sold them and installed them as well. The focus in the initial period was not looking at where money was, but rather looking at what

the success level of the technology was and if people would accept it…. When you have no money, you tend to be more innovative.

Obviously, these 'affordable losses' would not be same for all entrepreneurs. They are very much dependent on the context of each entrepreneur's own unique personal situation, and the nature and stage of the venture. There are two important implications of this principle. First, entrepreneurs focus more on the execution, on 'doing things' than on a detailed and systematic planning; the plan emerges from their learning-by-doing. Second, instead of taking grand bold actions, entrepreneurs actually take many small steps, which, even if they fail, will cause no or minimum loss. Each step also opens up new insights and possibilities of potential markets and partners.

3. **The crazy quilt principle.** Even though it may sound counter-intuitive, successful entrepreneurs seem to focus more on forming collaborative relationships, than on beating the competition. Identifying and building relationships with potential partners, supporters and stakeholders are critical aspects for developing a venture. Scott (2015) noted that

> There's a stereotype of the entrepreneur as a lone wolf, single-mindedly pursuing his mission on the way to glory. But the most successful entrepreneurs understand that strong convictions aren't mutually exclusive to working with partners. For social entrepreneurs, partnerships are particularly important because most social issues don't exist in a vacuum, and therefore can't be solved without the cooperation of different stakeholders.

One obvious reason for this is that in the beginning, their ideas are at such a nascent stage that doing a competitive analysis of the sector does not make any sense. Even when they study the other players, the potential competitors in the field, it is more to learn from them and to pick up their best practices. They actively seek people and agencies with whom they can bounce off their ideas and who would help them to give shape to their as-yet nebulous plans and designs. According to Rosen (2015), 'entrepreneurs are not only good at sharing information and ideas, they are often eager for the opinions and reviews of others and include the best ideas of others into their own thinking.' In fact, Napoletano (2012) suggested that entrepreneurs should actively bounce off their ideas with a diverse set of people such as their target customers, their potential supporters and even other entrepreneurs, and act on their feedback.

The other reason is that building partnerships works alongside the Affordable Loss Principle. When entrepreneurs share their ideas with others and modify and refine them on the basis of the feedback, they also reduce the risk by finding out the lacunae in their ideas as well as by discovering newer perspectives which they may not have thought of earlier. Often many people they interact with also become their key stakeholders, and potential funders, customers and suppliers. These pre-commitments by others in terms of time, money and/or other kind of support also reduce the uncertainty in the early stages of the venture.

4. **The lemonade principle.** As is evident, this principle derives from the adage which is often attributed to Dale Carnegie, 'If life gives you lemons, make lemonade.' Successful entrepreneurs have a talent for converting adversities and contingencies into opportunities. This is especially so since unlike causal reasoning which tries to avoid uncertainties by meticulous planning, an entrepreneur lives in an open-ended and imprecise reality; in such a state, surprises and contingencies are not only more likely to occur, but are also more likely to be noticed. As

Sarasvathy observed that 'Great entrepreneurial firms are products of contingencies.'

For instance, Richard Bronson, the founder of **Virgin Atlantic** airlines, described how the airlines got founded due to an entirely accidental event. In a blog on the airline's website, he wrote (Branson 2015):

> ...the whole reason we got into the airline industry was based on an unplanned situation, which at the time was very unfortunate but turned into the opportunity of a lifetime. I was trying to get to the British Virgin Islands to holiday with my then girlfriend/now wife, Joan, when my flight was cancelled. Desperate to meet Joan, I chartered a plane, borrowed a blackboard and wrote Virgin Airlines on the top of the blackboard, $39 one way to BVI.... I rounded up all the passengers who had been bumped, and filled up my first plane. Annoyed by the experience, I later called Boeing to find out if they had any second-hand 747s for sale, and the rest, as they say, is history!

Similarly, Sunil Mittal, the founder of **Airtel**, one of India's largest telecom company, described how he entered into phone business in the 1980s (Mittal 2008). Till then, he had built a successful business of importing and selling diesel generators in India, but then,

> ...you could call it an accident, because the government banned the import of generators. One fine day, there was no business. All the business that I had developed was gone.... I went back into those areas looking for a new product. And one of the theories that I'd built around my entrepreneurship was to do things that have not been done before. Because if you are competing with the big boys in areas where they are strong, there's no chance for you to succeed. My quest to look for the next big

breakthrough product, which also didn't need too much capital, was met in Taiwan at a trade fair when I saw push-button telephones. I brought India's first telephone set replacing the rotary phone.... That became a huge success, and my romance with telecom started thereafter. So, it went onto cordless phones, answering machines, fax machines, and then India's first mobile phone.

This ability to see the proverbial silver lining in the dark clouds also helps explaining how entrepreneurs identify opportunities. It is also important to note that the opportunities identified by entrepreneurs are always visible to most other people as well; however, entrepreneurs seem to have a talent for deriving something more, an actionable meaning, from the same situations, incidents and information which others also encounter but ignore. Ray and Cardozo (1996) described this predisposition as 'entrepreneurial awareness' and defined it as, 'a propensity to notice and be sensitive to information about objects, incidents, and patterns of behavior in the environment, with special sensitivity to maker and user problems, unmet needs and interests, and novel combinations of resources' (p. 10).

Why are entrepreneurs able to recognize the opportunities in the same situations which others seem to miss out? Many studies (e.g., Kirzner 1997; Ronstadt 1988; Shane 2000) have attributed this ability to recognize opportunities to the 'prior knowledge' that the entrepreneur have. In his study, Shane (2000) found that this 'prior knowledge' consists of three specific dimensions which facilitate opportunity identification: prior knowledge about the existence of the markets, knowledge about the needs and problems of the potential customers, and prior knowledge of ways to serve markets. As we discussed earlier, prospective entrepreneurs' focus on learning by experimenting and doing, and on building partnerships help them to acquire this 'prior knowledge' to connect the dots and identify opportunities.

5. **The pilot-in-the-plane principle.** This principle summarizes the implications of the previous four principles: entrepreneurs, using effectual logic, operate from the stance that the future is not out there to be predicted and discovered; rather, it is not only unknown, but is also unknowable. However, they also believe that through their actions they can control and create it. Like the pilot flying through the turbulent and unpredictable weather, they focus on what they can do in their given situation and act on things which are in their control. Like Alan Kay, the computer scientist whose work was seminal to the growth of the computing industry, they believe that 'the best way to predict the future is to invent it.'

Consequently, entrepreneurs rarely rely on attempts at predicting future and distrust formal market research. In fact, there is also a reasonable amount of empirical evidence that formal market research and expert forecasts, despite their sophisticated methodology and analysis, often fail in predicting how markets will respond to new ideas and technologies, or in identifying new markets (Christensen 1997; Mintzberg 1994). Many studies (e.g., Goll and Rasheed 1997; Hart and Diamantopoulos 1993; Priem et al. 1995) have also shown that there is no relationship between using market information or rational decision making and the performance and growth of the firm.

So how do expert entrepreneurs negotiate the future? As we saw in the examples of the entrepreneurs in this section, they do so by focusing on factors which they can influence, and thus determine and shape the future. They undertake activities on which they have control, for example, they take small steps using the means and resources they have available with them, reduce their risks by betting on things they can afford to lose, share their ideas with others and co-opt them in their ventures, and respond to the unexpected by identifying opportunities in them. As Sarasvathy describes it, their actions are based on the premise, 'to the extent we can control the future, we do not need to predict it'.

Two Sides of the Same Coin

But does this mean that causal reasoning has no use for entrepreneurs at all? Actually, no. To be successful, entrepreneurs need both. Once the venture has matured, causal reasoning becomes essential for managing and sustaining it. Entrepreneurs need to use it for many routine operational decisions to keep the organization running efficiently.

However, effectual reasoning is an essential prerequisite for any entrepreneurial activity for establishing the venture; it contributes to key entrepreneurial activities such as opportunity identification, innovating solutions, managing risks, mobilizing support and resources, etc. In fact, Sarasvathy found that even in later stages of the venture (e.g., in taking decisions about scaling up, diversifying and attracting investments), successful entrepreneurs have a propensity of falling back on effectual reasoning for taking key decisions.

SOCIAL AND COMMERCIAL ENTREPRENEURSHIP $\qquad$ 4

The organizations set up by social entrepreneurs defy pigeonholing. They cannot be lumped easily into the non-profit or for-profit worlds that we cling to. Increasingly, social entrepreneurs are setting up their organizations as for-profit entities, though most are still constituted as not-for-profits. The point is that the legal form chosen for the entity is simply a strategic decision based on how best to achieve the mission.

—*Hartigan and Billimoria (2005, p. 19)*

The Dynamics of Wealth Creation

As we discussed in Chapter 2, wealth creation is the hallmark of any kind of entrepreneurship. Unlike the other economic actors such as businessmen or managers, who primarily maintain or transact the wealth, the entrepreneurs create wealth by innovating and leveraging new patterns of production, which result in new product and services, improved competitiveness, job creation and economic growth. This understanding of the entrepreneurship phenomenon, however, also raises a basic question: If both social and commercial entrepreneurs impact the society by creating new wealth, what makes them different from each other?

To understand this difference, we need to look at the nature of wealth and how it gets created.

In classical economics and in common parlance, the term 'wealth' refers to material possessions, money, property or anything which has an economic value. However, it is being increasingly realized that as an indicator of human well-being, only economic wealth is an inadequate measure. A society with high per capita income may still be torn by social strife, host unhealthy populace or suffer from pollution and environmental degradation. Even at an individual level, it is a well-known experience that a well-paying job is not necessarily the most satisfying or healthy job.

In the recent years, many global initiatives have aimed to develop a more comprehensive definition of wealth. For instance, in 2012 United Nations Conference on Sustainable Development (also known as Rio+20) launched the first Inclusive Wealth Index to measure the progress, well-being and long-term sustainability of nations. This index defined a country's wealth as the social value (not the monetary price/value) of all its capital assets, that is, human capital (e.g., education, health and employment), natural capital (e.g., forest resources, agricultural land, minerals and fisheries) and produced/manufactured capital (e.g., output, assets and investments). Similarly, many other global measures and protocols, for example, UN Global Compact, Global Reporting Initiative (or Triple Bottom Line reporting) and Equator Principles, highlight more diverse and extensive parameters to capture the wealth and progress of organizations (see Box 4.1 for some details).

These initiatives and measures differentiate between two lenses for understanding wealth: the conventional understanding of wealth in economic terms (income, profits, GDP, etc.) and a more diverse and encompassing definition which also includes the social and environmental well-being and growth. The key difference between the commercial and social entrepreneurs is the operational definition they use between these two notions of wealth, and correspondingly the nature of wealth they strive to create. This determines the differences not only in their mission and goals, but also in their strategic and operational choices, systems and processes of their ventures, and the impact they make. To appreciate what distinguishes social entrepreneurs from their commercial counterparts, we need to look at two dimensions of wealth creation, namely, the nature of wealth they aim to create or enhance and for whom do they aim to create this wealth.

BOX 4.1 GLOBAL INITIATIVES WHICH PROMOTE MORE INCLUSIVE AND SUSTAINABLE WEALTH CREATION BY BUSINESS ORGANIZATIONS

UN Global Compact: UN Global Compact was launched in 2000 by the United Nations to encourage sustainable and socially responsible business practices among businesses worldwide, and to link company's bottom-line with their social and environmental impact. To be a member of the network, the business organizations have to commit to upholding 10 principles which relate to human rights, labour rights, environment and anti-corruptions, incorporate them in their strategies, policies and procedures, and report their progress annually. By 2017, close to 10,000 businesses across about 160 countries had committed to these principles.

Global Reporting Initiative: Global Reporting Initiative (also known as Sustainability Reporting and Triple Bottom Line Reporting) is a standard of measuring and reporting organizational performance on financial as well non-financial parameters. It provides a framework for assessing the economic, social and environmental impacts of organization's day-to-day activities, setting goals on these parameters and devising strategies to achieve them. Launched in 2000, GRI is used by more than 12,000 business and non-governmental organizations worldwide and is a mandatory requirement for joining the UN Global Compact.

The Equator Principles: The Equator Principles for project financing were developed in 2007 for assessing the environmental and social risks in funding a project above $10 million. These 10 principles provide guidelines for evaluating and monitoring any infrastructure project on issues such as pollution, impact on human settlements and health, effects on local culture and biodiversity, governance of project (e.g., stakeholder engagement, grievance mechanisms, monitoring and reporting), etc., in addition to the financial feasibility of the project. By January 2018, more than 90 global financial institutions and banks across 37 countries, representing more than $8.3 trillion (more than 70% of international project finance funds) had adopted these principles.

The Nature of Intended Wealth

By the very definitions, the focus of commercial entrepreneurs is on creating economic or financial wealth, while the social entrepreneurs focus on enhancing the diverse components of societal wealth. Even if they operate in similar markets and offer similar product or service, this difference in the wealth they intend to create will determine the goals and strategies of their respective ventures. To understand this difference, let us consider how commercial entrepreneurs and social entrepreneurs will approach and build their ventures on the same opportunity: providing low-cost affordable healthcare to low-income segment.

While both commercial and social ventures may contribute to improvement in the health of the community, they will differ significantly in terms of the nature of their goals, operations and outcomes. Since the goal for the commercial entrepreneur is to generate financial wealth for self and the venture, the success of the enterprise will be measured in terms of profits, turnover, market share, etc. The social entrepreneur, on the other hand, will measure the success of the venture in terms of improvement in health parameters of the community, decrease in loss of working days due to ill-health, savings on healthcare expenditure, etc.

This distinction in their goals and measures of success is critical since it would also define the performance parameters of the venture and determine the choices the entrepreneurs would make or not make. The commercial entrepreneurs, for instance, will focus more on those ailments which give high margins for treatment, even though they may be less prevalent. They will also not offer service to the ultra-poor since they cannot pay for the treatment, even though they may need the healthcare more. In contrast, the social entrepreneurs will focus on the treatment of the ailments which are more prevalent (e.g., waterborne diseases), since they cause loss of working days and income for more people, even though they have low margins. They will also try to reach the ultra-poor segment by other means, such as raising donations, cross-subsidization, seeking funds from government schemes, etc.

Intended Beneficiaries of the Created Wealth

The second critical distinction between the commercial and social entrepreneurs is about the envisioned recipient(s) of the wealth created by them. The efforts of commercial entrepreneurs are directed towards creating and accumulating wealth for themselves or their enterprise. Correspondingly, their primary accountability is to themselves, their shareholders/investors and their enterprise. They focus on profit maximization to ensure the sustainability of their enterprise and increasing economic gains for themselves and their shareholders/investors. Since the focus is on maximizing their share, they also look at the markets as a competitive landscape in which they need to win against other players. The benefits derived by their customers and suppliers are incidental to their aim, and largely a means to their financial goals. In fact, if forced to make a choice between their financial goals and gains to their customers/suppliers, they are more likely to choose the former at the expense of the latter.

In contrast, the mission of the social entrepreneurs is to serve their community/society by finding solutions to their problems. Not only do they focus on creating more inclusive and diverse wealth, but they also try to ensure that their served community is the prime beneficiary of that wealth. Since their purpose is to enhance the benefits for the community/society, they see other participants and agencies in the space as potential partners and try to forge collaborative relationships with them. For them, besides the sustainability of their venture, the sustainability of the impact on the community is an equally important and larger goal. To achieve this, they focus on strengthening and empowering the community by building capacities, sharing resources and forming partnerships. To ensure the financial sustainability of their venture, they too (like the commercial entrepreneurs) try to generate surplus. However, their aim is not profit maximization, but to remain profitable so that they remain self-sufficient and autonomous. Additional surplus is mostly reinvested in their programmes to increase the impact on the community. For instance, in response to allegations of low profitability of Grameen Bank, Professor Yunus had stated:

> Grameen's central focus is to help poor borrower move out of poverty, not making money. Making profit is always recognised as a necessary condition of success to show that we are covering costs. Volume of profit is not important in Grameen in money-making sense, but important as an indicator of efficiency. We would like to make more profit so that we can reduce interest rate—and pass on the benefits to the borrowers. (Yunus 2001/2010)

There are two significant implications of the preceding discussion for understanding social entrepreneurship. First, the nature and purpose of wealth-creation is the key differentiator between social and commercial entrepreneurs. As discussed above, the primary focus of commercial entrepreneurs is to generate financial wealth for themselves and their shareholders. They measure their success in terms of profits, turnover, market share, etc., and make efforts to increase these by competing against other market players.

In contrast, the efforts of social entrepreneurs focus on enhancing not just financial but also the social and environmental wealth. To achieve this aim, they devise strategies and 'business' models to ensure the dissemination of this wealth to the community/society they serve. Correspondingly, they tend to build partnerships with agencies and people with similar mission and measure their success in terms of their impact on the society (see Table 4.1 for summary).

TABLE 4.1: Difference between Commercial and Social Entrepreneurs

COMMERCIAL ENTREPRENEURS	SOCIAL ENTREPRENEURS
Driven by motive to generate financial wealth.	Driven by mission to create inclusive wealth (financial, social and environmental).
Benefits of wealth are accrued by the entrepreneur, shareholders and investors.	The purpose of wealth creation is to benefit the community/society.
Measure success of enterprise in terms of profits, turnover, market-share, etc.	Measure success of the venture in terms of the impact it has on the lives of community.
Focus on 'Profit-Maximization' to increase personal wealth.	Focus on being 'Profitable' (or revenue-surplus), to maintain autonomy and self-sufficiency of the venture.
Strive to overcome competition from other players to maximize their share of the market.	Strive to build partnerships with other participants in the space to increase benefits to the community.

Second, the uniqueness of social entrepreneurship lies in its social mission and value proposition. In addressing the critical social problems, social entrepreneurs aim to change the social dynamics and relationships and thus create new value for the society/community. As Martin and Osberg (2007) observed:

> ...[T]he social entrepreneur aims for value in the form of large-scale, transformational benefit that accrues either to a significant segment of society or to society at large. Unlike the entrepreneurial value proposition that assumes a market that can pay for the innovation, and may even provide substantial upside for investors, the social entrepreneur's value proposition targets an underserved, neglected, or highly disadvantaged population that lacks the financial means or political clout to achieve the transformative benefit on its own.... Ventures created by social entrepreneurs can certainly generate income, and they can be organized as either not-for-profits or for-profits. What distinguishes social entrepreneurship is the primacy of social benefit. (p. 35)

This 'primacy of social benefit' is an important distinction, especially since debates about defining social entrepreneurs often centre on the organizational models of their ventures.

Organizational Models for Social Entrepreneurial Ventures

It is important to appreciate that the dichotomy of the mission-driven social ventures and the profit-maximizing commercial enterprises (as described above) actually represent two idealized poles of a continuum. In reality, they describe the range and diversity of entrepreneurial ventures with varying degrees or mix of focus on social mission and financial profits. Appreciating this continuum of organizational forms is important for two reasons. First, because the discussions on social entrepreneurship on the basis of whether the venture is grant-based or for-profits, its revenue strategies and legal entity ignore the fact that organizational models are merely a means to achieve the venture's mission. And second, because they describe the range of possible organizational forms/models available to the social entrepreneur in planning and organizing his/her venture.

The following paragraphs describe some broad organizational models across this continuum (see also Box 4.2 for summary):

BOX 4.2 RANGE OF ENTREPRENEURIAL FORMS ACROSS THE SOCIAL-COMMERCIAL SPECTRUM

VENTURE MODELS	DESCRIPTION
Mission-driven social ventures	Mission driven not-for-profits. Mostly NGOs with primary focus on their programmes; rely on grants and donations from public, government and donors; do not have any revenue models, but often have robust fund-raising strategy.
Revenue surplus social ventures	Not-for-profits, but have a revenue stream from sources such as user/membership fee, training, consultancy and publications, implementation of projects, etc.; often tie up with government or CSR departments as implementation partners for their programmes; may also depend on grants.

VENTURE MODELS	DESCRIPTION
Hybrid ventures	Split into two complementing and connected entities—one which focuses on improving the social benefits for the served community, and the other which is market-facing business.
Social enterprises/ social businesses	Mission-driven for-profit commercial ventures which address the critical needs (e.g., healthcare, low-cost housing, clean drinking water and clean energy) of the un-served/under-served segments of the society at affordable price.
Socially responsible commercial ventures	Business ventures which are ethical in taking care of their responsibilities to their immediate stakeholders, such as employees, customers, suppliers, etc. (e.g., pay fair wages, ensure quality product, follow environmental norms and invest in CSR).
Profit-maximizing commercial ventures	Pure-play commercial ventures. Business ventures with primary purpose to exploit a market opportunity and increase entrepreneur's wealth.

Mission-Driven Not-for-Profits

Many social entrepreneurial ventures offer a service or product which cannot be monetized, either due to its nature or because of the population segment which they serve. To meet their costs, they primarily rely on grants and donations from public, government and/or donors. They do not have a revenue earning model but have a robust fund-raising strategy. For instance, many social ventures, such as Childline India, CRY, Goonj, Helpage India, etc., raise their programme costs through individual donations, grants from government and donors, public events, such as fund-raising marathons, crowd-funding platforms, etc. Even if they have an earned-income strategy, it contributes to a miniscule of their budgets. While they manage their operations efficiently to keep their overhead costs low, they are also innovative in mobilizing and managing resources. For instance, they may partner with other organizations to receive in-kind support for their programmes to keep their operational costs low. For instance, Childline India partners with government, multilateral agencies, educational institutions, corporates, to receive support for training, infrastructure, programme evaluation, volunteers, etc. Similarly, Goonj has run many nation-wide campaigns with large corporate partners such as Raymonds, Johnson and Johnson, Safexpress, for collection drive for clothes, books and toys, etc.

Revenue Generating Social Ventures

These too are not-for-profit ventures but have revenue streams which can come from a variety of activities. Many producer collectives, cooperatives, farmer producer organizations, etc., generate sufficient income through sales of their produce (e.g., handicrafts, poultry, honey and agricultural produce) to carry on these programmes with minimal external support. Similarly, some such ventures generate income for their programmes by tying up with government and CSR departments as the implementation partners for their schemes and projects. For instance, **Pratham**, one of the large social ventures in the field of primary education, partners with government to implement the Sarva Shiksha Abhiyan scheme for universalizing primary education. Similarly,

Akshaya Patra, which has a mission to eradicate child hunger and malnutrition, works with government's Integrated Child Development Services (ICDS) programme to provide wholesome meals in anganwadis and schools.

In some cases, the social ventures charge a user fee for the services they provide. For instance, **Milaap** is an online crowd-funding/micro-loaning platform which connects individual donors and lenders with low-income people who are in need of financial support. It charges 0–3 per cent on donations for philanthropic causes and 8 per cent on microlending, which takes care of the cost of processing the donation, maintaining the platform, due diligence of the NGOs and other administrative costs.

Hybrid Ventures

Hybrid models aim to combine the social mission with commercially sustainable income by splitting into two complementing and connected entities with separate legal identity—a not-for-profit which focuses on improving the social benefits for the served community, and the other for-profit which is market-facing business (Battilana et al. 2012). Often the not-for-profit arm holds equity stakes in the for-profit, allowing the profits to get reinvested in the social programmes. On the other hand, the for-profit arm sources the produce from the not-for-profit entity, thus providing it easy access to the market.

For instance, Bengaluru-based **Industree** focuses on creating rural livelihoods and saving the traditional crafts by helping the communities to establish their own enterprises which use their traditional skill sets. It operates through two separate legal entities. Its not-for-profit wing, Industree Crafts Foundation, works with the communities to organize them into production units, assist the artisans to access micro loans, build their capacity and develop marketable products. The foundation is supported by its for-profit arm, the Industree Crafts Pvt. Ltd, which interfaces the market and manages the sales and marketing of the products under Mother Earth brand.

This model has at least three major advantages for the venture. First, it enables the venture to focus on its core social mission, while having a revenue stream to fund its programmes. Second, since serving a community or cause and running a business require different competencies, this model also enables the venture to manage its talent in a more focused manner. And last, it allows greater flexibility to the venture in accessing different sources of funds; while it can seek grants and donations from donors through its not-for-profit entity, it can also raise investments from the equity market through its for-profit arm.

Social Enterprises/Social Businesses

Social enterprises or social businesses are for-profit commercial ventures, but differ from a typical profit-making business on two counts. First, they have a clear mission to address a critical social need of the un-served/under-served segments of the market (e.g., affordable healthcare, low-cost housing, clean drinking water and clean energy). Second, while their aim is to remain profitable, it is not profit-maximization. Remaining profitable allows them to have autonomy in decision-making, as well as to generate surpluses to invest in expanding their market and serving a larger population.

For instance, Vaatsalya Hospitals (earlier Vaatsalya Healthcare Solutions) started in 2005 with the aim to bridge the gap in access to affordable and specialized quality healthcare in semi-urban and rural areas—since 80 per cent of specialty healthcare facilities are available only in large cities and are costly, they are often out of reach, both physically and financially, for many patients residing in smaller towns. Starting with a small 20-bed pilot hospital in Hubli (Karnataka), over the years, Vaatsalaya has been able to replicate the model across seven Tier 2 and Tier 3 towns in Karnataka and Andhra Pradesh. These hospitals provide only those specialty services (e.g., paediatrics, gynaecology, medicine and surgery) at affordable price, which are not available in these towns.

Socially Responsible Commercial Ventures

These are business ventures, which are ethical in taking care of their social and legal responsibilities. They ensure quality products and fair price to their customers, pay fair wages to their employees, take care of their shareholders' interests, follow environmental norms, invest in the well-being of the communities where they operate, pay their taxes and so on. Often they have a strong and autonomous CSR department or foundation, which has well-structured and focused programmes with a long-term vision.

Pure-Play Commercial Ventures

Lastly, there are business ventures established to primarily do business and maximize profits for the entrepreneurs. Often they are founded to exploit an emergent market opportunity rather than due to an inherent passion of the entrepreneur.

As can be seen from the above broad classification, there are at least four broad organizational forms or models, ranging from mission-driven not-for-profits to for-profit social enterprises, which have clear and explicit social mission. Social entrepreneurial ventures adopt any of these organizational forms. That is, there is no single organizational form or model which defines the identity of social entrepreneurial ventures; rather, the choice mostly depends on which form would be most appropriate to achieve the social goals of the venture. As Dees (1998) noted in his seminal paper *The Meaning of Social Entrepreneurship*:

> In addition to innovative not-for-profit ventures, social entre-preneurship can include social purpose business ventures, such as for-profit community development banks, and hybrid organizations mixing not-for-profit and for-profit elements, such as homeless shelters that start businesses to train and

employ their residents…. Social entrepreneurs look for the most effective methods of serving their social missions. (p. 1)

Thus, social entrepreneurs mostly select the organizational form of their ventures with consideration to their goal and context such as the nature of product or service they are offering, nature of population segment they serve, nature of financial ecosystem in which the venture operates, government regulations, etc.

Legal Entity Options for Social Ventures in India

It is also important to note that social enterprises/social entrepreneurial ventures are an artefact of practice, and not a defined legal entity. In fact, in India, as in many other countries too, there is no legal definition (or a specific legal entity option to register as) specifically for a social entrepreneurial venture. Rather, the Indian regulatory environment provides a wide array of legal options for registration, which are conducive to different kinds of for-profit and not-for-profit social ventures. Selecting and registering the venture as an appropriate legal entity is often a critical choice for the social entrepreneurs, since each legal entity defines the boundaries (e.g., nature of activities which the enterprise can undertake, sources of funding and credit, tax benefits and requirements for governance) within which the venture can operate.

The following legal entity options describe the choices available for registering the venture:

1. **Public charitable trust**

   Public charitable trusts are established for not-for-profit 'charitable purposes' under the India Trust Act 1882. Some states (e.g., Maharashtra, Gujarat, Rajasthan and Madhya Pradesh) have their own Public trust Acts. A trust can be formed by any two persons, the 'trustees' and a 'trust deed', which describes one or more of the following activities the trust will undertake: (a) relief of poor, (b) education, (c) medical relief, (d) preservation of environment, (e) preservation of monuments or places or objects of artistic or historic interest and (f) advancement of any other object of general public utility.

Since the trust is for public charitable purposes, its income from voluntary contributions, donations and property are exempted from tax, provided that at least 85 per cent of such income is used for the activities of the trust. Often trusts also earn some income through its activities, for example, in the form of fee, membership, sales of items, etc. This income is also exempted from tax, provided the amount received through them does not exceed 20 per cent of trust's total income.

As a legal entity, public charitable trusts also have a couple of constraints. First, once registered, the trust is not allowed to undertake activities which are not mentioned in the trust deed. Thus, for a trust it is not possible to diversify its activities to meet other emerging needs (though to overcome this, often the trustees include all possible activities which they may undertake in the future). Second, once registered, a trust becomes irrevocable, since there is no legal provision to dissolve and close it. It can, however, be merged with another charitable trust and its assets and liabilities can be transferred.

2.   **Registered society**

A not-for-profit organization can also register as a society under Society Registration Act 1860, which is an all-India Act. Many states, however, also have variants on the Act with some minor modifications. A society can be registered by minimum seven people by filing a Memorandum of Association (MoA), which should describe the details of the members and the governing body, the rules of the society and the purpose for which it has been formed. Besides charitable purposes, Societies can also be established for the promotion of science, literature, education and fine arts, diffusion of useful knowledge, establishing and main-taining libraries or reading-rooms, public museums and galleries of works of art, collections of natural history, mechanical and philosophical inventions, instruments or designs, etc.

Societies are similar to Charitable Trusts in that they are exempted from taxes on income from non-commercial activities. However, as a legal entity they are more flexible than Trusts. Societies are governed by a managing committee, whose members are often elected by the members. They also allow membership for not only individuals but also for institutions. Most importantly, it is also possible to change the purpose of the Society or even dissolve it, with the approval of three-fifths of the members.

3. **Section 8 (earlier Section 25) company**

A Section 8 company is not-for-profit company which can be formed for promoting 'commerce, art, science, sports, education, research, social welfare, religion, charity, protection of environment or any such other object'. It can be established by two individuals if it is a private company or seven individuals if it is public company. The company is registered under Indian Company Act as a limited-liability legal entity, that is, the members of the company cannot be held personally liable for the company's debts or liabilities (e.g., in case of bankruptcy).

Like the Trusts and Societies, a Section 8 company also enjoys tax benefits, but it can explicitly and solely carry out commercial activities. The income derived from such activities and operation, however, needs to be reinvested in the company and cannot be distributed among its members as dividends. In its internal governance, a Section 8 company is similar to for-profit companies, with its board of directors, requirements of filing taxes, etc., and is much more transparent in its operations. They also enjoy greater freedom in their governance issues, such as appointment and removal of directors, shifting of registered office, increase in capital, changes in their purpose and object clause, etc. Like Societies, Section 8 companies can also be dissolved, though the remaining funds and property must be given or transferred to some other section 8 company, preferably one having similar objectives.

4. **Cooperative society**

Often social entrepreneurs mobilize members of the communities they work with to form collectives to empower them. Cooperative societies are such mutual-benefit or member-based organizations which are established to mobilize and aggregate community efforts and enhancing the benefit sharing among grass-roots farmers, workers or artisans. They are registered under Cooperative Societies Act, 1912 or any other law in force in any State for the registration of cooperative societies.

Cooperative societies can be formed for a variety of activities, such as providing credit facility to members, establishing cottage industries of artisans, processing and marketing of agricultural and non-farm produce, purchase of agricultural implements, seeds, livestock, etc., fisheries and allied activities, marketing of milk, oilseeds, fruits or vegetables grown by its members, etc. Cooperatives have access to government subsidies, low-interest credit, tax exemptions and other benefits to promote their activities.

5. **Producers' company**

This is a legal instrument for registration which was introduced in 2002 by incorporating a new section in the Companies Act. Producers' Company is a for-profit entity with members who are necessarily 'primary producers' (i.e., farmers involved in agriculture including animal husbandry, horticulture, floriculture, pisciculture, viticulture, forestry, forest products, revegetation, bee raising and farming plantation products; produce of persons engaged in handloom, handicraft and other cottage industries; by-products of such products and products arising out of ancillary industries) and own shares in the company. Producers' companies have the advantage of aggregation of produce, bypassing the intermediaries to directly deal with the market, pooling of resources and domain knowledge, etc. In addition, they enjoy the same benefits as a Cooperative Society.

6. **Non-banking financial company**
   Most MFIs are registered as non-banking financial company (NBFCs) in India. NBFCs are registered under the Companies Act, 1956, and engage in business of loans and advances, purchase of shares, stocks, bonds and other securities of marketable nature. However, they cannot accept deposits or issue cheque drawn on themselves. Ventures and institutions whose primary activity is that of agricultural and industrial business, but are also providing microfinance, also cannot register as NBFC.

7. **Private or public limited company**
   Both these are for-profit legal entities, registered as commercial ventures under the Companies Act 1956. Private Limited company can be formed by minimum shareholders (with a maximum limit of 50 shareholders). However, it cannot invite subscription of share or debentures, or accept deposits from the public. Public Limited Companies are similar to private limited companies, except that the minimum required shareholders are 7, and have no restriction on maximum number of shareholders, transfer of shares and acceptance of public deposits.

8. **Limited liability partnership**
   This is a very recent legal form introduced in India from 1 April 2009. Like elsewhere in the world, an LLP combines the ease of running a Partnership as a separate legal entity with the limited liability advantage of a 'for-profit' company.

However, unlike corporate shareholders, the partners have a right to manage the business directly.

As is evident from the above descriptions, different legal entities allow and support specific activities and operations, while also restricting some options for operations and growth. For instance, for-profit social ventures have very limited access to soft funding, which is enjoyed by the not-for-profit ventures. Income and corporate tax laws do not distinguish between the for-profit social ventures and the purely commercial ventures. Similarly, for the not-for-profit Trusts or Societies, the rules for merger, dissolution or restructuring are quite cumbersome. Thus, as they grow in operations and impact, it becomes difficult for them to realign their governance and structure to emerging requirements.

QUARTER IDEALISM AND A POUND OF PRAGMATISM

5

Indeed, one of the primary functions of the social entrepreneur is to serve as a kind of social alchemist: to create new social compounds; to gather together people's ideas, experiences, skills, and resources in configurations that society is not naturally aligned to produce.

—David Bornstein (2004)

Social entrepreneurs, first and foremost, are agents of social change. They are passionate about solving critical social problem(s) of their community/society and use entrepreneurial strategies to develop and implement innovative and sustainable solutions. This requires from them the romantic optimism of a dreamer as well as the hard-headed pragmatism of a realist. They work towards realizing an imagined ideal future which does not exist, while at the same time negotiating the existing real conditions which are often the hurdles in realizing it. Indeed, the Schwab Foundation for Social Entrepreneurship defines social entrepreneur as '…a leader or pragmatic visionary who…combines the characteristics represented by Richard Branson and Mother Teresa.'

How do they achieve this blend or balance between seemingly opposite qualities? The answer seems to lie not in what social entrepreneurs are, but as we discussed in an earlier chapter, in what they do. Many studies (e.g., Barendsen and Gardner 2004; Bornstein 2004; Dees 1998; Mair and Noboa 2006; Martin and Osberg 2007) have described the distinctive way in which they address a social problem, devise and implement solutions and create a sustainable impact. The following sections define some of these key qualities of the social entrepreneurs.

Mission to Create Social Change

Social entrepreneurs are driven by a passion to change societal conditions which trouble them. Many studies (e.g., Ip et al. 2017; Shumate et al. 2014) have shown that their motivations are often rooted in certain antecedent conditions, such as family legacy and/or some transformative experiences in early adulthood. They often have a first-hand exposure to social problems which disturbed them; they go through experiences (e.g., through visits, internships, journeys, personal trauma and volunteering), which make them reflect about the causes and cures for such issues; they have often experienced hope by experimenting with some successful efforts or through interactions with inspiring role models and social leaders and so on. Such experiences make them empathetic towards the marginalized segments and feel morally bound to help them; their experiences also create confidence in the latent capacity of their target community to change their own lives, their own ability to facilitate such social change and make them aware of potential sources of social support for their efforts (Hockerts 2015; Mair and Noboa 2006).

The efforts of social entrepreneurs are distinct in that they are aimed at a more fundamental level of social change than merely addressing the symptoms. In the true Schumpterian sense, they aim to 'revolutionize' the social order by creating and establishing new patterns and norms for the society and community. This is an important distinction from other efforts to address social problems. For instance, running a night shelter for the homeless also addresses a social issue. However, it does not question the conditions why people are left homeless, nor does it offer a long-term sustainable solution. A social entrepreneur, on the other hand, will address the problem of homelessness not just by running shelters, but also, for instance, creating communes for them to live together, acquiring skills to earn a livelihood and get rehabilitated or by actively lobbying to for a regulation to make well-equipped night shelters a norm in all cities. As Bill Drayton, the founder of Ashoka: Innovators for the Public, described: 'Social entrepreneurs are not content just to give a fish or teach how to fish. They will not rest until they have revolutionized the fishing industry.'

For instance, Nalini Shekar and Shekar Prabhakar co-founded **Hasiru Dala** (which means 'green force' in Kannada), a Bangalore-based collective of waste pickers which works with more than 500 waste pickers to provide them social justice and improve their livelihood opportunities. Waste pickers are one of the most neglected and poor segments in urban India. Despite providing an essential service to the city by collecting, sorting, grading and recycling waste, they are exploited and mistreated. The efforts of Hasiru Dala are not limited to getting them included into government's social security schemes, getting them identity cards so that they are not harassed by police, providing them with safety gears, etc. Nalini Shekar saw them as potential entrepreneurs and service providers, and collectivized them into a for-profit waste management venture. Hasiru Dala takes up waste management contract with bulk waste generators (e.g., apartment houses, public events and wedding parties), which are franchised to waste pickers in different zones. Waste pickers collect the waste and get paid for the service. They also sort and grade the waste; the dry recyclable waste is sent to the recycling industries, and the wet or organic waste is converted into compost which is sold for urban gardens and parks. Not only has this increased the income of the waste pickers significantly, but also has transformed them from beneficiaries to entrepreneurs (Arakali 2018).

Overcoming and Bridging 'Opportunity Structures' to Create Change

In his book *Banker for the Poor,* describing his early experiences with the poor which led to the establishment of Grameen Bank, Professor Muhammad Yunus had written:

> People were not poor because they were stupid or lazy. They worked all day long, doing complex physical tasks. They were poor because the financial structures which could help them to widen their economic base simply did not exist in this country. It was a structural problem, not a personal problem. (Yunus 2007, p. 11)

What Yunus was describing was the concept of 'Opportunity Structures'[1]—that is, *the outcomes of a person's efforts are mediated by the extraneous factors which permit or prohibit one's access to opportunities.* Or in other words, the results of one's efforts are not necessarily determined by one's merit, diligence, ability, etc., but by the external context and conditions over which one does not have any control or influence. Due to such factors, opportunities are easily accessible for some people, while others are unable to avail them.

Powell et al. (2011) described three kinds of opportunity structures, which determine the outcomes of efforts by the individual or communities:

1. **Physical opportunity structure**: Physical locations differ in terms of the opportunities they offer to individual and communities. Some places are high-opportunity locations and provide easy access to facilities such as educational institutions, healthcare facilities, banks, markets, employment

[1] The idea of 'Opportunity Structures' was proposed by sociologist Merton (1938) in his paper, to explain why differing structural opportunities make some people successful, while push others towards delinquency.

opportunities, etc., while other locations are deprived of these (Dreier et al. 2014). For instance, farmers living in villages which are well connected to markets have better chances of improving their lives than farmers living in places which are isolated and distant from markets.

2. **Social opportunity structure**: One's social connections, that is, who one knows, how well one knows them, which group does one belong to, etc., play an important role in one's chances to access available opportunities. Individuals who know the decision makers or potential employers, belong to an influential group (e.g., an alumni network or a particular class, caste or community) or have friends or relatives who are well-placed, influential and/or knowledgeable, etc., have easier access to opportunities (e.g., employment opportunities, loans and financial help, market information, legal entitlements and services such as education or healthcare) compared to those who are not so well connected. Similarly, communities too differ in terms of their social opportunity structures. People from communities whose members are placed in influential positions are likely to have better access to resources, government schemes, social justice, etc.

3. **Cultural opportunity structure**: The shared norms, values and goals of one's community and family facilitate or hinder an individual's efforts towards certain aims. Communities which have traditionally relied on specific occupation (e.g., trade and commerce, farming and weaving) would have more resources, technical knowledge and inclination to support similar behaviours and efforts, and would discourage other pursuits. Similarly, differences in the gender norms of different communities may encourage or discourage girls' education, women to work outside home or men to pursue up supposedly 'feminine' occupation (e.g., dancing, cooking and fine arts). In many parts of India, the caste norms within the community also determine the differing access

to common resources (e.g., water resources, educational and healthcare facilities and common space) among the community members.

Differences in opportunity structures lie at the heart of social inequalities and problems. They determine and explain many deprivations within some segments of society, for example, why many intelligent children belonging to poor families have to drop out of school, why many rural producers (e.g., farmers and artisans) are unable to get decent price for their produce, why often informal sector workers do not get fair wages, why many people do not have access to basic services such water, electricity, healthcare, etc. Often, such inherently unjust social arrangements are also accepted as 'normal' in the society since these segments lack financial means, resources and/or social influence.

Martin and Osberg (2007) described such unequal opportunity structures as 'stable but inherently unjust equilibrium that causes the exclusion, marginalization, or suffering of a segment of humanity' (p. 35). Such unjust equilibrium blocks the formation and utilization of social wealth by depriving the society and its citizens to realize their full potential. Social entrepreneurs see an opportunity for change in these inequities of opportunities. They do so by 'reframing challenges' (Barendsen and Gardner 2004) or by using what Sarasvathy (2008a) described as 'the lemonade principle'. That is, they focus their efforts on identifying the positives which can be leveraged; they build capacities to develop more empowered participants in the social/market dynamics; they redefine/re-craft value chains which connect players and locations; they identify partners to access resources and increase the scale and impact of their efforts and so on. If successful, they replace these sub-optimal equilibriums with new ones which are more equitable and open up new opportunities for the segment they serve.

For instance, Susmita Ghose started **RangSutra** in 2006 with the aim to provide sustainable livelihoods to the rural handloom artisans and craftsmen. In her previous experience in the sector, she had noticed that despite being highly skilled and hardworking, these artisans were able to earn just about ₹500–1,000 from their craft due to lack of access to the market. Her initial attempts to create an enterprise for the artisans met with obstacles to raise funds: government schemes needed 3 years of records, banks required collateral which she did not have, donor funds were sceptical about the profit motive of the enterprise and so on. Instead of abandoning the idea, Susmita Ghose asked the artisans to invest ₹1,000 each in the venture as shareholders, and invested her own savings, to raise the seed capital to start the venture. She also negotiated with Aavishkar, a micro-venture fund, and Fabindia to invest (through its joint venture company, Artisans Micro Finance Pvt Ltd) in the venture. Beginning with three groups of artisans in 2006, by 2017 Rangasutra was working with more than 3,000 rural artisans in about 30 clusters across Rajasthan, Uttar Pradesh, Manipur and West Bengal, with a turnover of more than ₹90 million. By providing design support, more efficient production processes and market access, the venture was able to increase the income of the artisans and craftsmen to about ₹3,000–5,000 per month.

Continuous Learning, Innovation and Self-correction

Like any entrepreneur, social entrepreneurs are also innovative. Given the inequities of access and opportunities in India, besides new products or services, they often focus more on finding new and innovative ways to make the products and services accessible to the end user. For instance, the innovation of **SELCO** (described earlier, see Box 1.3) was not the solar lightning systems, which were already in existence; the innovation was in making it affordable to low-income customers by tying up the product with consumer finance. Similarly, Bengaluru-based **eVidyaloka** developed a model for delivering quality education to rural schools by creative combination of existing resources; the venture harnesses the knowledge resources of more than 800 working professionals who volunteer to teach for a few hours a week, ties up with local NGOs to manage the almost 140 rural virtual classrooms in school premise, uses the existing state syllabus to assign lessons to be taught and connects the classrooms with the volunteer teachers through internet enabled audio-visual screens.

Moreover, for the social entrepreneurs innovating is also not a one-time activity, but is a continuous process of exploring, learning and improving (Dees 1998). This is so because, as discussed earlier, their entrepreneurial models need to go through iterations and evolve as they discover new opportunities and hurdles, negotiate changing market conditions and form new partnerships. In case of Indian social entrepreneurs, this requirement to learn, innovate and self-correct is much more pronounced due to two reasons.

First, social problems are often multi-layered, and manifest themselves gradually in response to an intervention. For instance, in 1996 Vijay Mahajan established India's first commercial microfinance venture, **BASIX**, with the aim of alleviating poverty by providing low interest credit to the poor. Five years later, however, an impact assessment study showed that despite the growth in number of borrowers and high repayment rates, there was not much change in the lives of its customers: only 52 per cent of its customers reported an increase in income, and that too by only 10 per cent; 23 per cent reported no change while 25 per cent of its borrowers had actually slipped deeper into poverty. He realized that mere loans without supporting livelihood mechanisms (e.g., knowledge about how to use the loan, capacity building and institutional support) do not help the poor. That learning changed the way BASIX engaged with the poor, and started providing livelihoods support in agriculture, livestock and micro-enterprise development to its borrowers (Karunakaran 2010).

Similarly, when the founders of **SEARCH (Society for Education, Action and Research in Community Health)** Drs Abhay and Rani Bang started their work to bring healthcare to the remote region of Gadchiroli (Maharashtra) in 1986, they found that when they shared the results of their research and diagnostic surveys (which they thought were significant and worrisome), the local population would pay no attention to their findings. Soon, through interacting with them, they realized that health problems they were researching had little relevance to the health priorities for the people. Moreover, the research methodology, which they had learned through their rigorous training as public health professionals, contributed little to the adoption of the healthcare solutions by the local population. This made them to revisit and question their own deeply ingrained assumptions about nature of relevant public health research and the practice of public healthcare itself. Over time, this learning culminated in their vision of 'Arogya Swaraj' which allowed the community to take charge of their own health, and research became a participative activity based on the community's needs, and carried out by themselves (Bang 2018).

Bornstein (2004) noted that this 'willingness to self-correct' is an important quality of social entrepreneurs:

> This may seem a simple point, but it cannot be overstated. It is inherently difficult to reverse a train once it has left the station. It takes a combination of hard-headedness, humility, and courage to stop and say, 'This isn't working' or 'Our assumptions were wrong',…the entrepreneur's inclination to self-correct stems from the attachment to a goal rather than to a particular approach or plan. (p. 233)

Second, by their very nature the social problems are complex and multifaceted. Often the solutions to social problems lie beyond a single discipline or agency, and need the collaboration among diverse stakeholders. For instance, tackling the problem of maternal malnutrition in poor households would need addressing not only the nutritional intake, but also gender biases, education and awareness in the family, capacity building of local village level health workers and anganwadi workers, etc. Similarly, the reasons for poor educational performance in rural primary schools lie in a combination of factors such as quality and availability of teacher, nature and local relevance of syllabus, poor school infrastructure (e.g., classrooms, blackboard and library), nature of subsistence activity of family which may require participation of the school-going child, gender status of the girl child in the family, etc. To address such problems, social entrepreneurs need to work across disciplinary boundaries, bringing different stakeholders in, what Schumpeter described as, 'new combinations' to architect a viable solution. As Bornstein (2004) noted:

> Faced with whole problems, social entrepreneurs readily cross disciplinary boundaries, pulling together people from different spheres, with different kinds of experience and expertise, who can, together, build workable solutions that are qualitatively new. (p. 237)

Embedded in the Needs of the Served Community

A key difference between the commercial and social entrepreneurs is that for commercial entrepreneurs markets work well in providing feedback about their success or failure (Dees 1998). If more customers are buying the product or service and are willing to pay an adequate price for the offerings, the profits (or market share) of the venture increase—and correspondingly, more financial wealth is created for the entrepreneur. Markets also identify and eliminate ventures which continue to remain non-profitable, since they are unable to attract resources, talent and investments. Creation of private wealth is a reliable market feedback to show whether the entrepreneur is running the venture efficiently or not.

However, markets are inefficient in valuing social benefits and do not provide reliable feedback to the social entrepreneurs about how effectively they are creating social wealth. This is so because mostly the social problems are complex and multilayered, and defy simple cause-and-effect relationship between an intervention and its outcome. Often the impact of social interventions is not immediately visible. For instance, improvements in community health indices, easy access to credit or training in livelihood skills, etc., take time to show resultant increase in income and well-being. Moreover, indicators of social improvement also do not always or necessarily get translated into positive social outcomes. For instance, despite improved learning in schools, children may still drop out due to unaffordability of further education, need to earn for family or even lack of higher-grade schools in the vicinity. Similarly, increase in income can lead either to investments in productive assets or to unproductive behaviour such as gambling or drinking. Such complexities make it harder to conclude whether the social entrepreneur is creating social wealth or not, even though the number of customers/beneficiaries she/he is serving may keep on increasing. Thus, unlike in case of commercial ventures, mere survival and growth a social venture is no assurance of its effectiveness in creating social wealth.

Effective social entrepreneurs, therefore, create feedback processes and mechanisms which are more sensitive to the changes in the communities they serve. They use base-line surveys to compare progress on multiple parameters, have regular interactions with the community, co-create solutions with their customers, have robust monitoring and evaluation processes in place and so on. As Dees (1998) observed:

> Because market discipline does not automatically weed out inefficient or ineffective social ventures, social entrepreneurs take steps to assure they are creating value. This means that they seek a sound understanding of the constituencies they are serving. They make sure they have correctly assessed the needs and values of the people they intend to serve and the communities in which they operate. In some cases, this requires close

connections with those communities.... They assess their progress in terms of social, financial, and managerial outcomes, not simply in terms of their size, outputs, or processes. They use this information to make course corrections as needed. (p. 5)

BOX 5.1   THE ELEVEN QUESTIONS OF SEWA

Questions to explore 'Full Employment'

1. Have more members obtained more employment?
2. Has their income increased?
3. Have they obtained food and nutrition?
4. Has their health been safeguarded?
5. Have they obtained child-care?
6. Have they obtained or improved their housing?
7. Have their assets increased? e.g., their own savings, land, house, workspace, tools or work, licences, identity cards, cattles and share in cooperatives—and all in their own name.

Questions to explore 'Self Reliance'

8. Have the worker's organizational strength increased?
9. Has worker's leadership increased?
10. Have they become self-reliant both collectively and individually?
11. Have they become literate?

For instance, **SEWA**, discussed in the earlier chapters, started with the twin goals of providing 'Full Employment' and 'Self Reliance' for its informal sector women members. Over the years, with the participation of its members, it has developed a list of 11 questions which it uses to constantly discuss and monitor the impact of its programmes and interventions (see Box 5.1). According to the organization:

> In order to ensure that we are moving in the direction of our two goals of Full Employment and Self Reliance, constant monitoring and evaluation is required. In a membership-based organisation, it is the members' priorities and needs which necessarily shapes the priorities and direction of the organisation. Hence, it is appropriate that members themselves develop their own yardstick for evaluation. The following… (questions) have emerged from the members and continually serve as a guide for all members, group leaders, executive committee members and full-time organisers of SEWA. It is also useful for monitoring SEWA's progress and the relevance of its various activities and their congruence with members' reality and priorities. It also increases the accountability of SEWA's leaders and organisers, to their members.

Building for Sustainability

For social entrepreneurs, the definition of sustainability includes much more than just the sustainability of their venture. It is certainly important to create a sustainable venture which is financially viable and organizationally resilient with robust processes and systems and a strong talent pool. However, given their mission and goals, it is equally important for them to ensure the sustainability of the social benefits they have created for their target community (Cannon 2002). Successful social entrepreneurs plan to create such 'benefit sustainability' for their served segments/communities.

This is easier to achieve by those social ventures which can create desired impact on the community members through a single or a few transactions. For instance, a social venture which is selling affordable solar systems, or training marginalized youth and getting them placed in secure jobs, is able to create the intended and durable social benefits once the product or service has been delivered. However, ensuring sustained social benefits is a challenge when the problems being addressed are more complex and deep-rooted (e.g., malnutrition among women and children, conditions of landless ultra-poor, caste and gender discrimination and human trafficking), and requires long-term engagement by the social entrepreneur/venture. An ideal resolution of such conditions requires (a) creating solutions which will reach the benefits to these marginalized segments and (b) changing the socioeconomic equilibrium in such a way that they continue to accrue the benefits without (or minimally) depending on any external agency, including the social entrepreneur or the venture.

There are four distinct, yet interrelated, ways in which social entrepreneurs achieve such a change in the equilibrium:

1. **Promoting social institutions to empower the community:** Often the problems of inequity in access and opportunities are rooted in the fragmented nature of the community, for example, isolated small producers or service providers mostly lack bargaining power in the markets, or due to their small savings and loan requirements poor are unable to access banking services. A sustainable solution requires increasing their influence and power, which can be achieved by collectivizing them into groups and institutions (self-help groups, producer organizations, community-owned common services, etc.) which are owned and managed by them. For instance, as we earlier saw in the example of **Hasiru Dala**, by creating a community-owned organization the social entrepreneurs were not only able to shift the unjust socioeconomic equilibrium in favour of the rag pickers, but also created a solution which is self-sustaining. Similarly, to address the exploitation of the marginal subsistence farmers (mostly women) by the middlemen, SEWA trained the rural women to manage the entire value chain from production to marketing of agri-products (cereals, pulses and spices), and promoted member-owned **RUDI Multi Trading Company**

which operates across 14 districts of Gujarat. The processing centres of the company are run by the women who manage all post-harvest operations (procurement, processing and packaging, quality control, brand-promotion and sales and marketing). This provides not only better margins to producers, but also better quality and price to local customers.

2. **Leveraging affordable and enabling technologies:** Easy access to technology is an effective leveller of disparities and inequities. During recent years, the proliferation of low-cost user-friendly technologies (internet, mobile phones, low-cost equipment, etc.) has created new opportunities for social entrepreneurs for empowering the communities to become self-sustaining and self-dependent. For instance, while India has a vast network of agricultural extension services promoted by the government to provide latest technical know-how to the farmers, its reach and effectiveness are limited. **Digital Green**, a venture founded by Rikin Gandhi, bridges this gap by providing the farmers a platform to share locally produced videos of good agricultural practices. Instead of depending on the extension service, Digital Green trains the farming community members to produce their own short instructional videos of their best practices in local language. These are then disseminated across about 7,000 villages through Digital Green's NGO partners. Many of these more than 4,000 videos are also uploaded online in a video library, which allows the user to search by state, language and subject and view them (Basu 2015; Bornstein 2013).

3. **Creating an ecosystem of stakeholders:** Sustainability of social benefits increases when they are owned and supported by multiple stakeholders. Social entrepreneurs achieve this by creating partnerships across different agencies which have a similar mission. For instance, in the examples quoted earlier, **Hasiru Dala** partners with Bruhat Bengaluru Mahanagara Palike (BBMP), Plastics for Change Consortium, Earth Care

Equipments, Daily Dump, Shudh-Labh, Radio Active, etc., who bring complementary capabilities to strengthen the initiative. Similarly, **Digital Green** partners with large NGOs such as PRADAN, BAIF, ACCESS etc., as well as with government's National Rural Livelihoods Mission to increase its reach and impact. By forming an ecosystem of agencies which are part of delivering similar benefits, over a period of time the benefit delivery becomes a part of standard practice without depending on only a single provider.

4. **Crafting a sectoral norm/standard of practice:** Sometimes social entrepreneurs also architect such an ecosystem of stakeholder by promoting a standard of practice which delivers the social benefits. For instance, Nobel Laureate, Kailash Satyarthi founded **Bachpan Bachao Andolan** with the aim of ending bonded and child labour, human trafficking and to rehabilitate the rescued children. When he realized that his sole efforts to rescue child slave labour from the rug-making industry had limited long-term impact, he started focusing on creating a consortium across the entire value chain of rug manufacturing. In 1994, he promoted RUGMARK (now GoodWeave International) as the first voluntary labelling scheme to certify that rugs were produced without child labour in South Asia. He campaigned with the large carpet importers in US and Europe to endorse the label, and also ran advocacy campaigns and negotiated with the carpet manufacturers and exporters to adhere to the standards. Over a period, RUGMARK/GoodWeave has grown into an international consortium of NGOs, experts and advocates dedicated to ending child labour, forced labour and bonded labour in global supply chains (Osberg and Martin 2015).

Scaling for Social Impact

Like any entrepreneur, for social entrepreneurs too, scaling is an important requirement to maximize the impact of their efforts.

As a large and diverse country with varied and pervasive social problems, the imperative to scale is also relevant for social entrepreneurs to achieve their mission of social change. Scaling, however, poses two critical challenges for social entrepreneurs in India.

First, the size and diversity of the country make it virtually impossible for a single venture or solution to scale up across the country. Social ventures do not possess the resources and outreach which would be required to achieve scale of this magnitude. Moreover, often the same solution may not meet the context and constraints of the unevenly distributed diversity of India. Different regions of the country speak different languages, follow different belief and lifestyles, are subjected to different state laws, are at different levels of development and have different aspirations and needs, etc. Addressing the same social need in such diverse settings requires considerable customization to local context. Often the solutions to solve the problems are also so localized that they have limited relevance to other regions (Shukla 2010).

Second, the social problems are also not always unrelated with each other or are specific to different segments of the society. In many social segments, one may find them coexisting for the same set of people. For instance, the same community of poor often have concurrent problems of unemployment, lack of access to formal credit, large incidences of ill-health and malnutrition, poor access to basic amenities such as water and electricity, etc. Similarly, the same set of small and marginal farmers may lack access to water, credit for inputs, knowledge of better agricultural techniques, more remunerative markets, etc. For the social entrepreneurs, such coexistence of problems broadens the meaning of 'scale' beyond just servicing more number of people.

Correspondingly, in Indian context, one needs to understand the concept of 'scale' in a much more nuanced manner. For social entrepreneurs, scaling of their social impact is a more important goal than scaling of their ventures. For them, increasing the size and reach of the venture is one of the many ways to create a larger impact, and they creatively devise alternative strategies to achieve the same social goals. For instance, they may partner with other organizations with similar mission to enlarge their impact, or they may use advocacy to create new standards, policies and practices to achieve large-scale change. Many social ventures also remain small and confined to a small community, and yet scale up their impact by successively meeting different needs of the same community. As Coffman (2010) observed:

> A good deal of the literature on scaling focuses on a definition that refers to the replication (often with room for adaptation) of programs to new sites or locations. But the 'what' of scaling can go well beyond program, and the 'how' of scaling can include much more than replication. (p. 2)

Clearly, for social entrepreneurs and ventures, scaling has a far more complex and variegated meaning than the conventional interpretation of the term. This complexity offers different choices for scaling to social entrepreneurs, and needs a more extensive treatment. We will discuss these choices in Chapter 6.

6

STRATEGIES FOR SCALING THE IMPACT

Scaling up is every entrepreneur's dream—and nightmare. Hypergrowth is terrifying, and it's most often success that kills great companies.

—*Verne Harnish (2014)*

The Imperative to Scale

In an article in the *Forbes* magazine, Dr Fazel Abed, the founder of world's largest not-for-profit social venture BRAC (Bangladesh Rural Advancement Comittee), had noted,

> If you want to do significant work, you have to be large. Otherwise we'd be tinkering around on the periphery. (Armstrong 2008)

This imperative to scale up and become large is a dominant narrative in the field of social entrepreneurship. In the Indian context, with its pervasive social problems, the need to have large-scale solutions is relevant too. For instance, if more poor have access to affordable clean drinking water, it will significantly bring down instances of illness, increase saving from healthcare costs, and help increasing their income; or, if more farmers have access to timely market information, they will be able to make more remunerative choices for crops.

Scaling, however, means different things to different social ventures. Depending on the nature of problems they address and the communities they serve, social ventures use different strategies to scale their impact. Bradach (2010) described a variety of ways in which social ventures scale their impact, such as by building networks, using intermediaries to reach their markets/ beneficiaries, developing social leaders and changemakers who can replicate their model in other regions, using advocacy to create a pro-change policy environment, etc. Similarly, Rosenberg (2010) noted:

> Scaling takes different forms, from replication of an established program model, to a deepening of program efforts to achieve more measurable impact, to scaling components that have demonstrated success. The approach taken depends in large part on the needs and goals of the program being scaled. (p. 10)

For a venture which offers an affordable and socially useful product, for instance, successful scaling would entail reaching the product to large population and to new markets. If, on the other hand, the mission of the venture is to provide services such as maternal healthcare to rural women, scaling would also involve greater inclusiveness and care. For social ventures aiming at systemic social change, larger impact can be achieved only when policy makers and citizens start owning the 'idea'. Some ventures partner with other organizations to replicate their innovative solutions to other regions, while others scale their impact by servicing multiple needs of the same community.

Clearly, in the social entrepreneurial context, scaling has many nuances and manifestations. These nuances also provide a choice of strategies to the social entrepreneur about how they can maximize the impact of their efforts. In this chapter, we will discuss four broad strategies for scaling, which social entrepreneurs use. Though conceptually and technically different, in practice these are not mutually exclusive, and often the social entrepreneurs use one or a combination of these.

Scaling Up

For many social ventures it is possible to increase their outreach and impact by growing larger and serving more customers in new markets. Having established their operations in one region, they use the learning of the initial success to expand into other markets to service similar needs. There are a variety of ways in which they can scale up: they may grow organically by opening more branches and offices; they may grow by making acquisitions of similar operations and they may expand 'upstream' by increasing the reach of their supply chain or 'downstream' by reaching into new markets and territories. Often, as the ventures scale up they also innovate new allied products and services to their portfolios. Increased scale of operations helps them to use their existing resources more efficiently, bring down the per-unit cost and make their offering more affordable.

For instance, **Milk Mantra** was established in 2011 by Srikumar Misra to address the plight of small milk producers in Western Odisha region. Despite the high milk production in the region, the producers remained poor; a large proportion of milk produced in the villages remained unsold and went waste, or was bought from the milk producers at exploitative prices. On the other hand, the consumers did not get good-quality milk and milk products at reasonable prices. Milk Mantra aimed to address this issue by establishing collection centres in villages to source the milk from the producers at fair price and regular payment, and then processing and packaging it to reach the urban markets.

The venture started by sourcing milk from just two villages in Puri district in 2011, and by the end of next year it had scaled up to tie up with 20,000 milk producers across 500 villages in the region. By 2017, it had established a robust supply chain with more than 600 collection points to connect about 50,000 milk farmers across 10 districts of Odisha. Over the years, it also increased its market reach from a single city of Bhubaneswar to other cities in Odisha and other states. In 2014, it acquired Westernland Dairy, giving it access to markets in western Odisha and the states of Chhattisgarh, Jharkhand and West Bengal. In terms of its products too, Milk Mantra kept adding milk-based products, such as cottage cheese, curd, milkshake, etc. To achieve its mission of creating prosperity for the milk producer, Milk Mantra also added new services to increase their produce. It tied up with government and private agencies to provide them services, such as cow feed at subsidized price, farmer training, artificial insemination, veterinary services, cow loans, etc.

While Scaling Up is a preferred strategy among the for-profit social enterprises, it is also adopted by a few not-for profit social ventures to increase their reach. For example, **Agastya International Foundation**, which runs the world's largest science education programme for children from disadvantage backgrounds and government schools, uses an innovative hub-and-spoke model to reach out to 1.5 million children and 250,000 teachers annually. The venture develops its low-cost, hands-on and experiential science modules in the innovation hub in its central campus in Kuppam town in Andhra Pradesh. These modules consist of models and experiments which can be built using local material, and allow children to design and conduct experiments to learn about science. While the innovation hub is visited by thousands of children every year, Agastya has also extended its reach to 15 Indian states by establishing 75 Science Centres with similar science modules to expose children and teachers from that region. These Science Centres are further supported by more than 200 Mobile Labs and about 75 Labs-on-Bike which travel across more than 200 districts to take science education to remote places and schools.

As can be seen from the above examples, Scaling Up is an efficient strategy for extending the impact to other markets and regions. Success of scaling up, however, depends on a few conditions.

1. **Standardized offering:** Scaling Up strategy is most likely to succeed when the venture has a standardized cookie-cutter

product, service or model with established social impact. It is also an efficient strategy when the varying socio-cultural context of other regions/markets does not significantly affect the impact of the offering. Being unaffected by the local social and cultural norms and preferences allows them to use the same template to roll out their innovation in different regions.

2. **Financial investments:** Since Scaling Up involves opening new units and offices, building or hiring new infrastructure, employing more people, developing new supply chains and distribution networks, etc., it requires large financial investments. This is also a reason why Scaling Up strategy is mostly used by the for-profit social ventures, since they can depend on either their profits and saving or have easier access to external financing through institutional loans or investments.

3. **Managerial and organizational capabilities:** Besides having the right product/service and financial resources, the crux of successful Scaling Up actually lies in the organizational and managerial capabilities of the venture to scale. To scale up successfully, ventures need to have the strategic expertise to identify and enter relevant markets, build systems and processes to manage extended operations, induct and develop managerial talent to oversee the operations, etc. In addition, one of the major challenges of Scaling Up is the essential change in the entrepreneur's role. The growth in the size of the venture requires from the entrepreneur to let go off some of his/her decision-making role and delegate it to others. Many entrepreneurs find it difficult to make this transition in their hands-on control and nature of working.

4. **Balancing social mission with goals of scaling:** Given the required financial investments in Scaling Up, especially by the for-profit social enterprises, its success and sustainability depend on adequate returns on investments. This dependence can sometimes create pressure to compromise the social objectives of the venture. For instance, a social venture which

provides affordable solar solutions to slums and rural poor can successfully scale up by serving more remunerative segments, such as hotels and urban housing societies. While this may serve to meet the goals of scaling, it would not achieve its social mission. Mission-aligned scaling up often requires developing innovative models which can balance the social objectives with the need to remain financially sustainable.

Scaling Out

McDonald's, the fast food giant, has more than 37,000 restaurants and kiosks in about 120 countries. Unlike the scaling up strategy, the MNC has been able to extend its business, not by opening its own outlets, but by partnering with around 5,000 partner franchisees across the globe who operate 92 per cent of its outlets. Despite such diversity of operators, however, each outlet offers the same or similar core menu, maintains the same product quality and efficiency of service, has similar layout and ambience, uses identical kitchen equipment, etc. McDonald's has been able to extend its business in diverse markets by standardizing and replicating its products and processes, while leaving enough freedom to the franchisee to customize the offering to local tastes. The company has standardized the procedures and time taken for various operations (e.g., quality check on the inputs, processing orders, maintenance of the kitchen, preparation of food items, efficient layout design for maximum utilization and serving the customers) and trains the personnel on these to ensure uniformity of service quality standards. The franchisees, on the other hand, use their knowledge of the local market to decide on marketing and pricing-related matters, staffing and employment-related decisions, and making small changes in the product offering to suite the local tastes (UK Essays 2017).

McDonald's example shows how organizations can extend their reach into new regions and markets by Scaling Out through partnerships to replicate their innovation/model. While the goal of Scaling Up strategy is the growth and expansion of the enterprise, the Scaling Out strategy focuses on the replication of the innovation or intervention in other regions. Unlike the Scaling Up which requires large financial investments, Scaling Out is also a cost-efficient strategy. Given the scarcity of financial, technical and human resources, many Indian social ventures use this strategy by *promoting replication* of their model to spread the social impact. For instance, **Afforest**, a for-profit social venture, was founded by Shubhendu Sharma in 2011 with the mission to regenerate natural forests and increase the green cover. The venture uses the Miyawaki Technique (Schirone et al. 2011), which grows indigenous, multi-layered and maintenance-free forests in 2–3 years. These forests do not use any chemical fertilizers, are multiple times denser than conventional monoculture plantations, absorb up to 30 times more carbon dioxide and support local biodiversity. Starting with pilot in his own backyard in Uttarakhand, by 2018 Sharma had planted 111 forests across 38 cities in nine countries. The venture partners with local organizations, municipalities and communities to replicate its model, who also provide the land for afforestation. The local partners help in identifying and planting the native plant species, and then taking care of the plantation till the forest becomes self-sufficient.

Forging partnerships plays a critical role in Scaling Out, since the partners not only bring in their own resources and thus sharing the costs, but also are able to customize the innovations to local contexts and needs. Social entrepreneurs select their partners depending on the nature of innovation and the purpose of scaling. One of the partnering options they use is to tie up with other social ventures with similar mission. For instance, instead of scaling up across the regions, in 2012 **SELCO** (see Box 1.3) started an incubation centre to nurture young solar ventures in other regions who share its mission. The incubation process focuses on enhancing the capacity of the ventures by sharing the key elements of SELCO's model, providing mentoring and business process planning support, arranging access to seed capital, etc. to replicate its model. Post incubation, SELCO continues to work with these ventures as partners and provides guidance and advisory services for expansion and diversifications. These partnerships have enabled SELCO to replicate its model to other states, such as Madhya Pradesh, Manipur, Odisha, Rajasthan and West Bengal.

Some innovations, specifically those which require last mile reach to remote communities, can be effectively Scaled Out by partnering with members of the communities themselves. For instance, to spread the impact of its solar electrification model for off-grid villages, **Barefoot College** (see Box 1.1) partners with the communities. The model relies on training disadvantaged and illiterate rural women, aged 35–60, as solar engineers (or 'solar mamas') to fabricate, install, repair and maintain solar electrification systems, for example, LED Lamp, Home Lighting System and Solar Lantern. These women are selected by the villagers, which ensures their acceptance by and influence in the community. On completion of training, they return to their respective villages with equipment needed to electrify houses in their communities, and are paid salaries through the 'village fund' for providing repair and maintenance services. Besides its training centre in Tilonia, Rajasthan, the College has also opened 'Regional Training Centres' in other countries in Africa, and has trained more than 750 women from remote villages in about 70 countries directly impacting more than 0.5 million households.

In Indian context, replicating the innovations/interventions through partnering with community is particularly relevant and prevalent. As we had discussed in the earlier chapters, many useful and affordable solutions do not reach the remote and dispersed communities due to lack of last mile connectivity. By partnering with the community members and training them to become 'barefoot paraprofessionals', social ventures are able to reach their innovations to these communities. In addition, this option for scaling out has two other benefits: first, the involvement of the local member increases the acceptance and credibility of the product/service in the eyes of the communities; and second, by creating a resource within the community also empowers the communities to take care of their own needs (Kanitkar 2017).

Many social innovations, if they coincide with government initiatives, are also able to Scale Out by partnering with government agencies. In earlier chapters, we have seen how many social ventures (e.g., Akshaya Patra, Childline India, Digital Green and Pratham) partnered with government programmes to gain access and support for their mission. Successful social entrepreneurs look at government as a useful ally, which can provide both critical funding and infrastructure to extend their reach and impact. Partnering in government schemes provides the ventures both the outreach and resources to replicate their innovation in remote regions with minimal efforts and expenses. In fact, a study of 20 large social entrepreneurial ventures by Pandey et al. (2017) found that 17 of them had increased their reach by collaborating with the government.

Working with government as partner, however, has its peculiar challenges. By nature, government systems and procedures are conservative, cumbersome and inflexible. Partnering with government requires an understanding of how the system works, and working and negotiating with the policy makers. Since government is also a political entity, one of the challenges for social entrepreneurs is to maintain one's political neutrality for sustenance of the partnership.

Successful Scaling Out depends on two critical requirements.

1. **Identification of mission-aligned partner(s):** Finding the right agency to partner with is critical to the success of Scaling Out strategy (Harris 2010). The partner must have similar social mission as the venture and should be working with communities which have similar unmet needs which can be served by the innovation/intervention. In addition, partner's own technical expertise to replicate (and customize

if needed), and staff capacity to roll out the innovation plays an important role in Scaling Out.

2. **Clarity about the 'theory of change':** As a concept, Scaling Out seems a simple act, but in practice it is a complex process. Its success depends on entrepreneur's ability to identify and articulate which elements of the innovation/intervention need to be replicated. This requires clear articulation of the venture's 'theory of change' (Taplin and Clark 2012), that is, why the innovation/intervention was successful and which of its features (activities, skills, organizational systems, etc.) are essential for producing desired social outcomes. As Bradach (2003) noted:

> The objective is to reproduce a successful program's results, not to slavishly recreate every one of its features. At the heart of replication is the movement of an organization's theory of change to a new location. In some cases, this might entail transferring a handful of practices from one site to another; in others, the wholesale cloning of the organization's culture. (p. 19)

Since replication requires standardization, complexity of Scaling Out will depend not only on the number of features which need to be standardized, but also on how amenable to standardization those features are. Certain features (e.g., a system for door-step delivery of a service) are easy to articulate and standardize in a step-by-step manner. But if the replication depends on more complex requirements, then standardization of method and transferring it to the partner becomes more complex and difficult.

Scaling Deep

As we note earlier, in many market segments and communities, problems are not only multilayered and coexist, but they are also interrelated. Solving only one of them, even on a large scale, without considering others will have limited social impact on the community. For instance, providing access to clean drinking water to a community may bring down health-related expenditure of the poor, but it may still not have any substantial impact on their income and well-being if they lack marketable skills or access to labour market, or if the labour market itself is exploitative. In such contexts, achieving and scaling social impact would require deeper interventions which address these multiple and inter-connected needs of the same community (Srinath 2018). Scaling deep refers to such scaling of interventions within the same community.

Often, as the social entrepreneurs engage more with community, they discover these new pain points as they become manifest, and need to be addressed. For instance, the story of the **Mann Deshi Foundation** started when in 1986, Chetna Gala Sinha (Chetna), an activist who had earlier participated in the JP Movement, got married and came to the Mhaswad village of Mann division (Dist. Satara, Maharashtra). She observed that due to widespread poverty and government negligence, the place lacked basic amenities. Initially, she started working on issues, such as availability of water and electricity, building toilets, securing entitlements from government schemes, etc., but soon noticed the plight of women who were left behind when men migrated to cities in search of work. These women were mostly illiterate and tried to supplement family income by running small businesses. Realizing the need to build mechanisms for asset creation to reduce migration, in 1992 she started the *Mann Vikas Samajik Sanstha*, a credit cooperative society for small saving and lending for the marginalized women. Soon women needed other financial services, such as larger loans, to build their small businesses. Since local cooperative banks were not helpful, in 1997, Chetna started India's first women's rural bank, the **Mann Deshi Mahila Sahakari Bank** owned and managed by illiterate rural women.

As new community needs surfaced, new solutions and innovation were found to address them. When women shared that bank timings clashed with their income generating time, the bank introduced door-step banking and then later digital banking with biometrics. To enable the borrowers to use their loans productively, the Foundation started its Mann Deshi Udyogini programme to develop them as micro-entrepreneurs. Under this initiative, women were trained in basic functional literacy, computer literacy, business development, etc., and also in domain-specific expertise in areas such as goat rearing, weaving, tailoring, veterinary care, weaving, vending, etc. Since migration still continued due to regular droughts, Mann Deshi started its community programme which focused on building check dams, rejuvenating wells, collectivizing small and marginal farmers and connecting them with market, etc. To promote social solidarity and to share information, it also started Mann Deshi Tarang Vahini, a community radio which provided a platform for sharing information about government schemes and markets, promoting local talent, achievements of local women, culture and traditions, etc. While Mann Deshi also opened seven branches of its bank in other parts of Maharashtra, its primary focus remained on scaling its interventions to meet diverse needs of the communities in the Mann division.

Scaling Deep also often becomes necessary due to the success of initial interventions by the social entrepreneur. Sometimes when communities develop and change due to an intervention/solution, new needs and issues emerge which need to be addressed. For instance, when **Drishtee** was started by Satyan Mishra in 2001, the aim of the venture was to facilitate development of the village by providing e-governance services (e.g., land records, certificates for income, caste or domicile and driving licences) through internet kiosks, managed by local entrepreneurs (called *soochak*). Soon, to meet other local needs, more services (e.g., education, health, computer training and insurance) were added to the same platform. However, after 7 years, Mishra realized that while the venture had scaled up and won many recognitions and awards, it had limited impact on developing the villages, and people continued to migrate for livelihoods. While people had benefitted from the interventions, they found no local opportunities to use their newly acquired skills and knowledge. This led to change in Drishtee's vision and agenda to include microenterprise creation and supporting local livelihoods through access to credit, market linkages and skill development. The venture also started running a physical low-cost rural supply chain for direct delivery of agricultural inputs and items of daily needs to the rural enterprises (Mishra 2012).

In the literature and discourse on scaling of social ventures, Scaling Deep is largely a neglected strategy. In fact, since the accepted definition and metrics of scaling revolves around the size and number of population and regions, it is often not even considered a scaling strategy. It is, however, a significant approach for scaling the social impact for two reasons:

First, the concept of scale is a relative one. Compared to the policy makers, investors and funders, award-giving foundations, academic researchers, etc., whose concern is the size of the impacted population, meaning of scale of impact can be quite different for the beneficiaries of the change intervention. For instance, for a rural community whose entire existence is confined to a radius of about 100 km, if the interventions increased opportunities for secure livelihoods, made credit, health care, education, government entitlements, etc., accessible to them, changed their relationship with the power structures in their lives (government officials, landlords, money lenders, etc.) to have an influence, and made them feel secure and in control of their lives, then for them the interventions had the scale of impact which changed *their* world.

Second, in communities/segments with interrelated multiple problems, mono-thematic solutions (e.g., skilling, providing solar energy and strengthening primary education) have limited impact, because they do not change the deep-rooted 'opportunity structures' which we discussed in Chapter 5. In such communities, besides changes in individual behaviour, sustainable change can be achieved only by changing the deeply entrenched social norms, relationships and structures (Kumar 2019; Moore et al. 2015). Scaling Deep enables the social entrepreneurs to change and transform these ingrained and disabling patterns within the community.

For the social entrepreneurs, the key challenge for successful Scaling deep strategy is the ability to steadily craft innovative solutions to address the successive problems as they surface. This requires three abilities from them.

1. **Sensitivity to 'low-intensity signals':** Often many deep-rooted problems are not readily visible, or even articulated by the target beneficiaries/customers of the intervention. They show up as 'low-intensity signals' such as a stray comment or incidents, sudden fluctuations in the lives of community members, in community response to events in the external environment, etc. For instance, in 2012 when the region was experiencing a severe drought, one of the women approached the Mann Deshi Bank to mortgage her gold. When she told that she wanted the money to buy water or else her family will have to migrate, Mann Deshi realized that to leverage the benefits from the banking services, community also needed a robust and secure environmental infrastructure. This led the venture to start its community programme focusing on rejuvenation and protection of water resources, live stocks, farmers' collectives, etc. Social entrepreneurs need sensitivity and readiness to pick up such imperceptible signals from chance events and discern the problems.

2. **Ability to redefine the problems:** As the social entrepreneurs delve deeper into the community issues, the definition of the problem they need to solve also undergoes changes. For instance, setting up a community-owned clean water facility may surface the problems of caste and community divide which does not allow people to share common

resources. Similarly, an innovative school project may uncover the underlying gender discrimination in the community resulting in low enrolment and higher dropout among girls. Discovery of such underlying problems changes the required interventions and innovations which can solve them. Social entrepreneurs, therefore, need to regularly reframe and redefine the problems for themselves and the community. In their study of scaling strategies, Moore at al. (2015) found that successful deep scaling '… involved deliberately reframing predominant narratives that existed about the social issue participants sought to address. By changing the narrative, participants described how they could successfully begin to change cultural norms and beliefs about the issue.' (p. 79)

3. **Patience and long-term engagement:** Scaling deep is a slow process to create sustainable social change. Reeler (2007) in his paper 'A Three-fold Theory of Social Change' noted that deep-rooted social change requires addressing a number of aspects related to the community, for example, mobilization of the community to develop a cohesive and collective identity; strengthening of collaborative and mutually supportive relationships within the community; facilitating unlearning and leaning of norms, processes and practices which influence the interactions among members; co-creating solutions which are acceptable to and owned by the community; aligning community needs and activities to external players (e.g., government, markets and other service providers) in a supportive relationship and so on. Facilitating such changes in the community requires long-term engagement with the community from the social entrepreneur.

Scaling Vertically

Many social problems are so deeply embedded in the society (cultural values and practices, institutions, government policies, etc.) that they can be addressed only through systemic changes, which establish new acceptable norms and practices among people and institutions. In earlier chapters, we saw a couple of such instances of systemic changes, for example, changes in the national education policy to incorporate EVS through the efforts of Gloria de Souza (Chapter 2) and creation of RUGMARK/GoodWeave standards to stop use of child labour in carpet making industry by Kailash Satyarthi (Chapter 5). In all such changes, the beginning was made with an innovative idea which had the potential of changing an existing sub-optimal societal equilibrium (Martin and Osberg 2007) by working with multiple stakeholders at individual, institutional and policy levels.

Scaling Vertically refers to such 'scaling of ideas'. According to EdelGive Foundation's report on *Growing at Scale: Best Practices in Scalability* (EdelGive Foundation 2018):

> Vertical scaling-up refers to the policy, political, legal, regulatory, budgetary, or other systems changes needed to institutionalise an innovation at the national or sub-national level through advocacy (public sector), strategic alliances, and collaborations (private/NGO sector). Vertical scaling-up calls for an understanding of the existing policy concerning the theme on which the organisation is working. (p. 4)

Scaling Vertically is often the most appropriate approach when the social entrepreneurs are trying to solve rights-based problems of equity, human right and justice. Such problems are complex and their solutions are not easily amenable to being expressed in quantifiable goals or well-defined interventions; these are 'wicked problems' (May et al. 2016) which 'have no definitive formulation—you just know it when you see it.' (p. 4). Solving such problems requires changes at multiple levels in societal practices, norms and policies, and use of a very different set of strategies and methods than the other three kinds of scaling.

To understand the nature and process of such scaling, let us look at the story of **NASVI** (National Association of Street Vendors of India, earlier National Alliance of Street Vendors of India):

> NASVI was formed in 1998, when some of the NGOs and civil society organizations, which worked with urban poor and informal sector workers, met in Ahmedabad to discuss how to collectively address the problems of street vendors at a national level. Despite being an essential part of the urban economy, the street vendors and hawkers were not even part of official statistics or were considered in the urban planning; they were, in fact, subjected to harassment, extortion and eviction. There were some member-based vendor organizations and trade unions in different cities, and while they could secure short-term concessions for the vendors through protests and litigations, they were not very effective in getting the vendors their due rights.
>
> These discussions resulted in a loose alliance, NASVI, with Arbind Singh, the founder of Nidan (see Box 1.3) as its national coordinator. In the following months, NASVI organized regional consultative meetings in Bangalore, Delhi, Mumbai and Patna with street vendors, vendor leaders, municipal administrators, elected representatives and other civil society organizations and the media to develop a common agenda. Besides bringing many other organizations into the alliance, these meetings also provided a common platform where the different stakeholders listened to others' perspectives to develop a common understanding of the issue. These deliberations also highlighted that a national level legislation is essential for providing the vendors with their legal rights.
>
> NASVI also realized that a national level legislation can be achieved only if there is a change in the perceptions about the

street vendors in the minds of administrators, legislators, elected representatives, urban planners and the public at large. Besides other forms of advocacy, this also required evidence that the street vendors are significant contributors to urban services and economy. It commissioned a study 'Hawkers in the Urban Informal Sector: A Study of Street Vending in Seven Cities' which was published in 2001 (Bhowmik 2001). The study documented how despite long working hours, tough working conditions, meagre income and harassment by the civic authorities, street vendors provided low-cost services and products at convenient locations to urban dwellers, especially from the middle and lower middle categories. The study concluded that though the vendors and hawkers 'are viewed as a problem for urban governance they are in fact the solution to some of the problems of the urban poor. By providing cheaper commodities hawkers are in effect providing subsidy to the urban poor, something which the government should have done.' (Bhowmik 2001, 30).

The findings of this landmark study were shared and publicized through media, became the basis of public discourse for finding solutions for the problems of street vendors. NASVI also shared the findings with the Ministry of Urban Development, which resulted in formation of a National Task Force to draft a National Policy on Street Vending in 2001–2002 by the government—and subsequently, the adoption of the National Policy on Urban Street Vendors by the parliament. The policy was a major breakthrough which for the first time recognized hawkers and vendors as contributors to urban economy and not as illegal encroacher of the public space. It also specified providing legal status to vendors, formation of Town Vending Committees with representation for vendors, vending zones in urban, etc.

A National Policy, however, only serves as a guideline to the states without making it mandatory. Correspondingly, while the guidelines were being followed in a few urban bodies, there was a need to aim for an act of parliament to achieve its goals. NASVI kept working with a number of government bodies, for example, the National Commission for Enterprises in the Unorganized Sector (NCEUS), Ministry of Housing and Urban Poverty Alleviation, National Advisory Council, etc., to push for a central law for vending. Besides these efforts, from 2009 NASVI also ensured pressure from below on the policy makers through a number of measures to demand a central law. For example, it organized a series of demonstrations and protest meetings across the states, its affiliates lobbied with local members of parliaments to exercise pressure within their parties, it held regular consultative meetings with local bureaucrats and councillors, and it even got the vendors to send more than a 100,000 postcards to the concerned minister. These initiatives bore results when in 2012 the street vendor bill was tabled by the Union Minister of Housing and Urban Poverty Alleviation in the parliament, and finally the Street Vendors (Protection of Livelihood and Regulation of Street Vending) Act was promulgated in 2014.

NASVI's success in 'Scaling Vertically' was rooted in its ability to work multiple stakeholders. Besides working with people not only within the government, it also partnered with other stakeholders in civil society organizations, national and international bodies (e.g., International Labour Organisation [ILO], Women in Informal Employment: Globalizing and Organizing [WIEGO] and Fredrick Ebert Stiftung) and media. To change the public perception about street vendors, since 2010, it started organizing 'Street Food Festivals' across different cities in India, which offered the residents not only safe street foods, but also to make them understand the vendors' legitimate contributions to urban life.

More importantly, NASVI helped changing the perceptions of its own constituents, the vendors, about themselves to become more self-reliant in meeting their needs. For instance, in 2001 to meet the credit and financial needs of the vendors, it started the Sanchay Thrift and Credit Cooperative Society, which allowed the vendors to save, deposit money and take loans to meet working capital or family needs; it formed local market committees comprising street vendors to address the issues of market access and market information faced by the vendors; it arranged for training of the street vendors and their families by partnering with Hotel Management Institutes and National Urban Livelihoods Mission (NULM). In fact, in 2013 it also started NASVI Street Food Private Ltd, with street food vendors as shareholders, to enlarge street food business across India. These initiatives and successes also helped NASVI to grow, and by 2017 it had a membership of 707,695 of 1,054 organizations in 25 states.

From the above example (and other similar instances of 'scaling of an idea'), one can derive three critical requirements for Scaling vertically:

1. **Creating evidence-based shared understanding:** First and foremost, Scaling Vertically requires creating a shared awareness among all the stakeholders about the problem itself. Often, the policy makers, public and even members of the affected population do not appreciate that the problem exists, or have differing perceptions and understanding about it. For instance, as we saw above, when NASVI started street vendors were viewed by the public and policy makers as nuisance and encroachers and not as valuable service providers. Similarly, the poverty and indebtedness of the rural poor may be viewed, even by the poor themselves, as due to exploitation by the local moneylender and not due to the exclusionary structure and policies of the formal financial institutions. Since the rights-based problems are often fuzzy to define clearly, the social entrepreneurs need to develop an

evidence-based formulation of the problem to influence the public discourse.

2. **Collaborating across segments:** Collaborations and alliances across multiple stakeholders play an important role in Scaling Vertically. Such collaborations provide valuable platforms to the social entrepreneurs to seed their ideas across wider segments. However, these partnerships also bring in new perspectives, which may necessitate redefinition and broadening the understanding of the problem definitions and re-conceptualizing the goal. To leverage the benefits of collaborations, the social entrepreneurs need both the capacity to 'let-go' and openness to others' views, as well as the ability to work through constructive dialogue to resolve the differences.

3. **Engaging in advocacy:** Since the goal is social change by codifying the new innovative approach in the policy, institutions and practices, advocacy is an essential part of Scaling Vertically (Klugman 2011; Moore et al. 2015). However, advocacy for vertical scaling is more than just political or social activism. It requires both engaging with the policy makers as well as mobilizing the grassroots opinion to support the idea. Social entrepreneurs achieve this by using a mix of activities and strategies: on the one hand, they write white papers and studies on the issue, organize consultative meetings and conferences, engage with political and participate in policy dialogues, etc., to put the issue on political agenda; on the other hand, they also mobilize grassroots support through protests and demonstrations, educate and strengthen the capacity of individuals and groups of potential beneficiaries of change, strategically use media, etc., to build bottom-up pressure for change.

FIVE ARCHETYPES OF SOCIAL ENTREPRENEURSHIP

7

To sum up, poetic, philosophical, scientific or political progress results from the accidental coincidence of a private obsession with a public need.

—*Richard Rorty (1986)*

Why Taxonomy of Entrepreneurs?

Across the examples of social entrepreneurs quoted in the previous chapters, one finds that while they are similar in their motivations and qualities, they also differ from each other in a variety of ways. They differ in terms of the nature of social issues they address, in the constraints and resources which shape their efforts, in the approach and solutions which they devise to address similar problems, in the kind of organizations they establish, in the manner in which they try to scale the impact of their efforts, etc. Surprisingly, barring few isolated articles (e.g., Zahra et al. 2009), the research and discourse on social entrepreneurship has remained silent on these differences among the social entrepreneurs. Based on their analysis of social entrepreneurial phenomenon, Zahra et al. (2009) noted:

> …different types of social entrepreneurs exist, addressing specific social problems in their own ways and within their own realms. Some might be the grand visionaries who identify big or even worldwide social causes and mobilize forces to tackle these concerns…. Other social entrepreneurs might

be more adept at creating organizations that tackle these issues. Still, some entrepreneurs focus more on local issues. (pp. 522–523)

In fact, across the stories and case studies of well-recognized social entrepreneurs, one finds that while they all share the common features which characterize social entrepreneurs (i.e., a mission to solve a social problem, and use of entrepreneurial strategy to develop and implement innovative and sustainable solutions), it is conceptually difficult to club them into one single theme or type. This diversity and multi-faceted nature of social entrepreneurship, as we had noted in the Chapter 1, is also a reason why a precise and all-encompassing definition is not possible. However, across their stories, one can discern some recurring patterns which distinguish them from each other. Each of these patterns describes a distinct model or archetype of social entrepreneurial activity and approach. In this chapter, we will discuss five such archetypes.

Local Changemakers

Sebayan is a small NGO on a remote impoverished island of Sunderban Delta of West Bengal[1]. It was founded by H. S. Rauth who was among the few youths from the island who could avail free education and get a decent job in Delhi. Having achieved a certain level of success in life, the founder was motivated to support the community of his native place. Sebayan is managed by his family members who live on island, and runs an assortment of small-scale programmes related to education of local children, biogas, horticulture, renewable energy, etc., to meet the needs of the local community of the

---

[1] This description is based on the notes taken by the author during an onsite assessment visit to the NGO as a part of India NGO Awards 2009.

island. Like similar small NGOs, it is largely funded by individual donations and some small grants from the government schemes in the region.

One of the problems faced by the island was its lack of connectivity with the mainland, which could be accessed only by crossing three contiguous islands. Since it took about 3–4 hours to reach the mainland, it deprived the local population from availing better opportunities. To overcome this constraint, Sebayan devised a simple but innovative solution using local resources. It mobilized the villagers to provide physical labour to make a jetty on the island where a ferry could dock, and take the locals to the mainland. This reduced the travel time to about 20–25 minutes, and had transformative impact on the economy of the island: the locals could now get better price for their produce (fish and vegetables) by selling it on mainland, they could earn more through wage employment, small shops on the island had easier and cheaper access to buy and sell items of local requirements, etc. Moreover, the easy accessibility of the island also increased the interaction of the community with the local government officials and counsellors, thus enabling them to influence their entitlements. What was remarkable about the 'Jetty Project', as it was called locally, was that it was entirely self-sustaining. The collection from the fare, which was just ₹2–3 per trip, was enough to meet the operational cost of the ferry, and also fund the annual repair of the jetty.

Sebayan's 'Jetty Project' represents countless similar highly localized, but high-impact, change initiatives, which remain conspicuously absent in the discussion on social entrepreneurship. This lack of acknowledgement of local initiatives and entrepreneurs is due to a variety of reasons. Mostly these change efforts are so small and localized that it is difficult to locate them. Often both the problems and their solutions are also relevant only to a locally unique condition, which makes it difficult to assess their impact in terms of size of the population or regions covered by them. Unfortunately, since the award-giving foundations, researchers, investors/funders and media emphasize scalability (in terms of size of population or regions) as an important criterion for defining and identifying social entrepreneurs, these Local Changemakers remain outside their search 'radar'. An unfortunate outcome of this sector/definitional bias is that despite being widespread and impactful, the contribution of such entrepreneurial individuals to social change does not get adequately recognized (see Box 7.1 for some examples).

BOX 7.1   SOME EXAMPLES OF LOCAL CHANGEMAKERS

Jan Swasthya Sahyog (JSS) located in the village Ganiyari, Bilaspur (M.P.), was founded in 1996 by four doctor couples from the All-India Institute of Medical Sciences (AIIMS), New Delhi. The founders left their jobs with AIIMS to pursue their dream of changing the rural healthcare situation by developing an effective, low-cost, high quality community-based healthcare system. They particularly selected Ganiyari because it was a low-resource area, and provided a laboratory for developing a model for the delivery of healthcare, which could be easily accessed by the rural poor. Starting with modest beginnings, JSS now serves more than 100 villages has more than 200 full-time staff mostly drawn and trained from local community, and treats more than 50,000 rural and tribal patients every year. It also provides free nursing courses to local dalit and tribal girls, and has created a cadre of village level health workers who make primary healthcare accessible to villagers locally.

Kalamandir works in the villages in and around East Singhbhum district of Jharkhand with the mission of preserving and promoting the local tribal art and craft

---

(e.g., music, dance, painting and metal art). It started in 2000 when the founder, Amitava Ghosh observed that the tribal artists and performers were abandoning their craft due to their single crop land and high indebtness. There were no locally sustainable livelihoods which could support the artists to continue performing. This led to interventions in livelihood promotion such as agriculture and water conservation, forming self-help groups of women for saving and inter-loaning, training in craft skills for product development, micro-enterprise development of artists and craftsmen, opening an outlet in the city to market their products, and so on. Over the years, the venture started promoting rural art tourism built around artisan-owned *kalagrams* (artists' villages) which provide livelihoods to the villagers while at the same time promote the local craft forms.

Protsahan is a small social venture in Uttam Nagar colony of New Delhi, which works with at-risk adolescent girls, providing them care, education and rehabilitation. It was founded in 2010 by then 24-year old microbiologist-cum-MBA Sonal Kapoor when, during a photo-shoot, she was shocked to find that many young girls were sent for sex trade to earn a living by their own family. Protsahan empowers and mainstream such girls through creative education and entrepreneurial skills training so that she can break the extreme cycle of poverty and abuse. It does so by using its '5 pillars of creativity model' (design, art, digital stories, photography, technology & cinema) to revolutionize the education delivery mechanism for children at the bottom-most of the social pyramid. Over the years, Protsahan had rescued and mainstreamed about 800 girls, and many of the girls had exceled and won awards in studies and sports.

Even when these entrepreneurial innovations are scalable and/or replicable, often the entrepreneurs lack resources and/or aspirations for scaling them beyond their limited local contexts. However, they remain committed to and engaged with their communities and scale their intervention deeper to address their multiple and emerging problems. It is also important to note that many social ventures start as a localized initiative to solve an indigenous problem. Over a period of time, some of them also gain recognition when their model is seen as replicable. For instance, over the years, Jan Swasthya Sahayog has been acknowledged for its successful model, and has become active in advocacy for healthcare as a basic right at national policy level.

Zahra et al. (2009) called such entrepreneurs *social bricoleur* 'who act on locally discovered opportunities with locally available resources.' (p. 524) The area of their change efforts remains geographically limited, which may be just a village, a district or a specific small region. In their limited local context, they solve pressing social problems which would otherwise remain unrecognized and unaddressed. In fact, they are uniquely positioned to do so, since they leverage the highly contextual, and often tacit, local knowledge to identify critical social problems, mobilize local resources and develop a solution which is relevant and viable in the local context.

Public Goods Providers

For any society to function efficiently and effectively, provision of certain basic services and amenities to its members is essential for building stronger communities, and promoting equity and social justice. People need education, affordable housing, electricity, road, food and nutrition, etc., in order to live a productive and healthy life. Provision of such public goods is mostly seen as the responsibility of the state, or as a part of charity done by many local NGOs and religious organizations.

In the conventional literature on social entrepreneurship, providing social goods and provisions is mostly considered as an act of philanthropy rather than that of entrepreneurship (e.g., Martin and Osberg 2007). This is also true for many initiatives which distribute socially useful goods and services to those who need them. However, in a resource-starved country like India, reaching such services and amenities to people also offers an entrepreneurial opportunity. Many social entrepreneurs create models of delivering these services and goods which are different than the conventional ways of doing charity; they are innovative, sustainable and create visible impact. To appreciate this point, consider an example (see Box 7.2 for some more examples):

BOX 7.2   EXAMPLES OF SOCIAL SERVICE PROVIDERS

GreenSole: GreenSole is a Mumbai-based venture which refurbishes used footwear into trendy slippers and distributes them to the underprivileged kids. It was founded by two young athletes, Shriyans Bhandari and Ramesh Dhami in 2013, when they realized that they wore out and discarded 3–4 sports shoes every year. However, the soles of the shoes remained in good condition and could be recycled to make slippers. Using the money from business-plan competition, they put up a unit. GreenSole conducts collection drives in colleges and schools, and has installed drop boxes in public places to collect discarded shoes. To make the venture sustainable, it also partners with a number of companies who conduct collection drives in their offices and pay GreenSole to refurbish the shoes and donate them in villages. People can also purchase shoes for themselves or donate to others. By 2018, GreenSole had distributed more than 100,000 refurbished footwears.

ToyBank: ToyBank is a Mumbai-based organization, founded by Shweta Chari in 2004, when she noticed that while children from underprivileged backgrounds have some access to clothes and books, they were deprived of toys and games which are necessary for their enjoyment and holistic development (e.g., social and emotional skills, intellectual abilities, motor skills and imagination). The venture collects donated toys and games and partners with about 70 organizations (e.g., NGOs, slum and rural schools, shelter homes, hospitals and pediatric care centres) and sets up play centres, equipped with educational toys and games, for children. These toys and games are stocked keeping in mind the developmental needs of the children, and are regularly replaced. It also partners with corporate, Rotary Club, NGOs, colleges and schools, etc., for volunteers who manage the play and story-telling sessions at the centres. By 2018, ToyBank was reaching about 50,000 children every year through it 285 play centres in Mumbai and other cities of Maharashtra.

Operation ASHA: Operation ASHA was founded by Dr Shelly Batra and Sandeep Ahuja in 2006 to bring diagnosis and treatment of tuberculosis (TB) to poor communities in India and Cambodia at their door-step. TB patients are largely from disadvantaged backgrounds (slum-dwellers, daily wagers, rural poor, etc.), who are unable to access government hospitals, both due to distance and time, and the social stigma attached with the disease. Operation ASHA establishes small specialized clinics in accessible places, such as businesses, pharmacies, temples, etc., which open at timings convenient to local people (early morning and late evening), and are managed by local community person (mostly women and youth) who are employed and trained as TB-specific health workers. In rural areas, a community health worker travels from village-to-village on a motorcycle/scooter carrying with him anti-TB drugs, supplies and equipment. By 2018, Operation ASHA was serving over 15 million people in India and Cambodia, with a team of over 250 field workers, 150 community partners and over 4,000 village workers.

Pune-based entrepreneur, Pradeep Lokhande started the **Gyan-Key Library** initiative in 2010, when he visited some rural schools in Maharashtra. He found that the children wanted to read books apart from their textbooks, but the schools were cash-strapped to have a library. Lokhande knew that reading in early age opens up the mind to new ideas, builds curiosity and ability to ask questions, and decided to establish libraries in the rural schools.

To set-up such libraries on a scale across the rural schools, Lokhande set up a well-oiled system. He searched the book markets in Pune and found that a set of about 180 reasonably-priced books in local language (on subjects such as personality development, self-help, communication skills, Indian consti-tution, drama, fiction, inspiring autobiographies, etc.), if bought in bulk, would cost just ₹5,000. This was sufficient to start a school library, which could benefit children from four to eight adjoining villages. He ensured that each library was managed by one of the students, called the Gyan-Key monitor, who was trained in managing the library.

Initially he approached his contacts to mobilize funds for the book, but later developed the Non-Resident Villagers (NRV) strategy to raise donations. He started writing to the villagers who had migrated and settled in the cities and abroad to fund the library. Most donated willingly, since they themselves had studied on those schools. To build donors' trust in the initiative, Lokhande used a novel method. Every donated book had a postcard with the donor's address. He would ask the children to write and post their comments about the book and what they learnt from that. This feedback to the donors brought in more donations. By 2018, he had established about 3,800 libraries in rural secondary schools, cumulatively containing 850,000 books from a donation ₹26.5 million, which benefitted about 1 million children (Menon 2014; *Pune Mirror* 2017).

As can be seen, the entrepreneurial initiatives to provide public goods differ from similar programmes by government and NGOs in significant ways. In fact, the entrepreneurial public goods providers are distinct in that they incorporate the three key features which characterize any entrepreneurial venture:

1. **Identifying opportunity in a neglected problem:** These entrepreneurs identify a gap in the nature of services which are being provided by the government and the NGOs. These needs are either not being serviced or are being serviced in an inefficient manner by the existing service providers. For instance, Anshu Gupta founded **Goonj** when he realized that among the three basic universal needs of 'food, shelter and clothing', clothes were neglected by almost all programmes, and were seen only as a relief material during natural calamities (see Box 1.3). Similarly, as the examples of such ventures show, they focused on social needs, such as children's library, toys, last mile treatment of TB, or shoes, etc., which are widespread and critical but are not adequately addressed.

2. **Crafting innovative solutions:** Like any entrepreneurial venture, these entrepreneurs devise innovative solutions to leverage the opportunity they have identified. As the examples in Box 7.2 show, they design their service innovatively, craft new ways to reach their target segment, devise creative models

to deliver the service on a large scale, develop methods to mobilize resources to make the initiative sustainable, and so on. For instance, **Akshaya Patra Foundation** started in 2000 with a mission to decrease the malnourishment among the school going children and increase the learning outcomes. To reach its mission to feed nutritious meals to millions of children, it did many innovations in its processes and 'business' model: it designed its kitchens like 'food factories' which can cook 6,000 kilos of rice, 4.5–5 tonnes of vegetables and 6,000 litres of sambar, in under 4 hours and make 40,000 rotis per hour; to save energy it devised automated gravity flow to move items in the kitchen; to reach out to the highly dispersed target segment, the venture created a network of centralized kitchens capable of cooking food up to 100,000 mid-day meals a day, and decentralized kitchen to provide meals to children in the remote areas; to mobilize resources and increase its outreach, it entered into public–private partnership in the Mid-Day Meal Scheme of the government and so on. These innovations enabled it to grow from a single kitchen serving just 1,500 children in five schools in 2000 to serving 1.7 million children in about 14,000 schools in 12 states in India.

3. **Focusing on scale and sustainability:** Though many such ventures start as a small prototype covering a small population, they are based on the perception of a need which is pervasive, and a larger vision by the entrepreneurs. This spurs, as well as provides opportunity to, the social entrepreneurs to plan how to scale up the impact of their efforts in a sustainable manner. For instance, **Pratham**, which is the largest non-governmental initiative to impart primary education in India, was co-founded by Madhav Chavan in 1995 as an educational initiative for children in Mumbai slums. Over the years, it developed high-quality, low-cost educational interventions which could be replicated across different contexts. It also invested in educational innovations, such as

Learn to Read programme which could improve learning outcomes in a short time span, use of volunteer-based model for scaling up of delivery at local level, innovative teaching-learning material and measurement methods, use of technology, programme for dropout students, etc. In 2006, Pratham also pioneered a nation-wide annual survey to assess the state of primary education in India. Its *Annual Survey of Education Report* (ASER) is used by the government as an input in policy formulation. Over the years, these innovations enabled the venture to scale up across the states of India.

Constructive Opportunists

Constructive opportunists represent the very prototypes, which dominates the definitions, research and discourse on social entrepreneurship (e.g., Dees 1998; Johnson 2003; Martin and Osberg 2007, Prabhu 1999). They actively identify opportunities to address social needs, which are widespread but are not addressed either by the government (due to neglect, lack of political will or inefficiencies) or by the business (due to lack of commercial incentive). Since these needs are extensive and prevalent, they hold the potential to build a scalable venture across regions and markets.

Consider the following example:

In India, offering of flower in temples is a common religious practice. To meet the growing demand for flowers, the farmers use large quantities of chemical fertilizers, pesticides and insecticides, which remain as residue on the flowers. Once used, these flowers are dumped in the rivers and water bodies, and contaminate them. Estimates suggest that at least 8 million metric tonnes of such chemical-ridden floral waste ends up in the rivers from these temples. These hazardous chemicals seep into the ground water causing threat to health; mix with the river water, thus affecting the fragile ecosystem of water bodies; and, decomposes along with the faecal coliform bacteria giving rise to waterborne diseases, such as diarrhoea, cholera, dysentery, hepatitis, etc.

Disturbed by this, but also sensing an opportunity, two young Kanpur-based entrepreneurs, Ankit Agarwal and Karan Rastogi came up with the idea of collecting and recycling (or 'flowercycling' as they termed it) the floral waste. After exploring various options for 18 months, they decided to make organic fertilizer from the waste using vermicomposting, which could be sold. They used the ₹72,000 they had received through various business-plan competitions, and in 2015, established their for-profit social enterprise, **Help Us Green** to put their idea into practice. Soon, besides the compost, they also developed a technique to make carbon-free incense sticks from the waste, and started employing local rural women— mostly the scavengers from the marginalized community—to collect, clean and recycle the flower waste to hand-roll the sticks. Besides providing these women with a regular job, they also helped them with opening bank accounts, insurance, providing vocational training to their children, etc.

By 2018, the venture was collecting as much as 800 kg of waste flowers every day from the temples in Kanpur, and was providing employment to about 1,200 rural women. They had also developed a product using the flower waste which could replace thermocol, a polystyrene packing material which normally takes about 80 years to degrade. In contrast, their product would self-degrade in less than 6 weeks. With funding from the Tata Trust and Echoing Green had started putting up facilities in Mathura and Varanasi to manufacture these.

The social entrepreneurs in the above illustration are a typical example of Constructive Opportunists. As the term suggests, they are sensitive to, and actively seek opportunities in, the unattended markets and then leverage them to create ventures to address a social problem on an ongoing basis. Mostly these ventures are for-profit in nature, or at least have an earned-income strategy. However, their focus remains on their social goals and aim at remaining profitable rather than on profit maximization (see Box 7.3 for some examples).

BOX 7.3 EXAMPLES OF CONSTRUCTIVE OPPORTUNISTS

Ekgaon Technologies Pvt Ltd: Ekgaon is a for profit enterprise, which was founded by Vijay Pratap Singh Aditya in 2002 to provide customized IT-enabled advisory services to small and marginal farmers to increase farm productivity and reduce cultivation costs. Ekgaon provides customized information such as local soil and its nutrient, crop and weather conditions, disease alerts and market prices, etc. for a fee of ₹150/cropping season. These services which are delivered via SMS in local language and phone calls at planned intervals are subscribed by about 300,000 farmers across the country. In 2015, Ekgaon scaled up to develop a supply chain which connects the farmers directly with the market, thus providing better prices. The venture directly purchases organic produce from the farmers and sells them online under Ekgaon brand. In 2018, Ekgaon had about 190 organic products in its portfolio which it was sourcing from 20,000 farmers across different states.

3S India: 3S India, a brand owned by Pune-based SaraPlast Pvt Ltd, was founded by Rajeev Kher to address the need for dignified and clean sanitation for the under-served segment. He noticed that most public toilets are either not used due to poor maintenance and cleanliness, or are often not available at places where they are required for short duration. To meet this need, 3S provides end-to-end portable sanitation and waste management solutions which includes installation of toilets, cleaning, maintenance, disposal and treatment of waste treatment and recycling the sewage water. These toilets are made of recyclable material and can be leased or purchased from the company with the entire service package. Though the primary focus of the company is to service low-income segments, for example, slum-dwellers, migrant labour, construction workers, etc., it also provides toilets at public places (e.g., bus stands and petrol pumps) religious and political gatherings, events (e.g., weddings), tourist sites, etc. The venture also provides hand-wash stations, biodigester-based eco-toilets, urinals and containerized solutions (which include toilets, urinals and wash basins) and septic tanks. 3S India operates across 10 Indian states and annually recycles 155 million litres of liquid waste, saving over 104 million litres of fresh water.

I Say Organic: Delhi-based I Say Organic Pvt. Ltd was founded by 25-years old Ashmeet Kapoor in late 2011, to promote organic agriculture by incentivizing farmers with fair price for their produce. The venture sources organic produce directly from farmer groups in different Indian states at a price 25%–40% higher than the local *mandi* prices. Unlike other aggregators/retailers, I Say Organic buys the perishables every day, helping the farmers to have a steady cash-flow. The items are sorted, graded and packed, and sold to the customers in the National Capital Region who can order by phone or on the venture's website for home delivery. By analysing the demand pattern, the venture is able to both procure right quantity of different products, and also counsel the farmers about the market preferences. Starting with a few farmers in UP, Haryana and Himachal Pradesh, by 2017

I Say Organic was sourcing from 12 certified organic farmer groups, consisting of about 10,000 growers, across 12 Indian states. Its portfolio too had enlarged from just a few items (e.g., fruits, vegetables and pulses) to more than 200 fresh and processed organic items, and it was servicing more than 150 deliveries per day. In addition, the venture had also started off-line sales by opening two stores in Gurgaon and South Delhi.

One of the major challenges that Constructive Opportunists face is in maintaining a balance between their social mission and commercial goals. As they grow, they are often confronted with the mutually competing institutional goals of making a social impact and also maintaining a healthy bottom line. As they expand into new markets and activities, they are subjected to an entirely different set of internal and external pressures, such as demands from the funders and investors, need for greater operational efficiency and control, requirements of greater profits to fund scaling up in the new market, and even the lure of financial gains, etc. In adjusting to these conditions, social ventures often become susceptible to 'mission drift' (Cornforth 2014; Jones 2007), that is, they diverge from, or dilute, their primary mission and purpose. For instance, to scale up a microfinance venture may be tempted to increase the average loan size to decrease its transaction costs, while neglecting small borrowers. Similarly, a social venture, which is providing an affordable high-quality product or service to marginalized segments, may diversify into more lucrative markets to increase its margins, while ignoring its original segment.

For the Constructive Opportunists, the mission drift can happen on either side. Not only the focus on commercial goals can make them neglect their primary social objective, but an over-involvement with social mission can also make their venture financially non-viable. Many researchers (e.g., Cornforth 2014; Ebrahim et al. 2014; Rabi 2016) have identified the actions which successful social entrepreneurs take to counter the possibilities of mission drift. Following are the key strategies for combating mission drift:

1. **Diversification and due diligence of funding sources:** Social ventures need external funds from donors and investors to operate and scale up. However, often this financial support comes with conditions which represent the priorities of the funder, which may not be aligned to the mission of the social entrepreneur. For instance, the investor may want the entrepreneur to diversify into markets which while increasing the revenue (and returns to the investor) may deviate the enterprise from its core purpose. Similarly, the funding from government or donor may require the entrepreneur to enter into activities which are unrelated to their mission.

   To counteract such pressures, entrepreneurs are often selective in choosing their donors and/or investors, and may even decline funding if accepting it would cause mission drift. They also work actively to widen their portfolio of funders and partners so that they can refuse those funding options which would compel them to digress from their core purpose.

2. **Strengthening the governance mechanisms:** Governance plays a critical role in ensuring that the venture is able to resist internal and external pressure to drift away from its purpose. The composition and functioning of the board is a key area for ensuring good governance practices and remaining committed to the purpose of the venture. Board members bring in their expertise, advice and connections, which influence the direction of the enterprise (Santos et al. 2015). Effective social entrepreneurs are careful in selecting their

board members to ensure a balance between the expertise and commitment to the mission, and to sustainable management practices.

Often the donors or investors demand a seat on the board and influence the decisions of the enterprise. If the entrepreneur has chosen his/her funders judiciously, their nominees on the board can also provide a more holistic approach to management. In many cases, however, this does not happen when the goals of the funder and enterprise are not aligned. A strong and committed board then is able to provide the balance and avoid a mission drift.

3. **Mission-aligned HR practices**: The role of human resource practices is often understated in discussions on social entrepreneurial ventures. HR practices and systems (e.g., recruitment and selection, training and performance management) are essential for aligning the efforts of people towards the same goal. While in the initial phase of the venture when the founding team is small and shares the same vision, these practices may not be important. But they become critical as the ventures scale up and more people join the team.

For social enterprises, this is even more challenging due to their twin social and commercial goals. As they scale up, they need not only people who are functionally competent to manage the operational requirements of efficiency and integration of activities, but also people who share the social vision and values of the venture. To cope with such demands, these ventures need to use innovative human resource practices in hiring, induction and socialization, performance management systems, compensation, etc., which can align the people with the twin goals of the venture.

4. **Loosely coupled hybrid structures**: Another way in which Constructive Opportunists cope with the potential hazard of

mission drift is by compartmentalizing the commercial and social activities in different parts of the organization. For instance, as we saw in some examples in the earlier chapters (e.g., Industree and Hasiru Dala), the venture may operate as a hybrid venture with a commercial arm which interfaces the market and manages the financial risks, and a not-for-profit entity which pursues the social mission of the venture.

Social Transformers

As discussed about Scaling Vertically in the last chapter, many social problems are so deeply entrenched in society that they cannot be solved within the existing social institutions, cultural practices and regulatory systems. For instance, despite the recognition of issues, such as child labour, caste-based discrimination, gender violence, exploitation of poor and marginalized, etc., they persist in the society. The reasons for the continuance of such problems can be varied, for example, the institutions and regulations to manage them are inadequate, those affected by these problems lack voice and influence in the society, or the privileged in the society, government and business lack incentive to solve them (or even actively prevent solutions through reforms). The only way in which such social issues can be addressed is by changing the very nature of institutions and systems.

Social Transformers are the special breed of social entrepreneurs who address and eradicate such deep-rooted problems by trying to bring about *systemic* change. Their mission is to replace the unjust existing social/bureaucratic institutions, regulations and social practices with more efficient and fair systems and institutions. By nature, they are ideologically inclined social activists and advocates for causes. While some researchers (e.g., Martin and Osberg 2007) have distinguished them from social entrepreneurs, there is sufficient literature and acknowledgement which treats them as a distinctive type of social entrepreneur. Zahra et al. (2009), for instance, described them as 'social engineers' who 'identify systemic problems within the social systems and structures and address them by bringing about revolutionary change.' (p. 526)

Compared to other kinds of social entrepreneurs, Social Transformers, if successful, bring about far more dramatic and radical transformations in the society. To understand how Social Transformers operate (and how social transformations happen), let us look at the story of **Right to Information (RTI)** movement, which finally resulted in the RTI Act (Bakshi and Kuti 2000; Roy 2018; Roy et al. 2001; Sharma 2014):

The campaign for Right to Information had a rather inconspicuous beginning in protest rallies by villagers in four blocks of Beawar district in Rajasthan during 1994. These protests were organized by Mazdoor Kisan Shakti Sangathan (MKSS), which was established by Aruna Roy along with Nikhil Dey and Shankar Singh in 1990 as a non-political people's organization to empower peasants and workers in their struggle for livelihoods and sustenance[2]. The protests were against the corruption in spending of government funds allocated for various projects and schemes in these blocks. What was distinctive about these protests was that instead of traditional *dharnas* (sit-ins), they used *jansunwai* (public hearing) to cross-validate the official records of funds and expenditure by the beneficiaries. These records, which were procured by the

[2] Aruna Roy had served in the Indian Administrative Service from 1968 till 1975, when she resigned and joined Social Work and Research Centre (SWRC)—also known as Barefoot College, a rural development agency in Rajasthan by activist and her husband, Bunker Roy. There she met Shankar Singh, a member of the Centre, who had a talent for mobilizing people through drama and had understanding of rural politics and exploitation, and Nikhil Dey, a young fellow who had given up his studies in United States to work at the grassroots. During their discussions, they realized that instead of being a 'catalyst' of social change, they would like to be a 'participant' in the process, and shifted to a village near Beawar in 1983, where Shankar Singh had a small plot of land. After many years of participating in people's struggles for their rights, MKSS was founded in 1990.

organizers from the local officials (gram sewaks, sarpanches, BDOs, etc.), were publicly read out, and the villagers were invited to comment and verify them. These public audits brought out many instances of corruption, such as missing names in muster rolls, false billing, benami sales of public land, bribery cases, etc. The uniqueness of protests received publicity through coverage in local and state-level newspapers, and also led to suspension of some local level officials. More importantly, these public audits made the people realize that access to information is an important requirement in their fight for justice and equity.

Realizing the consequences, the local official stopped sharing the records, claiming that they were accountable only to the higher officials and not to public. This, however, only intensified MKSS' struggle further, and Aruna Roy threatened to launch a state-wide agitation for right to information. As the pressure built up, in April 1995 the state chief minister announced in assembly that photocopies of records, such as muster roll, bills, vouchers etc., will be made available to public. This assurance, however, was not met, and the government kept on delaying and watering down the promise.

To renew the demand, in April 1996, MKSS went on a 40-day *dharna* at Beawar to demand transparency of public accounts with the slogan 'Hamara Paisa, Hamara Hisab' (our money, our accounts). By now MKSS' cause had captured the imagination of the local public, and they contributed money, grains, vegetables, etc., to the protestors, and helped spreading the word about the protest. With no response from the government, MKSS organized similar *dharnas* in Ajmer, and then in Jaipur. The organizers also used their contacts to keep the media, activists and other public persons informed, and invited eminent journalists, lawyers, retired and serving government officials, activists, artists, etc., from other places including from Delhi and Mumbai, and who also spoke for the constitutional legitimacy of the demand.

With wide media coverage in state and national papers, by now the right to information had changed from local issue of Beawar to a national policy discourse. Aruna Roy also used her contacts to involve larger bodies to support the cause of the struggle. Many well-known organizations, such as Press Council of India, the Press Institute of India, Gandhi Peace Foundation and even the Lal Bahadur Shastri Academy of Administration, Mussoorie took a lead in giving shape to a law for the right. During July 1996, while the protests were still going on, the Shastri Academy organized a series of consultation meetings with individuals from different professional backgrounds. Aruna Roy too was invited to be part of these consultations. These meetings led to the formation of an advocacy group, the National Campaign on People's Right to Information (NCPRI), consisting of activists, senior media persons, serving and retired bureaucrats and members of the bar and judiciary, etc., and culminated in framing of the first draft legislation for the right to information.

In August 1996, the Press Council of India convened a meeting under the chairmanship of Justice P. B. Sawant to finalize the draft of the legislation, while the Press Institute undertook to issue monthly bulletins on the progress of the campaign. The final version of the Press Council's draft was circulated to the then Prime Minister H. D. Deve Gowda and his Cabinet Ministers, Members of Parliament, and was covered widely by the press. The draft was also sent to all State Chief Ministers, and some states enacted their own right to information laws, for example, Tamil Nadu and Goa (1997), Rajasthan, Maharashtra, Karnataka (2000), Delhi (2001), Assam (2002) and Jammu and Kashmir (2003).

The first national legislation, the Freedom of Information Act 2002, however turned out to be a diluted watered-down version of the original draft. It did not contain a penalty provision, which meant that the information can be indefinitely delayed—and in fact, it was never notified. As the pressure from the stakeholders continued, a comprehensive legislation for right to information also got incorporated in the National Common Minimum Programme of the UPA government which came to power in 2004. After more than a decade of struggle, the Right to Information Act was enacted in the Parliament in 2005.

It is important to note that while all Social Transformers resort to social activism, all social activists are not necessarily social entrepreneurs. Often social activism remains confined to creating pressure through protest, and attempting a symptomatic solution to the problem. Such social activism fails to ameliorate the problem since it only achieves a temporary sub-optimal solution and the problem returns once the pressure dissipates. Social Transformers, on the other hand, practice a distinctive kind of activism which is characterized by three qualities:

1. **Focus on social justice:** Social Transformers do not aim at incremental changes, but at replacing an unjust and inefficient societal equilibrium with a new one (Martin and Osberg 2007). This focus on systemic change arises out of the unique way in which the Social Transformers perceive the problem they are attempting to solve. They see the social problems as arising out of the way the larger system works, that is, manner in which the multiple participants and stakeholders in the system (e.g., policy makers, government officials, public and business institutions, local leaders and community members) interact and take decisions. Since the problem lies in the norms, practices, cultural values and/or rules and regulations which govern the behaviour and decisions of the participants, they aim to change these 'rules' by which the system operates and replace them with more just and fair ones.

2. **Multi-stakeholder perspective:** Since the aim of the Social Transformers is to change the way the social systems operate,

they focus on bringing in all the stakeholders to co-create the solution. This is also important since, by nature, efforts to change the system require going against the dominant institutions, prevailing practices and entrenched incumbents, and are quite likely to be seen as subversive and against establishment. This lack of perceived legitimacy of their efforts, as well as the nature of deep and widespread social change they aim at, requires them to mobilize and harness social and political support for their mission. They often do so by mobilizing the masses, innovatively using the media as a strategic resource to put the issue in public discourse, creating alliances with like-minded people and policymakers, forming partnerships with institutions which will help them shape new social systems for resource allocation and service delivery and so on.

3. **Institutionalizing the change:** The multi-stakeholder app-roach of Social Transformers also paves the foundation to make the change sustainable. Any social transformation is successful only when the new norms get ingrained the policies, structures and practices of the society and are co-owned by everyone. By involving stakeholders across the spectrum, the entrepreneur is able to create multiple co-owners/leaders in change process, and thus make the change agenda a 'people's movement'. Often the change initiated by Social Transformers results in institutional changes in policies, structural arrange-ment, norms and standards, etc., which can sustain without the interventions from the entrepreneur. This is a critical difference between the change process initiated by the Social Transformers and some other social movements which revolve around the personality of the founder.

Ecosystem Builders

While entrepreneurial ventures capture the limelight in the media reports and academic case studies, they actually co-exist as a part of host of other organizations and agencies which form the ecosystem of the sector/industry. Besides their own capabilities, the success or failure of the ventures also depends on the support systems and services (e.g., funding, domain expertise and advisories, pipeline of talent and policy guidelines) which are provided by these organizations. These other participants in the ecosystem are essential for the growth of both the mainstream ventures, as well as the sector/industry. To appreciate the role and importance of ecosystem in the growth of the ventures and the sector, let us look at the growth of Indian Telecom sector.

In 1994, government of India announced the National Telecom Policy and opened up the sector for private participation to meet the growing need and demand for communication. The new opportunity attracted many entrepreneurial organizations, such as Bharti Telecom, HFCL, Modi Telstra, Reliance, Shyam Telelink, Skycell, Tata Teleservices, etc. Though not all of them succeeded, it was their collective initiatives which shaped the growth of the sector. The opening up of the sector also created space for many other organizations and agencies to provide services and support to the mainstream telecom players. For instance, the growing demand for telephony brought in telecom manufacturers (e.g., Beetel, BPL, Onida, SEPL and Videocon) to make the basic equipment available; there was a spurt in the telecom software firms, which developed the required software for switching, routing, high-speed networking, etc.; specialized investment funds got formed to support the growth of the eco-system incumbents; new consultancy and advisory services emerged, which specialized in telecom sector; to meet the talent needs of the sector, new and existing recruitment agencies started offering specialized services; sensing an opportunity, media houses launched new sector focused news magazines, such as *Voice&Data, Communications Today, TelecomLive*, etc., which collected and shared industry information and trends, and so on. An important role in the growth of the industry was played by the Telecom Regulatory Authority of India (TRAI) which developed regulatory framework for tariff, service norms, interconnections among operator, etc., to ensure fair competition as well as service to the subscribers. In addition, industry bodies, such as Confederation of Indian Industries (CII), Cellular Operators Association of India (COAI), Federation of Indian Chamber of Commerce & Industry (FICCI), etc., provided knowledge-sharing platforms for the stakeholders in the industry through conferences and seminars, and also advocacy support for influencing the policies through industry studies and white papers, etc.

As one would notice, the growth of the mainstream telecom enterprises could not have been possible without the web of these allied organizations. While each was an independent entity, they were all loosely coupled in a network through co-dependence, and formed the industry ecosystem. The role and nature of industry ecosystem and its constituents is only recently being acknowledged in understanding the entrepreneurial phenomenon (see Box 7.4 for key domains of an enabling entrepreneurial ecosystem). As Isenberg (2010), in his seminal article 'How to Start an Entrepreneurial Revolution', noted:

> The entrepreneurship ecosystem consists of a set of individual elements…that combine in complex ways. In isolation, each is conducive to entrepreneurship but insufficient to sustain it…. Together, however, these elements turbocharge venture creation and growth. (p. 3)

Describing the nature of relationship among the ecosystem players, Tukiainen et al. (2014) defined the entrepreneurial ecosystem as:

> …a set of companies (large and small) from different industries that want to work with each other because they have complementary economic, knowledge and/or capability interests, usually based on technological or business interdependencies. The firms are loosely or tightly coupled in order to co-create value, but largely independent of geographical location. Firms may sometimes compete and sometimes collaborate. (p. 8)

BOX 7.4   KEY ELEMENT OF ENTREPRENEURIAL ECOSYSTEM

Based on an analysis of nine different frameworks used by different agencies and organizations (e.g., Babson College, Council on Competitiveness, OECD, World Economic Forum and World Bank), Aspen Network for Development Entrepreneurs (2013) identified/synthesized eight key domains of an enabling ecosystem for entrepreneurs:

Financial support: Access to angels, debt, venture capital, grants, etc.; Banks, government funds, MFI, public capital markets, development finance institutions, etc.

Business Support: Incubators and accelerators; legal/accounting services, business mentors and technical consultants and advisers; industry networks, etc.

Human Capital Providers: Universities and other educational institutes, technical and professional training institutes, community colleges, etc.

Social Support Systems: Media and publications, citizen bodies, professional associations, social organizations that support a culture of entrepreneurship, etc.

Policy support: Government policies and schemes; tax rates and incentives; regulatory systems for starting and sustaining a venture, etc.

Market Systems: Existing distribution, supply chain and retail networks; customer awareness and demand; existing players, etc.

Infrastructure Availability: Roads, electricity and communication (phone, mobile and internet); utility providers, for example, gas, water, transport, etc.

Scientific and Technical Support: Public and private research centres and laboratories; technical advisory and support; access to inventions and prototypes, etc.

As we discussed earlier in Chapter 1, the growth of social entrepreneurship in India too is accompanied by establishment of organizations which specialize in providing ecosystem support (e.g., trained talent, funding, incubation and network support). Being a new sector/discipline, many such organizations are themselves established by entrepreneurs, the Ecosystem Builders, who contribute to social change by enabling the mainstream social ventures to perform more effectively and efficiently. In many ways, Ecosystem Builders are similar to the Constructive Opportunists. However, unlike the Constructive Opportunists, they do not directly address the social problems. Rather, they build their ventures to address the unattended gaps and opportunities within the social entrepreneurial ecosystem. They are also different than other elements in the ecosystem (e.g., government, banks and mainstream media), in that their services are specialized and focused only for the social entrepreneurial ecosystem. To appreciate the nature of contribution of these social entrepreneurs, let us consider one example (see Box 7.5 for some other examples):

BOX 7.5 EXAMPLES OF ECOSYSTEM BUILDERS

GiveIndia: GiveIndia is India's, and perhaps world's, first 'philanthropy exchange', which was started by an IIM Ahmedabad graduate, Venkat Krishnan N. in 2000. It provides an online platform to connect individual and corporate donors with over 200 not-for-profit social ventures and causes related to education, health, livelihoods, women and children, etc. Donors can select the venture they would like to support. The ventures are listed after due diligence through site visits on legal compliance, governance, programme implementation, financial information, etc. GiveIndia retains maximum of 10% from the donations to meet its operating costs (e.g., website maintenance, human resources and site visits), which allows it to sustain without relying on grants. Starting with just ₹2.5 million for a handful of organizations, within a decade GiveIndia had channelled over ₹1.3 billion to more than 270 ventures. By 2018, GiveIndia was disbursing more than ₹250 million of targeted donations annually to the ventures.

Start Up! was co-founded by Manisha Gupta in 2009 to provide comprehensive support services to social ventures across different stages in their lifecycle—early, growth and mature. It provides incubation and impact acceleration services which are immersive and long-term, i.e., the Start Up! team works on the ground with the entrepreneurs for a period ranging from 3 months to 2 years, and helps them in refining their products/services to match the market needs, building their capacities, formulating strategy, financial modelling and developing operational plans, fundraising, etc. The incubatees also get mentoring from domain and functional experts, as well as from leading social entrepreneurs. Start Up! also provides consultancy services to mature social ventures and other social sector organizations in areas such as market research, scaling up, impact assessment, strategic planning, teambuilding, etc. It has also been conducting the outreach, due diligence and jury presentation for the India Social Entrepreneur of the Year Award, which are jointly co-hosted by Schwab Foundation for Social Entrepreneurship and Jubilant Bhartia Foundation.

The Better India: The Better India (TBI) was started by a couple Anuradha Kedia and Dhimant Parekh in 2009 to share positive news about the work of grassroots heroes and social entrepreneurs which had significant on-ground impact. Though originally intended as a media portal, TBI has evolved into a repository of grassroots change initiatives and innovations, and provides visibility to many young social ventures.

It also acts as a catalyst by inspiring people to volunteer, donate, share resources, form partnerships and even replicate the social innovations. In a more active role, TBI has also partnered with the Government of Delhi in designing a school level entrepreneurship course, and with the Government of India (Atal Innovation Mission and NITI Ayog) to organize Innovation Marathon 2018 for young social innovators to take their ideas and prototypes to the next level of implementation. Over the years, it has created a large outreach with about 100,000 subscribers to its newsletter, 1.9 million followers on Facebook, 10,800 subscribers on YouTube and 35,000 subscribers to its WhatsApp channel.

Villgro (formerly known as Rural Innovations Network) is India's largest and oldest social incubator and was founded by Paul Basil, a mechanical engineer with a post-graduate degree in forestry management, in 2001. The idea of establishing the incubator came to Basil from his earlier experience of working with farmers and from the work done by Gujarat government's initiative Grassroots Innovation Augmentation Network (GIAN) and Honeybee Network in documenting the rural innovations. He realized that many villagers create innovations to meet their own needs, but these can also have significant impact on rural lives in other areas as well. However, they remain localized and are not replicated due to lack of technical, financial and marketing support. Villgro was established to incubate these innovations and transform them into enterprises, which can be run either by the innovator or by an entrepreneur.

While Villgro had developed its expertise in identifying grassroots innovators and reach to rural markets, it also partnered with other institutions and organizations to build an ecosystem which would support and fund these innovators. For instance, it tied up with Aavishkaar, a micro venture capital fund, to bring venture capital to the entrepreneurs; it partnered with IIT Madras and Lemelson Foundation (USA) to leverage on their technical knowledge and funding for the incubation; it took help from Rockefeller Foundation to create a pool of professionals who would mentor the grassroots entrepreneurs, and so on. Over the years, Villgro also enlarged its partnerships with many other organizations (e.g., Accion, Ankur Capital, Artha Venture, Omnivore Partners, Technology Development Board, Unitus Seed Fund, Upaya Ventures and USAID), and developed a wide range of incubation support services, which provide mentoring, technical support, market support, funding, institution building and human resources, etc.

Since 2009, Villgro started organizing 'Unconvention', an event to identify early-stage social start-ups/entrepreneurs to identify and incubate social start-ups which impact lives of the poor, specifically in the fields of education, health, agriculture, employability and energy sectors. These events also provided an opportunity to the entrepreneurs to connect with investors, mentors, service providers and other stakeholders, and pitch for support. By 2018, Villgro had organized about 130 such events across the country, had successfully incubated 279 social enterprises and had raised about ₹33 million as seed funding and almost ₹180 million as investments. Apart from India, Villgro had also started supporting social enterprises in Kenya, Philippines and Vietnam.

As these examples show, while Ecosystem Builders do not address the social problems directly, they create social impact through the services and support which they provide to the social entrepreneurs. They do so through strengthening the ecosystem in four inter-related ways (Shukla et al. 2012):

1. **Reducing learning curve for the new entrants**: The Ecosystem Builders mostly bring specific technical knowledge (e.g., about creating a business plan, marketing, fundraising and impactful sector practices), which a newcomer to the sector would otherwise learn through lot of time and effort.

By sharing these, the Ecosystem Builders enable the new entrants to take off faster and more efficiently.

2. **Increasing efficiency of the ecosystem**: Since the Ecosystem Builders service multiple players of the ecosystem, they are able to (and need to) create a databank of best practices and successful models of the sector. By collating and disseminating this repository (e.g., through incubation or consultancy support, conferences and publications), they are able to reduce the need to rework and 're-invent the wheel' for the ecosystem players.

3. **Facilitating partnerships and innovations**: One of the major contributions of the Ecosystem Builders is that, consciously (e.g., through events and seminars) or inadvertently (e.g., through reports, status papers and publications), they connect different players in the ecosystem. This allows players with complementary needs and capabilities to form collaborative relationships, work together and to innovate new practices and models.

4. **Enabling the sector to respond to new demand and challenges**: By connecting the sector and domain players, the Ecosystem Builders also bring together people who share common concerns, problems, or passion for the sector. This often enables them to respond proactively and collectively to new market or regulatory demands when they arise.

As can be seen from the above, social entrepreneurship manifests itself in a variety of forms. This is particularly true for India, where social problems exist at multifarious levels. Some can be solved only at a localized level, some require large-scale changes in the institutional and policy framework, and still others can be addressed by creatively applying business principles, and so on. The fivefold typology, discussed above, also describes five different approaches used by Indian social entrepreneurs. Appreciating this diversity of approaches and forms is important to understand the nature of social entrepreneurship in India.

UNEQUAL ACCESS: 'MARKETS OF THE POOR' 8

> *In understanding poverty and how to reduce it, there are two*
> *starting points.... One is the perceptions and priorities of*
> *those who define poverty—normal, non-poor, urban-based*
> *and numerate professionals. The other is the perceptions and*
> *priorities of the poor themselves... Most professionals plunge*
> *into the debate...without questioning their mindsets or*
> *the basic framework; and the poor are not much consulted*
> *anyway.*
>
> —*Robert Chambers (1988)*

In 2006, K. V. Kamath the then CEO of ICICI Bank gave an interview at The Wharton School of the University of Pennsylvania, Philadelphia, PA, USA (Knowledge@Wharton 2006). The entire interview was about ICICI's planned forays into the global and rural banking and the strategies and capacities the bank was building to meet these goals. At the end of the interview, the interviewer asked Kamath, 'As you look ahead over five years, many things can go wrong. What do you most fear in the Indian economy and the global economy that could derail your plans?' Mr Kamath's response was unexpected, but significant. He said:

I guess in the Indian context, I would say something that is unforeseen, like social strife, because *we are living in a world of haves and have nots. And there is a divide.* Now is this going to be something that could bother us? To me, this is the single most important thing which could impact business. (italics added)

Kamath's observation about the haves and have-nots was prescient of the inequality in Indian society, which was becoming increasingly visible and has continued to grow. While inequality and disparities had always characterized Indian society and economy, they had increased during the post-reform period (Pal and Ghosh 2007). Since the opening of the economy in the early 1990s, India has undergone a remarkable economic turnaround to leapfrog among the ranks of increasingly prosperous and fastest growing nations. During this period, India witnessed unprecedented growth in GDP, industrialization, productivity, per capita income, etc. The gains of this progress, however, have not reached equitably across different strata of the society, leading to widening disparities in lifestyles and access to basic services, resources and opportunities. This uneven growth has given rise to stark contrast between the 'two Indias', which is apparent in various parameters of development. For example[1]:

- As an economy, India ranks 6th in terms of nominal GDP, and 3rd in terms of purchasing power parity (PPP). However, globally it also ranks 130/189 on Human Development Index, which measures society's standard of living, health and education.
- Indian pharmaceutical sector is the largest provider of generic drugs globally, and supplies over 50 per cent of global demand for vaccines for different diseases. However, 85 per cent of India's public health problems are due to preventable water-borne diseases, and every year about 55 million Indians plunge into poverty due to out-of-pocket healthcare expenses.
- India has become a food-surplus nation and is the world's largest exporter of rice and wheat, largest producer of milk and second largest producer of fruits and vegetables. However,

[1] The figures quoted here are taken from various government and industry reports published during 2014–2019.

an Indian agricultural household has an average monthly income of ₹6,426, and 52 per cent live in debt with an average outstanding loan of ₹47,000 (2016).

- India has 0.33 million High Net Worth Individuals (HNWI, whose wealth is more than $1 million) whose combined wealth is $8.2 trillion. However, it also ranks 103/119 on Global Hunger Index (2018), and an estimated 195 million Indians go hungry to bed every day.

- The real estate market in India is valued at $120 billion, and is expected to grow to $1 trillion by 2030. However, 43 per cent of Indian population lives in kuccha or semi-pucca houses, and there is also a shortage of about 19 million houses to provide a dwelling to the homeless population (people living on streets, pavements, railway stations, etc.).

- India has the world's third largest educational system with about 900 universities, 40,000 degree colleges, and 75 other institutions of national importance (e.g., IIMs, IITs and NITs). However, 58 per cent Indians are educated up to primary level or below and only 4.5 per cent have a graduate or above degree and so on.

As these contrasts highlight, while the changes in the policies had spurred economic activities and wealth creation, a large segment of the society still has limited or no access to basic essentials (e.g., education, healthcare, energy, livelihoods and markets) required for a decent and productive life. The challenge and opportunity for social entrepreneurship in India is to devise innovative solutions to address these underserved gaps in the society. These are the 'markets of the poor'.[2] Before discussing

---

[2] The term 'poor' is used here in a wider sense than used in the official definition while calculating the 'poverty line', which only defines the subsistence levels. It also refers to the large low-income segment which exists slightly above the poverty line, but lacks access to basic amenities and services as common citizens. Another common term 'Bottom of Pyramid' (Prahalad, 2004) is avoided since

the innovative models used by Indian social entrepreneurs to serve this market, it is important to appreciate the unique nature of this market segment.

A Different Kind of 'Market'

The term 'markets' conjures up the image of a space where rational transactions take place for exchange of goods and services. Markets also consist of different segments (e.g., young–old, educated–uneducated and rural–urban), each with their specific and different sets of needs, aspiration and behaviour. Just like each of these segments behaves and responds to the same value proposition differently, the 'markets of the poor' are also characterized with the idiosyncrasies of the needs and constraints of the poor.

For instance, in 2002, Gillette (now a division of Proctor & Gamble) launched a razor blade, Vector, which was specifically designed for Indian rural users. It was an inexpensive model, with two blades and a sliding bar which could push the hair from the blade which met the requirement of the thick and dense growth among Indians. Gillette had also tested it with the Indian population in USA and had received positive feedback. However, when introduced in India, the product failed to take off. It was only when the Gillette executives visited Indian villages later, that they realized that the rural Indians do not shave every day, and therefore have a much denser growth than the razor was designed for. Moreover, they also did not have access to running water which was required for washing off the hair from the blade (Srinivasan 2004).

Similarly, it is 'well-known' that using biomass for cooking in Indian rural households causes indoor pollution and consequent respiratory disorders among the rural women and children. Moreover, using wood as fuel also has adverse impacts of the environmental conservation. To tackle these problems, many

---

it has been used to describe poor primarily as consumers of goods and services, and not also as productive economic members of the society.

years back, villagers were distributed and/or sold smokeless stoves at subsidized rates. However, soon it became evident that despite their obvious benefits, the villagers were not using the stoves. When a survey was done to find out the reasons, it turned out that the stoves were not being used because they did *not* emit smoke! The villagers wanted stoves which would emit smoke sometimes when they wanted it to—since the smoke killed the insects in the thatched roofs of their huts (Segran 2009).

As such examples show, poor often use products and services very differently than what they were intended for. In addition, often their buying decisions and behaviour defy what one would normally assume to be their needs. Karamchandani et al. (2009) report a study which explored what the village poor aspired to buy from the microfinance loan they would take. More than 80 per cent respondents were interested in buying items which were related to status, entertainment and daily convenience (e.g., gold coins, TV and clothes). Socially and personally beneficial items (e.g., livestock, water filters, solar lanterns, insurance and fertilizers), which would improve their life circumstances, figured very low in the priorities of the potential borrowers. Clearly, what the poor *want* is often unrelated to what the poor *need*.

Like any other market segment, the poor too assess and use a product or service within the context of their lives, aspirations and requirements. More often than not, as the above examples show, the rationality of their decisions belies the common sense understanding of those who designed those products and services. Often the poor do not (or are unable to) avail well-designed and useful products and services, since they do not match with the peculiar constraints and opportunities in which poor live their lives. Many studies (e.g., Banerjee and Duflo 2011; Chambers 1988; Collins et al. 2009; Karamchandani et al. 2009; Narayan et al. 2000; National Commission for Enterprises in Unorganised Sector, 2007) provide insights into the world of the poor which are useful in designing offerings to suit the markets of the poor.

UNEQUAL ACCESS: 'MARKETS OF THE POOR'

Poor Are Not a Homogeneous Segment

Poverty is not a binary, poor/not-poor phenomenon. Among the poor communities, people differ widely in terms of their income, nature of poverty, needs and aspiration, opportunities, access to resources and support, etc. Working with poor requires an appreciation of the nuances and shades of poverty.

National Commission for Enterprises in the Unorganized Sector (2007), for instance, highlighted that the poor and low-income groups live and work outside the formal economy. The report classified poor into six categories based on their daily expenditure: (a) *extremely poor or ultra-poor*, (b) *poor*, (c) *marginally poor*, (d) *vulnerable group* (e) *middle-income* and (f) *high-income groups*. Both the ultra-poor *and* poor fall below the official poverty line, and lack the means and resources for basic subsistence. The ultra-poor, in addition, lack any productive assets and savings which they can leverage on, depend primarily on manual work such as begging, physical labour, etc., for subsistence, and are extremely susceptible to food and health insecurity. The marginally poor and vulnerable group consist of segment which is slightly above the poverty line; they sometime own some productive asset (e.g., a couple of goats, a sewing machine and a small piece of land), have irregular income, are mostly casual labour and are vulnerable to minor adverse changes in their environment. The middle- and high-income groups, though not categorized as 'poor', are the low-income segment. Mostly, these are self-employed with some marketable skill, have a reasonably steady source of livelihood, and assets and savings which they can leverage to enhance their opportunities and earning.

Across the income spectrum, poor also vary widely in terms of their occupations. To illustrate, the classification of poor in terms of the nature of their informal/unorganized sector by the International Labour Organisation (1993) portrays the eclectic diversity of their livelihood activities: (a) *the own-account workers* in survival-type activities, for example, vendors of vegetables, fruits, meat and fish, and of non-perishable items like locks, clothes and vessels; garbage collectors, rag and scrap pickers; head-loaders, construction and agricultural workers, rickshaw-and cart-puller, etc., (b) *the paid domestic workers*, for example, maids, gardeners and chauffeurs, (c) *the home-based workers*, for example, garment makers, embroiderers, incense stick rollers, bidi-rollers, paper bag makers, kite makers and food processors and (d) *the self-employed* in microenterprises, for example, road-side mechanics, barbers, cobblers, carpenters, tailors, bookbinders and owners of small stalls and kiosks.

As is evident, each of these occupations is characterized by different opportunities, requirements and vulnerabilities. For instance, the own-account workers mostly earn on a day-to-day basis, which can get disrupted due to daily and seasonal exigencies such as rains, strikes, etc. This makes it difficult for them to make long-term financial commitments. In comparison, the paid domestic workers have a relatively more stable and assured income; depending on their relationship, they often also have access to easy loans from their employers, which allows future planning and asset building. Likewise, while both the micro-entrepreneurs and home-based workers produce goods and services for the customer, their relationship with market is very different; while the former have a direct interface with the market, the home-based workers connect with the market through intermediaries, and therefore, are susceptible to exploitative arrangements and so on.

Poverty Is Not Just about Income

Much of the policy discourse and the consequent interventions revolve around the premise that poor are poor because of low income, therefore low purchasing capacity. While that is true, it only partially reflects the reality, and is inadequate to understand the life and world of the poor. Poverty is a complex phenomenon, and it is being increasingly realized that it is multidimensional in nature. Chambers (1995) noted that:

> The realities of poor people are local, complex, diverse and dynamic. Income-poverty, though important, is only one aspect of deprivation. (p. 173)

Similarly, World Bank's comprehensive study, *The Voices of the Poor* (Narayan et al., 2000), found that:

> Definitions of poverty and its causes vary by gender, age, culture, and other social and economic contexts.... Poverty never results from the lack one thing but from many interlocking factors that cluster in poor people's experiences and definitions of poverty. (p. 32)

The low income of the poor is further aggravated by lack of both tangible (e.g., land, livestock, equipment, vehicle and electricity) and intangible (e.g., education, health and nutrition) assets. For instance, lack of access to water or cooking fuel forces women in poor households to spend productive time in fetching these. Similarly, lack of education or poor health reduces the chances accessing gainful livelihood opportunities. Ownership of assets also improves access to credit, which can then be used for income-enhancing activities. Assets also act as a buffer against the vulnerabilities of the poor, by enhancing opportunities for them. Many studies (e.g., Carter and Barret 2006; Dutta 2013) have shown that asset-based poverty increases the vulnerability of the poor to remain trapped in cycles of poverty, while asset formation is an important prerequisite for long-term poverty reduction.

In fact, from 2010, the United Nations changed its money metric measure of poverty to Multidimensional Poverty Index (Alkire and Santos 2010). The MPI recognizes that poverty is also about being deprived of basic societal resources, amenities and assets. It complements the monetary measures of poverty, and identifies the degree of deprivations suffered by people on the dimension of health, education and living standards (see Table 8.1).

TABLE 8.1: Multidimensional Poverty Index

DIMENSIONS OF POVERTY	INDICATORS	MEASURE
Health	Child mortality	Child mortality within the household within the last 5 years
	Nutrition	Adult or child malnourishment
Education	Year of schooling	The absence of any household member who has completed 5 years of schooling
	School attendance	Disrupted or curtailed schooling up to the age when the child would complete class 8
Standard of living	Cooking fuel	Lack of access to clean cooking fuel
	Toilet	Lack of access to basic sanitation services
	Water	Lack of access to safe drinking water within 15-minute walk from house
	Electricity	Lack of access to reliable electricity

(continued)

(continued)

DIMENSIONS OF POVERTY	INDICATORS	MEASURE
	Floor	The household has a dirt, sand, dung or 'other' (unspecified) type of floor.
	Assets	Lack of basic modern assets (radio, TV, telephone, computer, bike, motorbike, etc.)

Poor Are Consumers as Well as Producers

Most government interventions and the 'bottom of the pyramid' businesses visualize the poor as merely lacking resources which need to be reached to them. The poor, as the profile of the unorganized sector above shows, are also producers of useful goods and services for the society. As producers, suppliers and workers across sectors (agriculture, construction, mining, manufacturing, trade, transport, etc.) they contribute to about half of India's GDP (Labour Bureau 2015) and about one-third of manufacturing output (Ministry of Micro, Small and Medium Enterprises 2018); small and marginal farmers who own less than 2 hectares of land contribute to about 60 per cent of total food grain production (Gururaj et al. 2017).

Despite being a productive resource, the productivity and price-realization remain low for the poor. Reports show that 85–95 per cent of casual and contract labour and self-employed workers have an income of less than ₹10,000 per month; even among the better-off salary earners, more than 55 per cent earn less than ₹10,000 per month (Labour Bureau 2016a). Such low income levels are due to several challenges faced by the poor. As self-employed or wage workers, the poor mostly have irregular jobs, erratic flow of orders for their goods and services and/or are employed on casual basis. Even when poor are employed with somewhat regular income (e.g., a security guard and employed household help), the terms of employment do not ensure predictability of the employment—the continuance of the job depends on the whims and fancy of employer, rather than a formal contract. According to Government reports (Labour Bureau 2016a), almost two-thirds of the salaried and contract workers do not even have a written contract (the number is 95% for the casual workers). In fact, only about 60 per cent workers reported that they could get work for all the 12 months of the year.

As producers, the poor also lack volumes or size, and are generally dispersed and hard to aggregate. Out of the more than 60 million MSMEs in India, more than 99 per cent are micro-enterprises, which are mostly operated by a single person, either from within the household or without a fixed location (Ministry of Micro, Small and Medium Enterprises 2018). These conditions have two adverse consequences for the businesses run by the poor.

First, such small volumes and widely dispersed and remote nature of enterprises of the poor reduce their bargaining power, as well as place them at a disadvantage due to lack of economies of scale. Moreover, their enterprises mostly fall at the end of supply chains, which are opaque and inefficient, and are characterized by lack of access to basic physical infrastructure (e.g., roads, electricity and equipment), institutional finance, social security or legal protection. Lack of direct link with the markets also creates information asymmetry and makes them vulnerable to exploitation by the intermediaries (Karamchandani et al. 2009).

Second, it also reduces their access to formal sources of credit, since they are perceived as a risk by the banks. In their study on financing of SMEs, Singh and Wasdani (2016) found that difficulty in collateral/guarantee, complicated bank procedures, lengthy processing time for the loan approval and high service fees for processing loan requests were some of the key challenges SMEs faced to access bank loans. In fact, MSMEs account for less than 20 per cent of all loans given by the banks (Borgohain 2018) and have to rely on informal credit sources at high interest rates.

Poor producers and service providers also lack marketable skills which are necessary to service more lucrative markets and customers. Government survey reports show that only 5.4 per cent of the workforce has received any vocational training; and even out of these only 2 per cent were trained formally—other 3.4 per cent got trained 'informally' (Labour Bureau 2016b). Thus, most rely on their traditional skills which are no longer relevant in the context of changing demographics, technology and markets. For instance, a traditional household help may not know how to operate electronic appliance, rural weavers and artisans may not be aware of the tastes and preferences of the urban customer, or a mason may be ignorant of the new construction technologies and so on.

Lives of Poor Revolve around Managing Short-Term 'Cash Flows'

Poverty is mostly described in terms of per capita low daily, monthly or annual income. In most cases, however, poor do not earn the same amount every day, month or year: the incomes of a daily wager, street vendor, a farmer or a small micro-entrepreneur, etc., fluctuate and are unpredictable due to many extraneous reasons (Collins et al. 2009). If the income were regular and stable, poor can plan their lives to suit their priorities (e.g., send the child to school, save for exigencies or start building a house). Even otherwise, despite having a job, often the low level of income does not allow them to save and build a cushion for sudden and large expenditures, such as a wedding in the family, an illness or annual expenditure related to child's education (fee, uniform, books, etc.) and so on.

This 'triple whammy' (Collins et al. 2009) of low, irregular and unpredictable income is further aggravated by the low access to credit available to poor. Formal institutional sources of credit (e.g., banks) are often not very poor-friendly due to their distance, attitude of staff or requirements of paperwork; informal sources such as local moneylenders are expensive and exploitative. Lenders also are more willing to lend to someone whose income flows are predictable.

Correspondingly, poor spend much effort to ensure that their lives keep running smoothly by getting food on the table and in meeting their immediate and urgent needs. Managing the cash flows in the face of irregularities and unpredictability of income flows, therefore, becomes a more urgent priority for them than long-term building assets. Collins et al. (2009) noted:

> Not surprisingly, poor households put a great deal of effort into 'cash-flow management'—making sure that money is on hand when needed to meet the basic expenses.... (For) patching cash-flow mismatches between income and expenditure...poor households more often turn to small-scale borrowing and lending with friends, relatives, neighbours and employers. It is often hard work, and it can carry high costs— some of which are social and psychological and not just economic. (p. 61)

Poor are, in fact, ingenious in devising their own money management systems for saving for their short-term needs, which they use frequently and intensively. In a study of a small village, Rutherford (2002) found as many as 33 formal and informal money management systems, which ranged from formal banks and NGOs to moneylender, savings clubs, buying on credit, loans from family, neighbours, employers, etc. On average, a household used 10 of these different systems to manage its savings to meet exigent needs.

Poverty Impairs Decision-Making Ability

A common, and popular, belief is that poor remain poor because they make wrong decisions and choices. Research (e.g., Mani et al. 2013; Sheehy-Skeffington and Rea 2017), however, shows that bad decisions and dysfunctional behaviour are the consequence, and not the cause, of poverty. For instance, in their study of Indian sugar cane farmers, Mani et al. (2013) found that same set of farmers showed diminished cognitive functioning before the harvest when they were under financial pressures as compared to the post-harvest season, when financial concerns do not dominate their lives. They concluded that:

> The poor must manage sporadic income, juggle expenses, and make difficult tradeoffs. Even when not actually making a financial decision, these preoccupations can be present and distracting. The human cognitive system has limited capacity.... Preoccupations with pressing budgetary concerns leave fewer cognitive resources available to guide choice and action. Just as an air traffic controller focusing on a potential collision course is prone to neglect other planes in the air, the poor, when attending to monetary concerns, lose their capacity to give other problems their full consideration. (p. 976)

Similarly, in their extensive review of psychological literature on poverty, Sheehy-Skeffington and Rhea (2017) found that the poor are more prone to taking decisions which are based on 'proximal' (i.e., based on immediate, actual and tangible situations) rather than 'distal' (i.e., distant and possible in future) conditions. This preoccupation with the immediate needs, arising from socioeconomic insecurity and social exclusions, impedes the cognitive capacity to imagine one's future life and self, and shortens the time horizons of the poor (Banerjee and Mullainathan 2010; Bernheim et al. 2013; Fieulaine and Apostolidis 2015; Mani et al. 2013). Poor find it psychologically difficult to commit to long-term efforts (e.g., building assets and long-term savings) even if they would lead to more resilient future for them. In selecting between the known and unknown devils, the poor prefer to live in the comfort of their present and past. It often seems counter-intuitive that the poor do not avail and let go opportunities for a better future life by making small present sacrifices: they often splurge their hard earned income on a wedding instead of putting it in their savings, do not take their children for immunization which would ensure a healthy future life, or buy a TV instead of spending it on better diet, etc. However, as Banerjee and Duflo (2011) observed:

> We are often inclined to see the world of the poor as a land of missed opportunities and to wonder why they do not put these purchases on hold and invest in what would make their lives better. The poor, on the other hand, may be more skeptical about supposed opportunities and possibilities of any radical change in their lives. (p. 38)

This tendency to psychologically disregard the future also leads to 'behavioural poverty trap' (Laajaj 2017) in which short-term focus and poverty reinforce each other. The lack of faith in the future often makes the poor sacrifice their long-term formal agreements in favour of short-term exigencies of their lives. They often neglect their agreed-upon commitments, even if that leads to loss of opportunity in the long-term (e.g., a household help goes absent without notice and a tailor or a plumber fails to deliver on time). Karamchandani et al. (2009) found that in the informal, unskilled work settings:

> …the decisions of low-income suppliers follow short time horizons and are usually unconstrained by long-term contractual relationships. The problem of retention is compounded by the phenomenon of 'side-selling'—suppliers trying to increase their income in the short-term by selling their produce or labor to third parties. (pp. 73–74)

An implication of this focus on present and immediate gratification, however, is also that the poor respond well to products and services which provide immediate incentives, or at least do not disrupt their present cash-flows and lives. Many examples discussed later in Chapter 9 (e.g., Rickshaw Bank, Janta Meals and Rent-A-Solar-Battery) show that poor do adapt to new products and services if they match their income-expenditure cycles.

Poverty Has Socio-emotional Dimensions

Viewing poverty as primarily an economic circumstance in one's life often blinds us from the raw psychological experience of being poor. While the researchers, marketers and policy makers understand poverty as lack of income and assets, for the poor, the meaning of poverty is far deeper and experiential. Poverty impacts both social and emotional lives of people.

Socially, poor experience exclusions and discrimination and loss of dignity on a regular basis. Being shouted at, driven away, ignored, publicly humiliated or even physically assaulted, etc., are part of recurrent experiences of their daily lives. Müller and Neuhäuser (2011) noted that:

[P]oor are marginalized, rejected and humiliated in many subtle ways. Single incidents and situations often do not seem to be humiliating as such, but taken together they give reason to see one's self-respect and human dignity violated. Examples of this are the inability to be as mobile as others, to dress in a proper way, to attend ordinary social events, or to spend money on goods for entertainment in general. (p. 168)

Moreover, due to their low social status their voices are rarely heard, they are often denied their basic rights as a citizen and they learn to live with the injustices and exploitation. Discrimination is more so in case of women, children, migrant workers, etc. (National Commission for Enterprises in Unorganised Sector 2007). These conditions of powerlessness, shame and exclusion tend to further aggravate poverty. In their multi-country study of the lives of poor, Narayan et al. (2000) found that:

Poor people understand their exclusion on a number of levels, cited as alienation from community events, from decision making, from opportunity and access to resources or to information (p. 134).... Social and economic factors reinforce each other in a cycle of alienation and powerlessness. Poverty deprives people of access to resources, to opportunities and to contact with those more influential. Without resources, opportunities and connections, economic mobility becomes extremely difficult.... (p. 138)

Emotionally, being poor is also a daunting and precarious experience, in which a single rainy day, a one-day *bandh*, a forced relocation, or an illness is enough to send one's existence over the edge to the other side. Poor live with a persistent sense of *insecurity* and *vulnerability* (Narayan et al. 2000). Insecurity results from the capriciousness of various factors of their lives, such as lack of finances, worries about food, shelter and health, scarcity of resources, unpredictability of job/livelihood, community and family relations, etc. In addition, poverty also induces a sense of vulnerability, which is experienced as being subjected to unknown forces, lack of control over events in one's life, helplessness in coping with sudden shocks and setbacks, etc. In their extensive review of studies on psychological perspective on poverty, Fell and Hewstone (2015) found that recurring and continuous stressful experiences make poor more prone to anxiety disorders and mood swings—and in extreme cases, even to psychiatric episodes. They concluded:

> A key causal factor in the onset of depressive or anxious symptoms appears to be the experience of stressful life events, the prevalence of which is significantly elevated for those experiencing poverty. (p. 4)

These socio-emotional conditions of poverty have important bearings on the decisions and choices poor make. Besides shortening of the time horizon which we discussed earlier, poverty also reduces the self-confidence of poor to move out of the known options and to take rational risks. Moreover, to compensate for their anonymity and helplessness in the larger society, poor mostly rely on the support and solidarity of their community to continue to maintain their personal identity, and a sense of their own humanity. While this community support provides them with psychological security, the community norms and pressure also become a barrier for them to change their behaviour and choices.

Challenges of Serving the 'Markets of the Poor'

As can be seen from the above discussion, the world of poor is a unique terrain with its own peculiarities. Besides the economic numbers which deprive the poor of many opportunities, their behaviour and choices are also shaped and constrained by the psychosocial and emotional context in which they experience their lives and options. Any initiative to offer products and services to the poor needs to factor in the challenges which these conditions create. From the preceding discussion, one can derive the following five critical challenges:

Awareness and Information

Due to reasons such as lack of education, distance from the markets, low exposure, etc., poor lack information and awareness about the more beneficial options available for them. For instance, farmers often lack information about more advanced agricultural practices or the market prices, rural artisans are often not aware of customers' design preferences, poor also often lack knowledge about the benefits of services such as education, nutrition, primary healthcare, etc., migrant labours do not have updated information about the remunerative urban labour markets and so on. Lacking access to such information, they normally rely on traditional practices, their community and other informal information sources. One of the major hurdles for any venture aiming to serve the markets of the poor is to address this knowledge gap. This may require considerable resources for creating awareness, customer education and skill building.

Affordability

Making the services and products affordable for 'poor as customers' has two different kinds of challenges. First, many poor have enough aggregate earning to pay for the products or services, but are unable to do so since the terms of payment do not suit their cash-flow cycles. For instance, farmers earn only once or twice a year after harvest, while the income of a rickshaw puller or a street vendor is on a daily basis. Moreover, these earnings are also often unpredictable since they are vulnerable to many extraneous circumstances. For ventures aiming to serve the poor, the challenge is to innovatively devise the pricing strategy and flexible payment schedules.

Second, there are also poor whose earning is too scanty and below subsistence level to pay for many offerings, even though they need them to move out of poverty (e.g., a productive asset or a marketable skill). Market-based offerings do not work for them since, being ultra-poor, they are not part of the market. Servicing this segment of poor is particularly challenging since it requires creative and unconventional business models which can service them and still remain sustainable.

Aggregation

Another key challenge of servicing the markets of the poor is the very concept of 'market', and the prerequisites of its formation. Mere transactions among a few isolated and dispersed buyers and sellers do not qualify to be called a market. Market has a social and/or economic identity, and it comes into existence when a reasonable number of potential customers or producers are aggregated into an identifiable group.

The poor however, as we saw, are mostly dispersed and/or unconnected. Even when they exist as a socially identifiable group, they are remotely located and scattered. They also often lack a minimum social and physical infrastructure (e.g., a group identity, proximity and/or connectivity and banking infrastructure) which are preconditions for aggregation, and for efficient delivery of products and services. These conditions pose a challenge for social ventures, since such fragmented and difficult-to-reach 'markets' add significantly to the cost of serving them.

Contextualization

Like any market segment, poor too have specific set of needs and require products and services which are tailored to those needs. However, their ability to avail these products and services is also dependent on many extraneous conditions and context of their lives. Often, as we saw in the beginning of this chapter, a well-designed and customized product (e.g., Vector razor blade) may become useless for the poor due to other contextual factors such as lack of running water. Similarly, an initiative to aggregate and connect small rural artisans to remunerative markets may become ineffective due to their inability to avail working capital loan or lack of storage space, or an SMS-based customized market information for farmers may fail due to lack of network or lack of vernacular language.

Servicing the markets of the poor requires both customization (i.e., meeting the needs) as well contextualization (i.e., tailoring the products/services to the external conditions in which poor live). Since the poor live in very diverse life conditions, contextualization poses a major challenge to make the product/service accessible and requires innovative designs in delivery.

Behavioural Change

More often than not, the poor also need to adapt new forms of behaviour to avail the benefits from new products and services offered by the social ventures. For instance, to participate in formal urban markets, the poor may need to learn how to deal with more sophisticated customers, maintain time-commitments, learn to operate new gadgets, etc. Similarly, a farmer may need to shift from traditional agricultural practices and crops to increase income, or a low-wage earner may need to develop financial discipline to avail loans. Poor, as we discussed in the chapter, often find it difficult to change their behaviours due to factors such as deep-rooted cultural learning, community norms, lack of immediate incentive from the change, etc. In addition, even when they are willing to change, they often require training, hand-holding and counselling to make this transition.

Market of Opportunities and Constraints

As one can see, the 'markets of the poor' are characterized by two contrasting aspects. On the one hand, the poor represent a valuable resource in terms of their contribution to society and economy: they produce items ranging from grains to artefacts, provide useful services as vendors, repairmen, domestic help, etc., participate in economic and social activities as labour, micro-entrepreneurs, entertainers, etc. On the other hand, they also represent a world in which deprivation, exploitation and humiliation are a regular feature. Their productivity remains low because they have limited or no access to basic public services such as credit, education, healthcare, energy, markets, etc. Devoid of access to these, they remain entangled in the cycles of poverty.

With their unique features and constraints, these 'markets' offer a challenge for the social entrepreneurs to develop venture strategies to service them. Over the years, the Indian social ventures have innovated many entrepreneurial models which successfully provide beneficial products and services to the poor. In Chapter 9, we will look at some of these models.

ENTREPRENEURIAL MODELS FOR PROVIDING ACCESS

9

Many enterprises have pushed offerings into the market only to see them fail. People living at the base of the economic pyramid should be seen as customers and not beneficiaries; they will spend money, or switch livelihoods, or invest valuable time, only if they calculate the transaction will be worth their while.

—Ashish Karamchandani et al. (2009)

As we saw in the past chapter, the world of poor constitutes a different universe which operates in different and complex ways. Not only do the poor lack access to various products and services, they also have different needs and resources at their disposal and respond to situations differently. Both as consumers and producers, they are not easily accessible and amenable to aggregation. Reaching them offers diverse challenges and requires innovative market-based strategies to service them.

It is important to recognize, however, that not all poor have the capacity to transact in or with the market. The poorest of the poor or Ultra-Poor[1] (e.g., the destitute, beggars, disabled, those with no assets or marketable skills), a significant segment, lack the ability and resources, and are largely disconnected from the markets. They need a different approach to move out of abject poverty and

---

[1] The term 'ultra-poor' was coined by Michael Lipton (1983) who defined them as those poor who spend 80% of their total expenditure on food and cannot attain 80% of their standard calorie needs.

become economically active before they can be integrated into the markets (see Box 9.1 which describes The Ultra-Poor Graduation Approach).

BOX 9.1   THE ULTRA-POOR GRADUATION APPROACH

Ultra-poor represent the poorest of the poor (e.g., beggars, destitute, unsupported aged and disabled), who lack any productive assets, skills or savings which they can use for a secure and sustainable livelihood. They suffer from chronic poverty and are vulnerable to food and health insecurity. Invariably they are uncovered by the social protection programmes of the government and remain out of the focus of the microfinance programmes.

To address their developmental needs, The Ultra-Poor Graduation Approach (Matin, 2002) was developed by BRAC (Bangladesh Rural Advancement Committee). Over the years, it has been adopted and scaled up by UN agencies and international NGOs such as TrickleUp to other countries. In India, Bandhan Micro Finance (now Bandhan Bank) has been a pioneer in using this approach to enable the poor move out of abject poverty.

The Graduation Approach is a time-bound programme, normally lasting 18–24 months, consisting of six complementary interventions which are designed to address specific constraints faced by the ultra-poor households:

1. **Transfer of productive assets**: Households are helped to plan their livelihood, and a one-time transfer of productive assets (e.g., poultry, livestock and agricultural land) is made to them based on their skills and local livelihood opportunities.

2. **Cash stipend for consumption needs:** A small weekly cash stipend is given for a limited period (normally 4–8 months) to meet the basic consumption needs based on the nature of chosen productive asset.

3. **Technical skill training:** Training is provided to manage the chosen livelihood through the asset and running a business.

4. **Requirement of savings:** Households are required to save a nominal amount (as low as ₹10/week) to develop fiscal discipline and build resilience.

5. **Hand-holding support:** A team from the implementing organization makes a regular weekly visit to provide counselling, support and to facilitate integration with local community.

6. **Healthcare support:** Regular health check-ups and referrals are provided to the households.

Many studies (e.g., Banerjee et al., 2015) show that the positive outcomes of the Graduation Approach extend beyond an increase in their income through self-employment: there was consistent increase in their food expenditure, enabling them to afford two meals per day; they were able to increase their household assets beyond the assets which were given to them (e.g., they could buy ore livestock); they started saving more than the mandatory requirements; and from being marginalized, they became more accepted and involved in their communities.

In their study of market-based models for the low-income communities, Karamchandani et al. (2009) identified seven such models which social entrepreneurs/enterprises have successfully used to integrate the poor into the markets. In this section, we will discuss some of these and other models which have been effective in providing them the access to markets.

Cross-subsidization

Aravind Eye Care System is world's largest and most productive eye care facility which includes ten hospitals, 50 vision centres, a research institute, an intraocular lens factory, an eye bank, research centre and a training institute. Established in 1976, Aravind has since performed close to 40 million eye surgeries, half of which are provided free to the poor. The cost of surgery for the non-paying poor patient is cross-subsidized by the patients who can afford to pay—who, however, do not pay more than what they would pay for similar treatment in any other hospital. Aravind is able to cross-subsidize the poor without charging the others more due to its large volumes, frugal operations and cost-efficient utilization of its resources. For example, its doctors perform around 2,000 surgeries as compared to the national average of 500, it selects and trains local girls from marginalized background to become ophthalmologists/paramedics and it has standardized patient flow (Shainesh and Kulkarni 2016).

Aravind's model provides a practical approach to provide high-cost essential services and product to the poor without compromising on quality. Cross-subsidization is not a new concept, but has been used frequently in more mature high-end markets. Social ventures use three different cross-subsidized pricing structures to make services and products affordable (or free) for the poor (Jahani and West 2015). One common version of cross-subsidization, as in the case of Arvind Eye Hospital, is by charging differential pricing of the same product or service for different segments. For instance, **Ziqitza Health Care**, which provides ambulances through its **Dial 1298** service, provides the service free for the patients going to the government hospitals (mostly the poor) through the fee it charges to those going to private hospitals (mostly the rich).

The second pricing model involves offering an upgraded product/service at higher price to cover the cost of providing discounted or free products/services with same functionality.

VisionSpring, for instance, uses this strategy to provide inexpensive eyeglasses to the urban and remote low-income communities (e.g., tailors, rug makers, bike mechanics, weavers and artisans) whose livelihoods suffer due to loss of their near vision. Venture's optical shops and field-level entrepreneurs offer a variety of frame options ranging from the most basic to more trendy ones with higher price and margins. The surpluses generated through the higher margin products are then used to subsidize the operational costs of providing the products to poor and remote customers.

The third variation of cross-subsidization strategy involves using the profits/surpluses from an entirely different high margin product/service to subsidize the costs of offering for the low-income markets. For instance, **Aga Khan Development Network (AKDN)**, which runs social welfare and developmental projects across 30 countries, has a commercial arm, the **Aga Khan Fund for Economic Development (AKFED)** with a turnover of more than $4 billion from a variety of businesses (financial services, tourism promotion, infrastructure projects, media services, etc.). While AKDN also gets funding from international and national donors, the surpluses from AKFED are also invested to subsidize its development projects. Similarly, many smaller hybrid social enterprises use the surpluses from their for-profit arm (e.g., consultancy, advisory and publications) to support the costs of reaching services or products (e.g., education and healthcare) to the low-income communities.

Product = Product + Finance

The second half of the 1980s saw a sudden spurt in the purchase of consumer durables among the emerging Indian middle class. Many people had started buying expensive items such as car, TV, scooter, etc. However, this abrupt growth in buying was not due to any drastic increase in the income of the middle class. Rather it happened because many banks and financial institutions (e.g., Bank of India, Canara Bank, Citibank and State Bank of India) and financial institutions (e.g., Nagarjuna Finance, Bajaj Auto Finance and Shri Ram Fibres Finance) had started giving out consumer loans which were multiple times the income and/or savings of the borrower. This convenience to 'buy now, pay later' had suddenly made these expensive products 'affordable' for the middle class (Joseph 1988).

For the low-income communities, many products and services remain 'unaffordable' because they often do not have access to easy loans, due to requirements of collateral, guarantee, documents, etc. Even when the loans are available, the repayment cycles often do not match the earning cycles of the poor (EMI, or equated monthly instalment, is more suited for salaried class whose earnings are monthly, but not for a road-side vendor who earns daily, or a farmer, whose income is tied to harvesting season). For the low-income communities, many products and services become 'affordable' when they come bundled with appropriate loan or lease (see Box 9.2 for some examples).

BOX 9.2   SOME EXAMPLES OF 'PRODUCT = PRODUCT + FINANCE' MODEL

SELCO Solar: SELCO Solar provides customized solar lighting and other systems to rural and slum households, which comes with after-sales maintenance and support. Though its customers need these products, given the pattern of their income cycles, they are unable to buy them by paying the full price all at once. To bring the products within their reach, SELCO has forged partnerships with regional rural banks, commercial banks, NGOs and credit cooperatives, which provide affordable and accessible credit to their customers. Customers typically make between 10 and 25% down payment, and pay the balance over a period of time.

PARFI Gurukul: PARFI (PanIIT Alumni Reach for India Foundation) runs vocational training centres, called Gurukul, across many states in India which provide holistic training and various technical skills like construction, medical services, logistics, electrical and others to youth from marginalized backgrounds. It is a demand-based model which trains the students according to the industry demand, and thus provides assured placement. Since most of these youth come from economically weaker sections, they are unable to pay the training fee upfront. To solve this issue, PARFI has developed a loan-based model, enabling the students to get loans from banks, which they repay once they get the job.

Rickshaw Bank: Almost 90% of India's millions of rickshaw-pullers do not own the rickshaw but take them on daily rent. They pay a major portion of their earning as rent (which does not include maintenance costs), which leaves them with an income just enough for a daily subsistence. Since they are mostly poor migrants, they also do not have the required documents and collateral to get loans from the bank to buy their own rickshaw. To address this problem, Dr Pradip Kumar Sarmah, founder of Centre for Rural Development, Guwahati, innovated 'Rickshaw Bank' which allows the pullers to take the rickshaw on lease, for which they pay a daily instalment equal to the rent they were paying earlier. On payment of the lease amount within 12–18 months, they start owning the rickshaw, which makes a quantum increase in their daily income. In addition, the members of the Rickshaw Bank also avail insurance, licence, photo ID cards, uniform, health check-up, fuel package (LP Gas with Stove), educational loan for their children, etc.

The design of this model requires some critical considerations for it to benefit the poor:

1. **Income-enhancing product/service:** By definition, the poor do not have surplus income to repay the loan. Therefore, the model is viable only when the product or service they buy on loan helps them to increase their productivity and income. The enhanced income enables them to pay back the loan and in due course they start owning the product.

2. **Easy, smooth access to loan:** The poor often find it difficult to take loan from the formal channels because the banking institutions are normally not poor-friendly. The entrepreneur/ venture plays a proactive role in making the loan accessible with minimum hassle in terms of efforts, delay, and need for copious documentation. Often the entrepreneurs/venture interface with the banks directly, stand the guarantee or provide the loan themselves.

3. **Customized repayment terms:** As mentioned above, the income cycles of the poor vary widely from daily to seasonal, as per their occupations. With low or nil savings, the poor can repay only when they earn. The model requires the repayment schedule and instalments to be appropriately customized to match the income cycles. This also implies additional responsibility for the entrepreneur/venture, for example, if the repayment is done daily, then required process, infrastructure and personnel would be needed for collection.

Pay-per-Use

Consider the taxi service which many people use to commute in the city. Even if one is not able to buy a car, a taxi provides the comfort and safety of travelling in a car without having to own and maintain one. By paying only for utilizing the service, it also gives one the flexibility to use it only when needed, or when one can afford to pay for it. In this way, for many people, the 'pay-per-use' model of taxi service makes it affordable to access the benefits of a car.

The 'pay-per-use' model uses the same principles as the taxi service to provide affordable access to necessary products and services for the low-income communities. The cost of ownership and irregular income deprives many people from availing the benefits of necessary product and services, which they may require only sporadically. One of the first proponent and pioneers of this model in India was **Sulabh Shauchalay**. While the need for a clean and hygienic toilet is almost universal, most people are unable to afford one due to cost, space and maintenance. Most public toilets, on the other hand, are poorly maintained and dirty. To address this need, Sulabh International pioneered community toilets in 1974 in Patna, and now Sulabh operates more than 6,000 community complexes in about 1,100 towns and cities (including about 100 railway stations) across India. Most of the Sulabh units are operated by a local entrepreneur and charge nominal fee per-use which is used for maintenance and the salary of the staff (see Box 9.3 for some more examples).

BOX 9.3   SOME EXAMPLES OF PAY-PER-USE MODEL

Sarvajal Water ATMs: Sarvajal, a social enterprise by Piramal Foundation, provides clean and affordable drinking water to underserved communities in slums and rural areas through automated water vending machines. The customers can buy water as per their requirement from these water ATMs for as low a price as 30–50 paise per litre. These 'water ATMs' are solar powered and cloud connected, thus enabling remote tracking of the water quality and of each pay per use transaction. Through a franchising model, Sarvajal has 570+ installations across 12 states and serves about 300,000 consumers daily.

Farm Equipment Rentals ('Fazilka Model'): Farm equipments are largely underutilized assets, since they are used seasonally. On the other hand, being expensive, small farmers are not able to afford them. To offset this asymmetry, Vikram Ahuja, the Founder and Director of Zamindara Farm Solutions, based in Fazilka, Punjab pioneered the farm equipment rentals. The model uses agriculture implements and machinery (e.g., tractors, harrow, spike, chisel plow, cultivator, rotator and rollers) which are lying idle with individuals, and provides them to small and marginal farmers on a pay-for-use basis by connecting the owners and users on a virtual platform.

Rent-a-Solar-Battery Entrepreneurs: Solar lamps/lanterns are cleaner, have lesser operational cost, and provide better lighting for the street vendors. However, they often do not use them since they cannot afford to buy the entire solar lighting systems (panels, batteries, etc.) to charge them. Many solar lighting entrepreneurs, supported by SELCO, provide solar energy to these vendors on a daily basis. They charge the batteries during the day using solar panels, and rent them out for the evening to the vendors. The vendors pay about ₹15 per evening for the 4–5 hours of light, which is equal or less than what they would have spent on the kerosene.

The design features of the pay-per-use models share certain key common principles:

1. **Flexible and accommodating terms:** The model allows the customers to use a product or service as and when needed and/or when they can afford them. There are possibilities of variations

in the terms of payment, which can be 'pay-as-you-use' (e.g., Sulabh Shauchalay), 'pre-paid cards' (e.g., Sarvajal's water ATMs or mobile charge cards) or rented (e.g., Fazilka's farm equipment rentals), etc.

2. **Common central infrastructure:** The model economizes by using the same facility or infrastructure to service to a large number of people. A central infrastructure enables higher efficiency in distribution, day-to-day operations and collection—and thus, lowering per unit cost.

3. **High demand/utilization requirement:** The model is viable only when the product/service is availed by a large number of people. This need for high utilization of the service has two implications for the venture: one, often and for certain offerings the demand would need to be 'pushed'. For instance, the poor are often not aware of the health benefits of clean drinking water or sanitation and may need to be educated/ informed about them. Second, to achieve high utilization, the facility needs to be located where the density of potential customers is high and is easy to approach.

4. **Scaling though third-party administration:** Scaling of the model is possible through replication in multiple locations. This is done by franchising the facility to a local entity, such as a local entrepreneur, a firm, community or an NGO to run it. Locally managed operations help in leveraging on the contacts of the operator and in customizing the model to suit the local conditions. Often the local operators also bring down the cost of operation by bringing in the required operational, financial and marketing expertise and resources.

No-Frills Offering

The cost of many products and services increase because they come bundled up with many features and functionalities, which may be desirable, but not essential, for the user. For instance, many of the functions which are built into a smart phone or the

Microsoft Office Suite are never used by the customer, even though they pay for these features. Similarly, the price difference between a cup of tea in a road-side eatery and an up-market restaurant is not necessarily due to the quality of the tea, but because the tea in the restaurant also includes the cost of the property, manpower, infrastructure, ambience, etc.

The 'no-frills offering' model re-engineers the products and services to meet the customized requirements of the low-income communities by economizing on the non-essential functionalities. For instance, people in villages have a need to keep their perishables (e.g., vegetables, milk and poultry products) cool to avoid wastage. However, the conventional domestic refrigerator is too costly for them and may not even be useful in many regions due to erratic electricity supply. Trying to address this need, Gopalan Sunderraman, the Executive Vice President of Godrej & Boyce, noticed that major cost in a refrigerator is the compressor. However, while the compressor is required to cool the refrigerator up to below the freezing temperature, such low temperature is not needed to store the perishables. The outcome of this insight was a stripped-down version of a refrigerator, **Chotukool**. Chotukool is a 45-litre plastic container that uses solid-state technology rather than a conventional, compressor-driven system. It runs on a 12-volt battery and can keep the temperature to around 8–10 °C, which is sufficient to keep the perishables fresh. Being battery-driven, it can also be used in remote places with low levels of electricity provision. This redesign also brought down the cost and made the product available at an affordable price of ₹3,000–3,500.

The 'no-frills offering' model also helps in bringing many services within the reach of low-income communities. For instance, by sticking to the core offering, the Gurgaon-based **Janta Meals** is able to provide hygienic and nutritious meals at affordable price to the migrant daily workers (e.g., construction workers, auto-drivers, rickshaw pullers, vendors, security guards and daily-wagers). The venture reaches out to its customers through about

SOCIAL ENTREPRENEURSHIP IN INDIA

202

30 franchisees which are run by local micro-entrepreneurs. The meals are supplied from a centralized kitchen, for which Janta Meals has formed partnership with Akshay Patra Foundation which runs centralized kitchens across India to provide mid-day meals to government schools; since the cooking in these kitchens gets over by mid-morning, Janta Meals uses the infrastructure, thus reducing its overhead costs. These measures enable the venture to provide wholesome, but standardized meals (dal, vegetable and roti/rice) for just ₹20.

Similarly, **LifeSpring Hospitals Pvt Ltd** (a chain of 17 hospitals and extension centres in and around Hyderabad) provides affordable maternal and paediatric healthcare to low-income community by focusing on bare-bone but high-quality service. To keep the costs low, the hospitals, which are simple 20–25 bed facilities on leased property, do not provide air-conditioned private rooms or canteen facilities. It also does not maintain facilities for testing laboratory or pharmacy, which are outsourced to partners. Since only 2–3 per cent cases require intensive care, LifeSpring refers them to other better equipped hospitals instead of maintaining an in-house intensive care unit. Through an effective outreach programme to attract customers, the venture has a high utilization of its facilities, enabling it to perform three times the deliveries in a month, as compared to hospitals of similar size. These measures keep the cost low, enabling LifeSpring to provide services which are 30–50 per cent of the market rates.

As can be seen from these examples, designing such offerings rely on some common core principles:

1. **Focus on core functionality**: Instead of offering a wide bouquet of choices, the product or service is designed or re-engineered to meet a very specific but widespread need of a segment. The value proposition of these products/services is narrow and by focusing on 'bare-bone' requirements, the venture is able to both economize on the costs as well as maintain high quality of the offering.

2. **Standardization and specialization**: By limiting the offering to a narrow array of services, the provider is able to standardize its processes and procedures, which can be documented and routinized. This enables bringing down the costs through economies of scale and through delivering of the services through lower-skilled (therefore, less-expensive) staff. For instance, Janta Meals is able to offer its meals through local micro-entrepreneurs by providing them minimal training in heating, serving and accounting. Similarly, LifeSpring Hospitals is able to train local women in standard procedures and use them as para-medical staff.

3. **High-throughput/high asset utilization**: The no-frills offering model can succeed only when its offering meets a specific need of a large segment. Since these products and services operate on thin margins, high customer volumes are essential to bring down the per-unit cost by providing economies of scale. This becomes possible when the service is easily accessible and are located near the customers. For instance, the LifeSpring Hospitals are located near the slums which makes it easy for their prospective customers to access them. Similarly, to reach out to its predominantly rural customers, Godrej & Boyce partnered with India Posts enabling the customers to purchase Chotukool through the local post offices.

Para-skilling

A major challenge for the pharmaceutical companies is to reach their product information to the thousands of highly dispersed doctors, who alone can prescribe the medicines. To be convinced about the medicine, the doctors also ask for technical information and clarifications, which can only be provided by experts, who are expensive to hire. Moreover, doctors have a very limited time to take away from seeing the patients, which is their main priority. To address this need, the pharmaceutical companies hire and train

Medical Representatives (MRs), who form a critical link between the company and the doctors.

Medical Representatives, however, are low-paid graduates and mostly have no pharmaceutical qualifications. They are trained in the basic features of the drugs, the tests which have been carried out on the drugs and some allied information. To interact with the doctors, they are given flip-chart booklets which contain the information, and the MRs are trained in the script to deliver that information, and answer some expected questions, in the limited time they will get from the doctor. MRs enable the companies a large-scale outreach through a cadre of low-cost paraprofessionals.

As is evident, the para-skilling model is useful where scales are required and the costs of last-mile delivering high-quality services are high. Providing such services require professional experts who are expensive and constitute the main component of the fixed costs. Para-skilling enables delivery of these complex services by disaggregating them into simple and standardized tasks, which can be done by less skilled workers. By reducing the costs, it also enables increase in the volumes and scale.

Para-skilling is a useful model for providing high-quality essential services, such as education, healthcare or financial services to the low-end markets of the poor at affordable costs. Many social ventures and initiatives have successfully trained and used such (often local) paraprofessionals to provide basic services to poor at large scale. For instance, many banks and financial institutions use Business Correspondents (or 'Bank Mitra') who are mostly local graduates to reach the basic banking services to the remote villages and slums. Similarly, public health initiatives such as **CORD (Chinmaya Organization for Rural Development)** in Himachal Pradesh, Jharkhand-based **Ekjut, Jan Swasthya Sahyog** in Chhattisgarh, etc., train and use local rural women to deliver a wide range of basic healthcare services to the remote communities (see Box 9.4 for some other examples).

BOX 9.4   SOME EXAMPLES OF 'PARA-SKILLING' MODEL

wPOWER: wPOWER (Partnership on Women's Entrepreneurship in Clean Energy) is a programme pioneered by Maharashtra-based organization Swayam Shikshan Prayog (SSP), which focuses on meeting the energy needs of deprived communities in rural households. To reach the last-mile, SSP has created a cadre of women entrepreneurs called Sakhis. These semi-literate women are selected from the rural communities and are trained to market and sell clean energy products like cook stoves, water treatment plants, solar water heaters, solar lanterns, biogas plants etc. In addition, SSP also trains local youth as energy technicians to take care of after-sales service. By 2016, wPOWER had trained more than 1,000 women entrepreneurs to reach out to over 200,000 households across eight districts in Maharashtra and Bihar by 2016 (Mishra, 2018).

Gyan Shala: Ahmedabad-based, Gyan Shala, started in 2000 with the aim of providing low-cost high-quality education to children living marginalized urban communities through single teacher schools. The venture was planned for scale by re-engineering and de-segregating the teaching activity. A small central curriculum design team develops high quality and standardized course content and learning material. The curriculum is delivered by an army of low-qualification class teachers, who are para-skilled to deliver the curriculum as per the standardize lesson plan. These teachers are selected from the local community, and are trained for 2 weeks in pedagogical skills. These para-teachers are also supported by specialist teachers with subject-matter expertise, who visit the classes once a week to answer children's specific queries which are not covered in the

SOCIAL ENTREPRENEURSHIP IN INDIA

standardized curriculum. This model allowed the venture to scale up and by 2016, its programme was running in about 1,630 urban and 7,300 rural centres in nine districts of Gujarat, Bihar and West Bengal, covering about 0.5 million children.

Jamkhed Project: The Comprehensive Rural Health Project, Jamkhed (popularly known as the Jamkhed Project) was started in 1970 with the aim to provide community-based primary healthcare to the rural communities. It provides comprehensive public healthcare across 2,000 villages through a network of health clinics, mobile health team, self-help groups, farmers' clubs, adolescent clubs, etc. The project relies on a large cadre of Village Health Workers (VHWs), mostly illiterate or semi-literate women who are selected from the local communities. Besides being the health educators and mobilisers in the community, the VHWs are trained to provide basic medical care (e.g. prenatal care, safe deliveries, infant care, family planning and treatment of minor illnesses). This enables the communities to take care of about 80% of their health-related problems and reduces their dependence on centralized healthcare services.

The design elements of the para-skilling model are same as the no-frills model with some additional features:

1. **Re-engineered, disaggregated core processes:** The model relies on remodelling the complex activities which require professional expertise so that they can be performed by lesser-skilled staff. To achieve this, the core processes are re-engineered to separate the low and high skill components of the activity, so that the former can be delegated to the paraprofessional staff.

2. **Simplified and codified protocol of activities:** The low-skill activities are arranged and codified in simple steps so that performing them does not require extensive skills and discretion. Developing this protocol is critical for training the paraprofessionals and ensuring consistency of quality in delivery. Moreover, routinizing of the activities also allows high volumes, thus lowering the cost of delivery.

3. **Developing the paraprofessional cadre:** Careful selection and training of the paraprofessionals are a critical element in the success of the model. Besides the basic required qualifications, often many other factors play a role in suitability of the staff. For instance, often non-financial motives (e.g., 'I am doing this for my community') and their acceptance by the community also play a major role in their effectiveness.

Shared Channels

In the early 1980s, Super Cassettes launched its T-Series brand for the large low-income segment of film music lovers, who were neglected by the existing high-end market players (HMV and Polydor India). Compared to the price of more than ₹40 per cassette which were sold by HMV and Polydor India, the 'version-recorded' low-quality T-Series cassettes were priced at just ₹16 with ₹1 margin. To reach the potential customers (who would normally not go to a branded store), Super Cassettes tied up with the road-side paan wallas and kirana shops who would sell its cassettes. Though often charged for its unethical practices and copyright violations, Super Cassettes' sales and distribution strategy offers a good example of a low-cost approach to reach the low-end customers. By piggybacking on the existing customer supply chains, not only the company could reach its highly dispersed market, but could save on distribution costs, and thus keep the prices low.

Poor, as we discussed earlier, constitute markets which are remote and highly dispersed. Reaching them is costly and adds to the end-price of the product or service. Moreover, distribution of socially beneficial goods and services in less accessible markets also pose a hurdle in the scaling up and viability of the enterprise. To offset this challenge, many enterprises use the existing customer supply chains to reach these markets. Such partnerships greatly reduce the distribution costs, as well as help in increasing the reach to the intended users.

In India, there are many existing channels (e.g., post offices, self-help groups, MFIs, grassroots NGOs and village-level shops) which reach into, and service, the remote markets of the poor. They provide a ready platform to the enterprises serving the poor through partnerships. For instance, **ChotuKool**, which was discussed in an earlier section, tied up with India Post which has 150,000 post offices across the country. This enabled the rural customers to book the product by paying the money, which would then be delivered through the Express Post Parcel services of India Post (see Box 9.5 for some examples).

BOX 9.5   EXAMPLES OF SHARED CHANNEL

Frontier Markets: Frontier Markets is a social enterprise which sources and sells solar products in rural areas. To reach its market, the enterprise partners with local village-level entrepreneurs (VLEs) who are normally owners of local shops and stores, and have the understanding of the local community. They are selected on the basis of their business experience and reputation, and are given training about the product and its marketing. Besides selling the products, they also help in providing information on product demand, servicing needs, and product feedback, and get a share of the margins of the sales.

Hrudaya Post: Hrudaya Post is a consultation service by **Narayana Hospitals**, a multi-specialty chain of hospitals with a mission of providing high-quality, low-cost services to poor. In 2007, it tied up with the Karnataka circle of postal department to provide free health consultations to the poor. This facility allows the rural poor to send their reports through the IT infrastructure at the post office for a small fee. On receiving the report, the hospital provides free consultation and expert advice through video conferencing within 24–48 hours.

Aakar Innovations: Aakar Innovations focuses on making high-quality, affordable and bio-degradable sanitary napkins to women in rural and under-resourced communities. Branded as Anandi pads, its model relies on its 'mini factory' which can be used by semi-literate women with little training, and uses locally available agricultural and plant waste as the raw material. Aakar partners with the local NGOs, government agencies and CSR departments to reach self-help groups who then become both the producers and customers of the sanitary pads.

Onergy: Onergy is a Kolkata-based social venture which manufactures and markets solar products in rural communities across India. To reach its potential customers, Onergy partners with local MFI who not only provide loans to the rural customers but their members also help in marketing the products. For instance in 2016, Onergy tied up with Belghoria Janakalyan Samity (BJS), an NGO and MFI with active presence across West Bengal. Through this partnership, Onergy could reach the NGO's self-help groups, and trained about 100 women in marketing and usage of solar lights (Chakraborty, 2016).

As can be seen from the examples, the success of this model relies on some critical design features such as:

1. **Selection of appropriate channel/platform:** Mostly, many channels and platforms (e.g., post offices, MFIs, SHGs, shop owners and other players) have presence in the same remote market, but all of them are not always active and functioning. For instance, the self-help groups may be dormant or too nascent to help, the MFI may lack credibility in the local community, or the post office may be poorly resourced, etc. Selection of suitable partner requires proper due diligence to ensure their capacity to deliver and service the local customers.

2. **Training/capacity building of the partners' staff:** The partnership brings new tasks and activities for the staff of the channel partner, for which they may not have the knowledge or skill. They would need to be trained for these new requirements, such as about the features of the product, selling and maintain the product, order taking, account keeping, etc.

3. **Incentives for the participants in distribution chain:** The partnership also adds additional responsibilities for the channel partner and their staff. They should have some incentive to provide the last-mile delivery. While often these incentives are monetary in terms of increased income for the partner and the staff, if the alignment of social mission of the enterprise and the partner also acts as a powerful incentive (e.g., often the SHG members or the local shop owners accept to participate in the delivery, even though the financial incentive is minimal or nil, because they feel that it is good for their community).

Aggregated Market Linkage

The **e-Choupal** initiative of ITC's Agri Business Division is an innovative e-enabled platform which procures a range of agricultural produces (soya bean, coffee, wheat, rice, pulses and shrimp) directly from about 4 million producers across 10 states. Spread across 35,000 villages, these more than 6,000 internet kiosks are managed by local farmers (*sanchalaks*), and facilitate informed decision-making by informing the agricultural community about the comparative market prices in local *mandi* (wholesale market) and that offered by ITC. In addition, the e-Choupals also provide information about weather and scientific farm practices and facilitate sale of farm inputs to farmers. Through aggregation of the produce, ITC is able to reduce its transaction costs. The farmers are able to improve their productivity and realize better price for their produce by bypassing the intermediaries and directly linking with the market.

The e-Choupal model provides an example of how aggregated and direct market linkages provide a cost-effective way to overcome the problems of the traditional supply chains for the poor, namely, low volumes of production, fragmented last-mile infrastructure, opaque and inefficient supply chains, lack of market information, exploitative intermediaries, etc. Many Indian ventures which work with small producers use similar models to overcome the distinctive problems of imperfect markets in which the poor producers operate (one of the pioneers in the use this model is Amul, which was described in Chapter 1). Karamchandani et al. (2009) describe two variants of this model:

- **Contract production** is an agreement of assured buy-back at pre-negotiated price between the producers and the enterprise. The price is usually above the minimum or spot market price, and in some cases, if at the time of procurement the market price is significantly higher, then the producers may get an additional mark-up. The enterprise provides the inputs and other resources (e.g., seeds and fertilizers in case of farmers or raw material in case of artisans and credit, technical advice), and the arrangement specifies the quality specifications at which the enterprise will procure the produce. For instance, **Jaipur Rugs**, India's largest exporter of hand-woven carpets, works with 40,000 rural artisans and contractors across five states, to whom the weaving is contracted. The company provides the artisans with raw material, designs and working capital. In addition, its non-profit arm, **Jaipur Rugs Foundation**, trains them with relevant skills, besides providing them with other social benefits such as education and healthcare, financial inclusion, insurance linkages, etc.

This model benefits the enterprise by making a regular supply of quality produce available at low transaction costs. For the low-income producers, it reduces the market risks and need for capital requirements by transferring them to the enterprise which has more capacity to absorb them. In addition, by directly linking with the demand sources, the small producers bypass the intermediaries and get better price for their produce. More importantly, by access to an assured and predictable cash flow, they are better able to plan the other priorities of their lives (e.g., savings, children's education and buying/building assets).

- **Deep procurement**: Being at the end of the supply chain, and often also due to their remote and dispersed location, a very small proportion (as low as 25%–30%) of the eventual market price of their produce reaches the small producers; a major portion of the value is realized by the numerous other intermediaries (e.g., transporters, commission agents, wholesalers and retailers). As we saw in the earlier example of e-Choupal, it is possible to provide the producer a larger share by dis-intermediating and collapsing the supply chain and source the produce directly from them. Deep Procurement strategy relies on buying directly from the producer by building one's own supply chain. The purchasing relationship is mostly informal and non-binding, but works since the producers get a better price than they would from the traditional channel. For instance, **Kaushalya Foundation** sources from about 20,000 small vegetable growers in Bihar and sells them through its for-profit arm **Knid Green Pvt Ltd** to urban vendors and institutional customers under *Samriddhi* brand. The collection and grading of the vegetables are done near the source, and payment is made on the spot. The enterprise also provides training, technical know-how and market information to the growers (Singh 2016).

Though the model does not rely on a mutually binding contract, but the purchasing relationship survives due to mutual benefit of the enterprise and producer: the enterprise is able to lower its costs by aggregation, and access to good quality produce since the sorting and grading is done at the point of purchase; and the producers get better prices than they would otherwise. Moreover, in almost all cases, the producers also get technical advice and information about the market requirements, which acts as an incentive to stay in the relationship. Often the enterprise also helps them in accessing various government schemes and entitlements.

In practice, there are many variations of these two approaches to aggregated market linkages. For instance, often the enterprises use 'shared channels' (e.g., local NGOs and partners and state machinery) to reach the producers and lower their costs. Similarly, many enterprises innovatively use online platforms to reach the producers and connect them to the market (see Box 9.6 for some examples). Despite their potential success, the model also presents certain challenges:

BOX 9.6   EXAMPLES OF AGGREGATED
MARKET LINKAGES

DeHaat: DeHaat is an initiative of the Green Agrevolution Pvt. Ltd, which works with small farmers to increase their income per unit area by providing capacity building, advisory and market linkage support. DeHaat are ICT-enabled kiosks at block level, which provide end-to-end agri-services (seeds, fertilizers, equipment, crop advisory and market-linkages) to the member farmers in Bihar, UP and Odisha. For the associated farmers, this results in savings in input prices, improved productivity and better farm gate prices of the produce, and overall 40%–50% improvement in income (Wangchuk, 2019).

Appachi Eco-Logic Cotton Pvt Ltd: Appachi is an organic farm-to-fashion enterprise located in Tamil Nadu, India. The venture works with about 2,000 small, marginal tribal cotton farmers, and weaves high-quality cotton products in its under brand-name, Ethicus. The cotton is sourced from the farmers on a pre-fixed price, which is decided by a committee formed with farmer representatives. The farmers, however, have a right to sell their produce to any other buyer. Appachi supplies the farmers with non-BT cotton seeds on interest free credit, and also provides support in sourcing organic inputs such as manure, neem oil, bio pesticides etc. To safeguard and improve lives of the farmers, the venture also provides crop insurance, and supports them with education, sanitation, etc. (Prabhu, 2013).

GoCoop Solutions Pvt Ltd: GoCoop works with about 285 handloom weaver cooperatives and 40 clusters, comprising of about 70,000 producers across 10 states of India to provide them access to urban and international markets for their products. It owns and operates an online marketplace, gocoop.com, which enable the handloom weavers to sell directly to buyers, including boutiques, designers, home entrepreneurs and large corporate players. While the venture charges a fee of 10%–15%, it has resulted in increased margins, regular orders and immediate payments, and sustainable livelihoods for the weavers (Dhamija, 2017; Vitta, 2017).

1. The model requires building and maintaining a new supply chain, which is a major investment for the enterprise. This is more so given that the producers are normally located in remote regions and are dispersed.

2. Even if the cost of establishing individual procurement centre may be low, maintaining a large network of them is a fixed cost. The enterprise would need sufficient scale and throughput of sourcing to make it financially viable. This becomes an even greater challenge since most of the agricultural produce are seasonal (even the rural artisans often do not work during certain seasons when they get involved in agricultural activities).

3. The model tries to bypass the intermediaries in the existing supply chain, who would naturally have interest in opposing and sabotaging the effort to displace them. It is also important to recognize that, besides their commercial (even if exploitative) role, often the 'intermediaries' also have a role and place in the community, in which they provide useful advice, mediate in conflicts, provide immediate loan in emergencies, etc. Moreover, they are often more knowledgeable about the local socio-cultural and political nuances of the producer community (successful aggregating enterprises often treat them as a resource and try to co-opt and absorb them in the new supply chain).

4. The model assumes that the enterprise has access to markets and buyers which can guarantee the sale of the purchased goods. If such markets/buyers do not readily exist, then maintaining and functioning such an end-to-end enterprise would not only require greater investments, but also a wide variety of skills and competencies.

5. Finally, as we discussed earlier, the poor are often prone to respond to their immediate needs and forsake their long-term contracts and relationships. Since this model depends on explicit (as in the case of Contractual Production) or implicit (as in the case of Deep Procurement) assurance of

regular supply from the producers, it is also vulnerable to such choices by the producers. For instance, the producers may resort to 'side-selling' (i.e., selling to some other party than the enterprise, even if there is a contractual arrangement), or the supply from an artisan's collective may get disrupted due to sudden new opportunities for earning (e.g., a construction project in the vicinity).

Supply–Demand Matching

Since they are dispersed, remote and often lack identity, poor frequently miss out on the potential economic opportunities available to them, such as possibilities of gainful work, or access to resources which would be beneficial for them. For instance, poor in the informal sector waste a lot of their productive time idle because they are unable to connect to those who need their services. A plumber, a cycle-rickshaw puller or a road-side mechanic, for instance, may lose as much as 4–6 hours of their workday waiting or searching for a customer. Similarly, a person looking for a job as a domestic help often does not know about the available opportunities for employment. They often have to rely on their acquaintances or pay a commission to agents to get this information. In fact, *The Report on Employment-Unemployment Survey 2013–2014* estimated that among the self-employed, casual and contract labour almost 30–40 per cent are not economically active during the entire year (Labour Bureau 2015).

Ironically, even the potential customers are similarly handicapped by lack of adequate and reliable market information. Most customers searching for a service provider normally rely on inefficient informal channels and referrals. Supply–demand matching model addresses this need by devising viable solutions to address this gap in the requirements and availability of service providers. For instance, many women from lower-income backgrounds look for a regular and safe job, which use their home-based skills such as cooking, washing, sweeping, etc.; on the other hand, the demand for trained and reliable household maid in middle- and upper-class families is a large 'market' in urban areas. Many ventures such as **Maid in India, kaamwalibais, bookmybai**, etc., address this gap by providing trained women with background check from marginalized background and ensuring them the fair wages and a safe working environment.

Given the magnitude and multiplicity of services which the informal sector workers provide, there are also a variety of niches which require more efficient, transparent and fair linkages between the service providers and customers. In recent times, many social ventures have come up, which address the underemployment and unemployment problems of the self-employed and the casual and contract workers. Mostly, these ventures leverage technology to find innovative ways to provide individuals from lower income backgrounds access to better employment opportunities and facilitate a quick, reliable hiring process for employers (see Box 9.7 for some examples).

Irrespective of their target segment, these ventures share some common design requirements which they need to meet:

BOX 9.7   SOME EXAMPLES OF DEMAND–SUPPLY MATCHING MODEL

EasyFix: EasyFix provides home repair services, for example, plumbing, electrical repairs, carpentry, etc., across five cities (Delhi NCR, Mumbai, Pune, Hyderabad and Bangalore) using the uber-like model of dial a taxi. The venture works with a large cadre of servicemen, who are affiliated to it; they are also trained to ensure quality of service. On receiving a booking, the nearest serviceman is assigned to the customer. Since there is a warranty on all repair work, it ensures quality for the customers; the servicemen, on the other hand, get regular business with fair payment.

BabaJob: BabaJob (now acquired by Quikr) is one of the largest online marketplace for informal sector jobs, and connects jobseekers in more than 20 job categories (e.g., maid, ayah, nurse, driver, security guard and data entry operator) to prospective employers across almost 25 cities. Since many of the job seekers do not have access to computers, it enables the jobseekers to create their profiles using their mobile phones free of cost, and they can receive daily messages potential job matches at a-rupee-a day charges. The venture charges higher amount to the hirers on a 'package basis' which allows them to access and connect to a specified number of profiles, which are provided matching with their requirements (e.g., role, education, experience, work timings and expected salary) from its 5 million registered job-seekers.

Ecocabs: Ecocabs is a dial-a-rickshaw venture which organizes, improves and promotes cycle rickshaw operations to provide greater usage and income to the rickshaw pullers, and more professional service to the customers. The venture provides membership to rickshaw-pullers, which connects them to the Ecocabs call-centres through mobile phones. The customers can phone their requirements to the call centre, which in turn connects them to the rickshaw puller. By aggregating the calls from different areas, the call-centre is also able to estimate demand from different areas and is able to advise the rickshaw pullers to move to high demand places. The membership also enables the rickshaw-pullers to access centralized maintenance service, health and accident insurance, low-interest loans from banks, etc. Starting in Fazilka, Punjab, the model has since been replicated across the towns in Punjab, and in three towns in Haryana.

1. **Identification and aggregation of customers and service providers:** To provide sufficient choice to the service provider as well as to the employer, it is critical for the ventures to operate on a scale. They need to co-opt and register a reasonable number of users on both demand and supply side for the venture to add value to either. While technology (e.g., use of web-based platform or SMS) makes this achievable, often the low-income service providers have limited access and skills to use technology. It is important to make the process of registering and accessing the opportunities inexpensive and hassle-free for them.

2. **Fair and transparent payment system:** The markets of the poor are customarily erratic and ridden with distorted pricing. Customers/employers often try to exploit, and the service providers also often charge unrealistically for their services. One of the challenges for the ventures would be to devise pricing which is fair to both, a mechanism which is transparent.

3. **Assurance of quality:** In connecting the informal workers to customers, there are twofold service quality requirements. First, while they may have the basic skills and know-how of the work, they may still need to be retrained to keep up with the customer requirements (e.g., a housemaid may need to be trained to use household gadgets, or a plumber may need to be updated on new fixtures and fittings). Second, besides the technical proficiency, often the individuals coming from marginalized backgrounds also need behavioural skills (e.g., communication, etiquettes and self-confidence) to provide a professional service to the customers.

4. **Enforcement of regulatory requirements:** Even though there are laws and regulations which protect the right of informal workforce (e.g., minimum wages for different kinds of work, working hours and insurance), the informal labour markets are largely unregulated in practice. Similarly, there are requirements for the users of services (e.g., verification of

domestic help) which are not only necessary but are also mandatory in some places. For the ventures, it becomes important to lay down processes to ensure these.

Micro-investing/loaning

As we discussed earlier, often the poor are unable to start, sustain and/or grow their businesses due to lack of access to formal low-cost credit. The quantum of loan which they require is often quite small, which can help them buy small productive assets such as a goat, sewing machine, or an equipment, etc., or invest in income-enhancing activities, such as buying seeds or other raw material. However, they are unable to access formal credit sources (commercial banks, regional rural banks, local area banks, etc.) due to a number of reasons such as being considered 'unbankable' by the commercial banks, lack of availability of nearby banking services, lack of collateral for taking loan, illiteracy along with cumbersome bank procedures, etc. (see Chapter 8). They largely also remain outside the services of the MFIs due to high rates of interest which range between 18 and 27 per cent to cover the high transaction costs.

On the other side of the spectrum, with a growing and prosperous middle class, there are also an increasing number of people who would like to use their surplus income for some social good. However, instead of donating to traditional charities, they expect to see their contributions make an impact, which they can track and verify.

During the last few years, a few micro-investing/loaning models have emerged to address this gap by connecting the individual 'social investors' directly with the poor through an online peer-to-peer lending platform (see Box 9.8 for some examples). The platform features the profiles and needs of the poor borrowers who are looking for financial help and provides flexibility to fund the need in full or part, and by more than one person. This gives the choice to the potential investors to select to whom and how much loan they would like to give. Since the investors are not looking for high

BOX 9.8   SOME EXAMPLES OF MICRO-LOANING/INVESTING

Kiva: Kiva, world's first P2P micro-lending platform, is a San Francisco-based charity which operates across 80 countries. Kiva crowdfunds loans for financially excluded borrowers (e.g., farmers, artisans and small business owners), who are identified and vetted by its field partners and trustees. Among other similar platforms, its uniqueness is that the entire amount committed to Kiva is given as interest-free loan, and it does not charge any processing fee either from the lender or from the borrower. Its own operating costs are supported by donations and grants from supporters and foundations. Kiva started its operations in India in 2012, and by beginning of 2019, Kiva had lent more than $3.5 million worth loans to more than a million borrowers in India, of about 75% were women.

MicroGraam: MicroGraam is a for-profit peer-to-peer investment platform which was founded by Rangan Varadan and Sekhar Sarukkai in 2010. The venture enables low-income mostly rural borrowers to avail affordable loans for education, agricultural inputs, livestock investments and micro-enterprises, etc., from social investors. The investors can choose their return between 0% and 9%, while the borrowers pay 9.5%–16.5% interest per annum. MicroGram disburses the loans through its partner NGOs in the rural regions, and charges a service fee of 7% on reducing balance to remain sustainable. It also measures the social impact of the loans by visiting and collecting reports on various parameters, including the increase in cash-flows after loans. By 2018, MicroGraam had channelled ₹ 300 million loans from about 3,500 social investors to around 17,500 borrowers.

RangDe: RangDe is India's first micro-investment platform founded by the couple, Ramakrishan N. K. and Smita Ram in 2008. Starting small, this not-for profit venture has raised investments worth about ₹600 million from close to 12,500 social investors, and has channelled more than 60,000 loans to micro-entrepreneurs. Borrowers repay back the loan on an interest rate which ranges between 6% and 10% within a fixed time, of which 2% is returned to the investor and 2% is retained by RangDe to cover its expenses. The remaining is shared with RangDe's field partners who provide outreach to the underserved segments in 18 states in India, and help the venture with identification and verification of the borrowers.

returns on the loans (which normally is in the range of 0%–4%), and by using technology, these ventures are able to provide financial help to the poor at very nominal interest rates. Investors also have the option of recycling their paid loans across other borrowers, thus amplifying the impact of the same loan.

While these ventures differ from each other in terms of the processing fee they charge, interest rates for the borrowers, etc., their success depends on a few key design features which they share in common:

1. **Transparent online interface which allows individualized tracking of loans:** Since the social investors are motivated by the outcomes of their loans rather than returns, sharing the information about the borrowers (e.g., their needs and pain points, the purpose for which they require financial help and the time they need to pay back the loan) is an essential element for attracting funds. Besides the profile of the borrower, the micro-lending platforms also have a 'ticker' below the profile which keeps the investors updated about the amount/proportion of loan which has been committed.

2. **Due diligence of the borrowers**: To ensure that the loans are reaching the right person, as well to eliminate/minimize repayment defaults, verifying the borrowers' details is a critical aspect of sustainability of this model. Micro-investment ventures do this through their on-the-ground network partners (local NGOs, MFIs and other organizations) who help them in both verifying the creditworthiness of the borrowers as well as in identifying them. In addition, the ventures also undertake field trips to places where their borrowers are located to verify the details and to assess the impact of the loans. Some micro-investing ventures also do a credit appraisal of the borrower on specific criteria and share the credit-risk grading with the investors.

3. **Clarity and communication of service/processing fee**: The revenue source for micro-investing ventures is mostly based on the fee they charge for servicing the transactions (investments and repayments) they handle. It is naturally important for them to develop a fair revenue model which clearly identifies how this revenue will be realized (e.g., the servicing fee it charges to the investor or borrower and whether it is upfront on the loan given or on the repaid amount). Moreover, since micro-investing is largely based on trust, a transparent communication of the revenue model to the investors is important for building and retaining their confidence.

Skilling for Inclusion

As discussed earlier in some previous chapters, India has a large low-income informal workforce which remains outside the more remunerative formal labour markets. One of the key reasons (though not the only one) for this exclusion is their lack of marketable workplace skills to avail the existing and emerging opportunities. In fact, with the changes in technology and work-place practices, many with traditional skills also find that they have become obsolete for emerging jobs. For example, traditional masons may find that skills do not meet the requirements of modern construction technologies, or the housemaid may find herself ill-equipped to handle new domestic appliances.

Since many of these opportunities exist in those parts of society which are alien to their own socio-cultural milieu, besides the specific vocational skills, this workforce also needs training in behavioural areas such as presenting oneself (e.g., dressing, grooming and communicating), interacting with customers, building confidence, self-discipline (e.g., holding emotions and punctuality) and so on. There are many innovative and inclusive models which target the most neglected segments of population (e.g., PwDs and rural youth who lack mobility to urban areas) and train and get them gainful employment. For instance, Chennai-based **v-shesh** (with presence in Bhopal, Bhubaneswar, Mumbai, Bangalore and New Delhi) provides vocational skill training and employment support specifically to people who are either disabled from backward regions or from disadvantaged socio-economic background. The venture has developed customized 1–3 week training curriculum for different kinds of jobs (e.g., hospitality, back-office and front-end), which are aligned to employers' requirements. Besides the job-related skills, the training also includes life skills, communication and interview skills, exposure visits to workplaces, live projects and domain specific sessions by experts. In addition, v-shesh also consults with employers to assist them design more inclusive hiring processes and workplaces (see Box 9.9 for some more examples).

BOX 9.9   SOME EXAMPLES OF SKILLING FOR INCLUSION

DesiCrew: DesiCrew was founded by Saloni Malhotra in 2007, establishing India's first rural BPO with the aim of reversing the rural–urban migration among rural youth. Starting with providing back-office data entry and transcription services, the venture now provides a range of services such as analytics, content support, testing, digital asset management, testing and even artificial intelligence and machine learning based offerings. Over the years, it has serviced clients across sectors such as insurance, media, FMCG, banking, retail, education, technology, government, etc. The venture selects, trains and employs rural youth in their data processing centres, with the aim to increase and provide steady income to rural youth. The focus of hiring is specifically on women, people from the socially and economically disadvantaged, minority communities and the physically challenged individuals. It also provides support for education, certification and career development of its employees.

RuralShores: RuralShores was co-founded by Murali Vullaganti with other associates in 2008 to provide the underprivileged rural youth with employability solutions and sustainable employment opportunities. It selects, trains and employs rural youth who are normally class 12th pass, and who would otherwise have had to migrate for jobs; about half of its employees are women. These youth are deployed to deliver services to corporate clients across RuralShores' 17 rural centres in 10 states, each of which employs about 200 youth from nearby villages. The venture offers three kinds of services: (a) technology-enabled/BPO services such as transaction processing, voice support, technical support, etc., (b) business-support services such as market intelligence and field surveys, running product campaigns, post-sales support, etc. and (c) skill development services, which trains the youth for ITES/BPO jobs.

Youth4Jobs: Youth4Jobs was founded by Meera Shenoy in 2012 and is India's largest vocational skilling venture for youth with disabilities. It has 32 centres spread out in 14 states, which identify, train and place both educated and less educated youth in rural and urban areas who suffer from locomotor, visual, and hearing and speech disabilities. The venture has designed customized programmes for people with disabilities (PwDs) in terms of the nature and degree of disability and education level. The training module is around 2 months in duration and covers English, soft skills and computer skills, beside the sector/job specific competencies. Youth4Jobs also partners with colleges and educational institutions to provide need-based orientation and employability training to students with disabilities and connecting them to companies. On the demand side, the venture works with a network of about 500 companies and MSMEs for placement, as well as conducting sensitivity workshops for them to create a disability-friendly workplace.

Some of the common design features for effective vocational skilling ventures are as follows:

1. **Demand-based holistic training**: Vocational skill training is useful only if those skills are required and can be absorbed in the labour market. To be successful, therefore, skilling ventures need to design their curriculum based on market demands, which may emanate from the potential employers, or from the local markets. Moreover, besides the job skills, the soft behavioural skills play a major role in both getting the job (e.g., interview or dealing with customer) and for being effective in the job. Successful vocational training ventures incorporate these skills in their training package.

2. **Post-placement hand-holding support**: Many newly placed poor drop out of their jobs because often their new job also exposes them to a milieu and lifestyle that they are not equipped to deal with. Experiences such as following a fixed

work schedule, following instructions, dealing with rude customers or superiors, living alone and away from the family, etc., cause stress and require support and counselling. To ensure the positive outcome of training, effective vocational training ventures track and assist their alumni till they transition into their new way of life.

3. **Certification of quality**: Certification is useful for both the employers and trainees as well as for the venture, since it assures the degree of quality of training. Instead of providing just a completion certificate, effective social ventures test the trainees on their knowledge and skills and provide this assessment. It is also possible to do third-party assessment of the trainees' capabilities, and during recent years the government has also started certification for skill sets in different vocational domains.

EPILOGUE

Societies differ widely in terms of the nature of social problems which are critical to them. They also differ in terms of the institutional resources and constraints within which viable solutions can be developed to address these problems. Correspondingly, the nature of social entrepreneurship across every society has its own unique and distinctive flavour and contours. The purpose of writing this book was to explore the unique nature of social entrepreneurship within the Indian socio-economic, institutional and cultural context.

Across the examples and descriptions, one can distil three key features of Indian social ventures which describe the distinctive characteristics of the social entrepreneurship phenomenon in India. Even though specific to India, these features also provide a model for many societies with similar socio-economic profile:

First, as we discussed in the book, while on an aggregate level, India is a resource-rich and prosperous country, it also hosts disproportionate number of people who lack access to basic education, primary healthcare, clean water and energy, linkages to markets, justice, and so on. The focus on bridging this widespread 'unequal access' to basic societal resources and amenities is a pervasive feature of Indian social entrepreneurship field. Identifying and solving these problems of access is also an opportunity for the budding social entrepreneurs to solve critical social problems.

Second, the Indian social entrepreneurial ventures come in different shapes and sizes: they are diverse in terms of their legal forms, as well as in the size of community and markets they serve; they range from for-profit ventures which provide products and services to social movements which impact the sociopolitical institutions; some achieve social impact by spreading across regions and markets, while some focus on deeper impact on a limited and localized community and so on. This wide diversity of ventures is a unique feature of Indian social entrepreneurship, and also provides a wide array of approaches to solve social issues.

Finally, India is often seen as a nation with poor record of innovations. Indian social entrepreneurs defy this myth. Their innovations, however, are not about new products and technology. Rather, they are 'social innovations', that is, they focus on finding new ways to make the existing products, technologies, services, etc., accessible to those who lack them. As we have seen through numerous examples in this book, their innovations revolve around developing new social processes, mechanisms and structures which ensure equitable access to societal resources. For instance, they create a pricing structure which can make high-priced quality products and services affordable to poor; they build value chains which connect the producers and services providers to more lucrative markets; they adapt and customize the existing products and services to suit the unique context of their served community; they develop new forms of organizations which empower people to solve their own problems and so on. In fact, as the numerous examples in the book show, Indian social entrepreneurship sector is a vibrant and active 'lab' for social innovations.

REFERENCES

Alkire, Sabina, and Maria Emma Santos. 2010. 'Acute Multidimensional Poverty: A New Index for Developing Countries'. OPHI Working Paper No. 38. Oxford, UK: Oxford Poverty & Human Development Initiative. Accessed on October 1, 2019. https://ophi.org.uk/acute-multidimensional-poverty-a-new-index-for-developing-countries/

Allen, Sarah, Anar Bhatt, Usha Ganesh, and Nisha Kumar Kulkarni. 2012. *On the Path to Sustainability and Scale: A Study of India's Social Enterprise landscape*. Mumbai: Intellecap.

Arakali, H. 2018. Hasiru Dala is Lifting Waste Pickers Up From the Dumps. *Forbes India*, May 30. Accessed on October 30, 2019. http://www.forbesindia.com/article/sustainability-special/hasiru-dala-is-lifting-waste-pickers-up-from-the-dumps/50337/1

Armstrong, D. 2008. Is Bigger Better? *Forbes*, May 23. Accessed on October 30, 2019. https://www.forbes.com/global/2008/0602/066.html#-16ff26604d72

Aspen Network for Development Entrepreneurs. ANDE Entrepreneurial Ecosystem Diagnostic Toolkit. December 2013. Accessed on October 1, 2019. https://assets.aspeninstitute.org/content/uploads/files/content/docs/pubs/FINAL%20Ecosystem%20Toolkit%20Draft_print%20version.pdf

Atkinson, J. W., and D. Birch. 1979. *An Introduction to Motivation*. Princeton, NJ: Von Nostrand.

Austin, James, Howard Stevenson, and Jane Wei-Skillern. 2006. 'Social and Commercial Entrepreneurship: Same, Different, or Both?' *Entrepreneurship Theory and Practice* 30 (1): 1–22.

Bakshi, Rajni, and Bapu Kuti. 2000. *Journeys in Rediscovery of Gandhi*. New Delhi: Penguin Books.

Banerjee, A., and Esther Duflo. 2011. *Poor Economics*. Noida: Random House India.

Banerjee A., and S. Mullainathan. 2010. The Shape of Temptation: Implications for the Economic Lives of the Poor. NBER Working

Paper No. 15973. Accessed on October 1, 2019. http://www.nber.org/papers/w15973.pdf

Banerjee, A., E. Duflo, and J. Shapiro. 2015. 'Graduating the Ultra Poor in India.' Accessed on October 1, 2019. https://www.poverty-action.org/study/graduating-ultra-poor-india

Bang, Abhay. 2018. 'Research for whom?' *India Development Review*, May 3. Accessed on October 1, 2019. http://idronline.org/putting-people-heart-research/

Banks, Joseph Ambrose. 1972. *The Sociology of Social Movements*. London, UK: Macmillan British Sociological Association.

Bannister, A. 2012. From Singer to Subway: The History of Franchising. *Elite Franchise Magazine*, September 18. Accessed on October 1, 2019. http://elitefranchisemagazine.co.uk/analysis/item/from-singer-to-subway-the-history-of-franchising

Barendsen, L., and H. Gardner. 2004, Fall. 'Is the Social Entrepreneur a New Type of Leader?' *Leader to Leader* 2004 (34): 43–50. Accessed on October 1, 2019. https://doi.org/10.1002/ltl.100

Basu, T. 2015. Farmers Star in Their Own Films. *The Hindu Business Line*, June 19. Accessed on November 4, 2019. https://www.thehindubusinessline.com/news/variety/farmers-star-in-their-own-films/article7333817.ece

Battilana, Julie, Matthew Lee, J. Walker, and C. Dorsey. 2012. 'In Search of the Hybrid Ideal.' *Stanford Social Innovation Review* 10 (3): 51–55.

Begley, T. M., and D. P. Boyd. 1986. 'Psychological Characteristics Associated with Entrepreneurial Performance.' In *Frontiers of Entrepreneurship Research*, edited by R. Ronstadt, J. A. Hornaday, R. Peterson, and K. H. Vesper, 146–165. Wellesley, MA: Babson College, Centre for Entrepreneurial Studies.

Bernheim, B. Douglas, Debraj Ray, and Sevin Yeltekin. 2013. 'Poverty and Self Control.' NBER Working Paper No. 18742. The National Bureau of Economic Research. Accessed on October 1, 2019. http://www.nber.org/papers/w18742

Bhatt, Ela R. 2006. *We Are Poor but So Many*. New Delhi: Oxford University Press.

Bhowmik, Sharit K. 2001. *Hawkers and the Urban Informal Sector: A Study of Street Vending in Seven Cities*. New Delhi: National Alliance of Street Vendors of India. Accessed on October 30, 2019. https://www.wiego.org/publications/hawkers-and-urban-informal-sector-study-street-vending-seven-cities

Borgohain, A. 2018. 'Economic Survey: Large Businesses Corner 82.6% of Credit, MSMEs Get a Paltry 17.4%'. *Economic Times*, January 28. Accessed on November 4, 2019. https://economictimes.indiatimes.com/articleshow/62693254.cms

Borland, C. 1974. 'Locus of Control, Need for Achievement and Entrepreneurship'. Unpublished Doctoral Dissertation, University of Texas, Austin.

Bornstein, David. 2004. *How to Change the World: Social Entrepreneurs and the Power of New Ideas*. New Delhi: Penguin India.

Bornstein, David. 2011. 'A Light in India'. *New York Times*, January 10. Accessed on November 4, 2019. https://opinionator.blogs.nytimes.com/2011/01/10/a-light-in-india/

Bornstein, David. 2013. 'Where YouTube Meets the Farmer'. *New York Times*, April 3. Accessed on November 4, 2019. https://opinionator.blogs.nytimes.com/2013/04/03/where-youtube-meets-the-farm/

Boschee, J., and J. McClurg. 2003. 'Toward a Better Understanding of Social Entrepreneurship: Some Important Distinctions.' Accessed on June 14, 2005. http://www.se-alliance.org/better_understanding.pdf

Bradach, J. 2003, Spring. 'Going to Scale.' *The Stanford Social Innovation Review*, 18–25. Accessed on October 1, 2019. http://www.ssireview.org/articles/entry/going_to_scale/

Bradach, J. 2010. 'Scaling Impact: How to Get 100x the Results with 2x the Organization.' *Stanford Social Innovation Review* 6 (3): 27–28.

Brandstätter, H. 2011. 'Personality Aspects of Entrepreneurship: A Look at Five Meta-analyses.' *Personality and Individual Differences* 51 (3): 222–230.

Branson, R. 2015, April 13. 'What Not to Do When Starting a Business.' Accessed on October 1, 2019. https://www.virgin.com/richard-branson/what-not-to-do-when-starting-a-business

Brockhaus, R. H. 1982. 'The Psychology of the Entrepreneur.' In *Encyclopedia of Entrepreneurship*, edited by C. A. Kent, D. L. Sexton, and K. H. Vesper, 39–57. Englewood Cliffs, NJ: Prentice-Hall.

Brodbar, G. 2009, Fall. 'Not Everyone's a Social Entrepreneur'. *Beyond Profit*, 30–32.

Business Standard. 2016. 'Affordable Women Hygiene Product Maker Saral Designs, Raises Angel Funding.' *Business Standard*, January 20. Accessed on November 4, 2019. http://www.business-standard.com/article/companies/affordable-women-hygiene-product-maker-saral-designs-raises-angel-funding-116012000585_1.html

Cannon, L. 2002. 'Defining Sustainability.' In *The Earthscan Reader on NGO Management*, edited by M. Edwards and A. Fowler, 363–365. London: Earthscan.

Carter, M. R., and C. Barrett. 2006. 'The Economics of Poverty Traps and Persistent Poverty: An Asset Based Approach.' *Journal of Development Studies*, 42 (1): 178–99.

Chakraborty, S. K. 1987. *Managerial Effectiveness and Quality of Work Life: Indian Insights*. Bombay: Himalaya Publishing House.

Chakraborty, A. 2016. 'ONergy Shows New Light in Solar Sector.' *Times of India*, January 16. Accessed on October 30, 2019. https://timesofindia.indiatimes.com/city/kolkata/ONergy-shows-new-light-in-solar-sector/articleshow/50639646.cms

Chambers, Robert. 1988, January. 'Poverty in India: Concept, Research and Reality.' Discussion Paper 241. Brighton: Institute of Development Studies. Accessed on October 1, 2019. https://opendocs.ids.ac.uk/opendocs/bitstream/handle/123456789/212/rc269.pdf

Chambers, Robert. 1995. 'Poverty and Livelihoods: Whose Reality Counts?' *Environment and Urbanization*, 7 (1): 173–204.

Chandler, Gaylen N., Dawn R. DeTienne, Alexander McKelvie, and Troy V. Mumford. 2011. 'Causation and Effectuation Processes: A Validation Study.' *Journal of Business Venturing* 26: 375–390.

Christensen, Clayton M. 1997. *The Innovator's Dilemma: When New Technologies Cause Great Firms to Fail*. Boston, MA: Harvard Business School Press.

Coffman, Julia. 2010. 'Broadening the Perspective on Scale.' *The Evaluation Exchange* 15(1): 2.

Cohen, Adam. 2003. *The Perfect Store*. New York, NY: Hachette Book Group.

Collins, D., J. Murdoch, S. Rutherford, and O. Ruthven. 2009. *Portfolios of the Poor: How the World Survives on $2 a Day*. Princeton, New Jersey: Princeton University Press.

Cornforth, Christopher. 2014. 'Understanding and Combating Mission Drift in Social Enterprises.' *Social Enterprise Journal* 10 (1): 3–20.

Dacanay, Marie Lisa M. 2006, September 14. 'Social Entrepreneurship: An Asian Perspective, Civil Society Forum, IMF-WB Annual Meeting.' Asian Institute of Management. Accessed on October 1, 2019. https://www.isea-group.net/isea_hub/filecontent/1245226720SE%20An%20Asian%20Perspective%20Updated%20113007.doc

Dees, G. 1998. The Meaning of Social Entrepreneurship. Accessed on May 10, 2010. http://www.fuqua.duke.edu/centers/case/documents/dees_SE.pdf

Dhamija, A. 2017. GoCoop's Business Model is Connecting Rural Artisans to Global Buyers. *Forbes*, January 17. Accessed on October 30, 2019. http://www.forbesindia.com/article/social-impact-special/gocoops-business-model-is-connecting-rural-artisans-to-global-buyers/45413/1

Dreier, P., J. Mollenkopf, and T. Swanstrom. 2014. *Place Matters: Metropolitics for the Twenty-First Century,* 3rd edition, Revised. Lawrence, KS: University Press of Kansas.

Drucker, Peter. 1986. *Innovation and Entrepreneurship.* London, UK: Pan Books.

Dutta, S. 2013. 'Poverty to Vulnerability in Indian Rural States: An Asset-Based Approach.' *Poverty & Public Policy* 5 (2): 146–161. Accessed on October 1, 2019. https://doi.org/10.1002/pop4.26

Ebrahim, A., J. Battilana, and J. Mair. 2014. 'The Governance of Social Enterprises: Mission Drift and Accountability Challenges in Hybrid Organizations.' *Research in Organizational Behavior* 34: 81–100.

Economic Times. 2006. 'Nobel for Grameen and Yunus.' *Economic Times* October 16. Accessed on March 28, 2016. http://articles.economic times.indiatimes.com/2006-10-16/news/27439769_1_grameen-bank-peace-prize-muhammad-yunus

EdelGive Foundation. 2018. 'Growing at Scale: Best Practices in Scalability.' Accessed on October 1, 2019. https://www.edelgive.org/documents/251134/0/Paper%204.%20A%20Synopsis%20-%20Skilled%20Futures-Best%20Practices%20in%20Capacity%20Building%20and%20Community%20Engagement.pdf

EnAble India. 2017. Media Kit. Accessed on October 1, 2019. https://s3.amazonaws.com/s3.enableacademy.cloodon.com/Enable+India/PDFs/Website+version_Enable+India+Media+Kit_+Jan+2017.pdf

Fell, Ben, and Miles Hewstone. 2015. *Psychological Perspectives on Poverty.* York, UK: Joseph Rowntree Foundation. Accessed on October 1, 2019. https://www.jrf.org.uk/report/psychological-perspectives-poverty

Fieulaine, N., and T. Apostolidis. 2015. 'Precariousness as a Time Horizon: How Poverty and Social Insecurity Shape Individuals' Time Perspectives.' In *Time Perspective Theory; Review, Research and Application: Essays in Honor of Philip G. Zimbardo*, edited by M. Stolarski, N. Fieulaine, and W. van Beek, 213–228. Cham, Switzerland: Springer International Publishing.

Gates, Bill. 1996. *The Road Ahead.* New York, NY: Penguin Books.

Ghate, P. 2006. *Microfinance in India: A State of Sector Report 2006.* New Delhi: Microfinance India.

Giersch, Herbert. 1984. 'The Age of Schumpeter.' *American Economic Review* 74 (2): 103–09.

Goll, I., and Abdul A. Rasheed. 1997. 'Rational Decision-making and Firm Performance: The Moderating Role of Environment.' *Strategic Management Journal* 18 (7): 583–591.

Gopalan, Krishna. 2007. 'No Poverty of Ideas.' *Business Today.* Accessed on May 14, 2015. http://archives.digitaltoday.in/businesstoday/20070225/current3.html#2

Gururaj, B., K. R. Hamsa, Ramesh, and G. S. Mahadevaiah. 2017. 'Doubling of Small and Marginal Farmers Income through Rural Non-Farm and Farm Sector in Karnataka.' *Economic Affairs* 62 (4): 581–587.

Hansemark, Ove C. 2003. 'Need for Achievement, Locus of Control and the Prediction of Business Start-ups: A Longitudinal Study.' *Journal of Economic Psychology* 24 (3): 301–319.

Harnish, Verne. 2014. *Scaling Up: How a Few Companies Make It…and Why the Rest Don't.* Ashburn, VA: Gazelles Inc.

Harris, Erin. 2010. 'Six Steps to Successfully Scale Impact in the Nonprofit Sector.' *The Evaluation Exchange* 15 (1): 4–6.

Hart, S., and A. Diamantopoulos. 1993. 'Marketing Research Activity and Company Performance: Evidence from Manufacturing Industry.' *European Journal of Marketing* 27 (5): 54–72.

Hartigan, Pamela, and Jeroo Billimoria. 2005. 'Social Entrepreneurship an Overview.' *Alliance* 10 (1). Accessed on October 1, 2019. https://www.alliancemagazine.org/feature/social-entrepreneurship-an-overview/

Hirsch, P. M., and D. Z. Levin. 1999. 'Umbrella Advocates versus Validity Police: A Life-Cycle Model.' *Organization Science* 10 (2): 199–212. Accessed on October 1, 2019. https://doi.org/10.1287/orsc.10.2.199

Hockerts, K. 2015. Antecedents of Social Entrepreneurial Intentions: A Validation Study.' *Social Enterprise Journal* 11 (3): 260–280.

Hospers, Gert-Jan. 2005. 'Joseph Schumpeter and His Legacy in Innovation Studies.' *Knowledge, Technology and Policy* 18 (3): 20–37.

Hulme, David. 2008. 'The Story of the Grameen Bank: From Subsidised Microcredit to Market-Based Microfinance' (1 November 2008). Brooks World Poverty Institute Working Paper No. 60. Accessed on October 1, 2019. http://dx.doi.org/10.2139/ssrn.1300930

International Labour Organisation. 1993. 'ICLS Definition of the Informal Sector.' ILO Report of the Fifteenth International Conference of Labour Statisticians, Geneva.

Ip, C. Y., W. Shih-Chia, H. C. Liu, and C. Liang. 2017. 'Revisiting the Antecedents of Social Entrepreneurial Intentions in Hong Kong.' *International Journal of Educational Psychology* 6 (3): 301–323. Accessed on October 1, 2019. https://doi.org/10.17583/ijep.2017.2835

Isenberg, D. J. 2010. 'How to Start an Entrepreneurial Revolution.' *Harvard Business Review*, June, 2–11.

Jahani, Mirza and Elizabeth West. 2015. 'Investing in Cross-Subsidy for Greater Impact.' *The Stanford Social Innovation Review*, May 27. Accessed May 2, 2019. https://ssir.org/articles/entry/investing_in_cross_subsidy_for_greater_impact

Johnson, Sherril. 2003. 'Literature Review on Social Entrepreneurship.' Canadian Centre for Social Entrepreneurship. https://www.research gate.net/publication/246704544_Literature_Review_Of_Social_Entrepreneurship

Jones, Marshall B. 2007. 'The Multiple Sources of Mission Drift.' *Nonprofit and Voluntary Sector Quarterly* 36 (2): 299–307.

Joseph, Tony. 1988. 'New Trend of Consumer Financing Catches on in India.' *India Today*, October 15. Accessed on October 30, 2019. https://www.indiatoday.in/magazine/economy/story/19881015-new-trend-of-consumer-financing-catches-on-in-india-797812-1988-10-15

Kanitkar, Ajit. 2017. 'Community Resource Persons are Torchbearers of the Resurgent Countryside.' *VillageSquare*, April 5. Accessed on October 1, 2019. https://www.villagesquare.in/2017/04/05/community-resource-persons-torchbearers-resurgent-countryside/

Karamchandani, Ashish, Michael Kubzansky, and Paul Frandano. 2009. 'Emerging Markets, Emerging Models: Market-Based Solutions to the Challenges of Global Poverty.' Monitor Company. Accessed on October 1, 2019. https://s3.amazonaws.com/PfP/Monitor_Emerging+Markets_Full+Report.pdf

Karunakaran, Naren. 2010. 'How to Fix Flaws in the Present Microfinance Model.' *The Economic Times*, November 12. Accessed on October 30, 2019. https://economictimes.indiatimes.com/industry/banking/finance/how-to-fix-flaws-in-the-present-microfinance-model/articleshow/6912025.cms

Kets de Vries, Manfred F. R. 1977. 'The Entrepreneurial Personality: A Person at the Crossroads.' *Journal of Management Studies* 14 (1): 34–57.

Kilby, P. M. 1971. *Entrepreneurship and Economic Development.* New York, NY: Macmillan.

Kirzner, I. M. 1997. 'Entrepreneurial Discovery and the Competitive Market Process: An Austrian Approach.' *Journal of Economic Literature* 35 (1): 60–85.

Klugman, Barbara. 2011. 'Effective Social Justice Advocacy: A Theory-of-Change Framework for Assessing Progress.' *Reproductive Health Matters* 19 (38): 146–162.

Knowledge@Wharton. 2006. 'ICICI's K.V. Kamath Shapes a Business Plan in Rural India's Uncertain Financial Terrain.' Accessed on October 1, 2019. http://knowledge.wharton.upenn.edu/article/icicis-k-v-kamath-shapes-a-business-plan-in-rural-indias-uncertain-financial-terrain/

Kuchimanchi, Ravi. 2003. 'Story of How AID Started.' Accessed on October 1, 2019. https://aidindia.org/about-aid/history-of-aid/

Kuhn, Thomas. 1962. *The Structure of Scientific Revolutions.* Chicago, IL: The University of Chicago Press.

Kumar, A. 2019. 'Are Social Change and Scale Mutually Exclusive?' *India Development Review*, April 11. Accessed on October 1, 2019. https://idronline.org/are-social-change-and-scale-mutually-exclusive/

Laajaj, D. 2017. 'Endogenous Time Horizon and Behavioral Poverty Trap: Theory and Evidence from Mozambique.' *Journal of Development Economics* 127: 187–208.

Labour Bureau. 2015. *Report on Employment in Informal Sector and Conditions of Informal Employment 2013–14.* Chandigarh: Ministry of Labour and Employment.

Labour Bureau. 2016a. *Report on Fifth Annual Employment-Unemployment Survey (2015-16),* Volume I. Chandigarh: Ministry of Labour and Employment.

Labour Bureau. 2016b. *Report on Education, Skill Development and Labour Force (2015–16),* Volume III. Chandigarh: Ministry of Labour and Employment.

Leadbeater, Charles. 1997. *The Rise of the Social Entrepreneur.* London, UK: Demos.

Lipton, M. 1983. 'Poverty, Undernutrition, and Hunger (English).' Staff Working Paper no. SWP 597. Washington, DC: The World Bank.

Accessed on October 1, 2019. http://documents.worldbank.org/curated/
en/892041468766760990/Poverty-undernutrition-and-hunger

Mair, Johanna. 2010, November. 'Social Entrepreneurship: Taking Stock
and Looking Ahead.' Working Paper WP-888, University of Navarra,
ISIE Business School.

Mair, Johanna, and Ignasi Martí. 2006. 'Social Entrepreneurship Research:
A Source of Explanation, Prediction, and Delight.' *Journal of World
Business* 41 (1): 36–44.

Mair, J., and Noboa, E. 2006. 'Social Entrepreneurship: How Intentions to
Create a Social Venture are Formed?' In *Social Entrepreneurship*, edited
by J. Mair, J. Robinson, and K. Hockerts, 121–135. New York, NY:
Macmillan.

Mallya, H. 2018. 'Husk Power Systems Raises $20M from Shell, Others to
Scale Renewable Mini-grids in Africa and Asia.' Your Story, January
16. Accessed on October 1, 2019. https://yourstory.com/2018/01/husk-
power-systems-series-c-expansion/

Mani, A., S. Mullainathan, E. Shafir, and J. Zhao. 2013. 'Poverty Impedes
Cognitive Function.' *Science* 341 (6149): 976–980.

Martin, R. J., and S. Osberg. 2007, Spring. 'Social Entrepreneurship:
The Case for a Definition.' *Stanford Social Innovation Review*, 5:
29–39.

May, Maria A., Faustina Pereira, and Arbind Singh. 2016, Spring. 'Tackling
"Wicked" Rights and Justice Issues.' *The Stanford Social Innovation
Review* (Supplement on 'Scaling Social Innovation in South Asia).
Accessed on October 1, 2019. https://ssir.org/supplement/scaling_
social_innovation_in_south_asia

McClelland, D. C. 1961. *The Achieving Society*. Princeton, NJ: Van Nostrand.

McClelland, D. C. 1985. *Power: The Inner Experience*. New York, NY:
Irvington Publishers.

McDaniel, Bruce A. 2011. 'Schumpeter's View of Market Distribution and
Redirection of Income and Wealth.' *Journal of Management Policy and
Practice* 12 (4): 23–26.

Menon, R. 2014. 'Building a Library a Day.' *India Together*, August 28.
http://www.indiatogether.org/pradeep-lokhandes-rural-school-libraries-
in-maharashtra-education

Merton, R. K. 1938. *Social Structure and Anomie*. Indianapolis, IN: The
Bobbs-Merrill Company Inc.

Ministry of Micro, Small and Medium Enterprises. 2018. 'Annual Report 17–18.' New Delhi: Government of India.

Mintzberg, Henry. 1994. *The Rise and Fall of Strategic Planning: Reconceiving Roles for Planning, Plans, Planners.* New York, NY: Free Press.

Mintzberg, Henry, and James A. Waters. 1985. 'Of Strategies, Deliberate and Emergent.' *Strategic Management Journal* 6 (3): 257–272.

Mishra, Satyan. 2012. 'Technology, Development and Inclusion.' 4th National Conference on Social Entrepreneurship, January 27–29, XLRI Jamshedpur, India. Accessed on October 30, 2019. https://economictimes.indiatimes.com/industry/banking/finance/how-to-fix-flaws-in-the-present-microfinance-model/articleshow/6912025.cms

Mishra, A. 2018. 'NGOs bring clean power to dark homes.' TheThirdPole.net, January 31. Accessed on October 1, 2019. https://www.thethirdpole.net/2018/01/31/ngos-bring-clean-power-to-dark-homes/

Mitra, Sramana. 2007. 'Social Entrepreneur: Harish Hande (Part 2).' Accessed on October 1, 2019. http://www.sramanamitra.com/2007/05/11/social-entrepreneur-harish-hande-part-2/

Mittal, Sunil Bharti. 2008. On Lessons of Entrepreneurship and Leadership. Knowledge@Wharton, July 10. Accessed on October 1, 2019. http://knowledge.wharton.upenn.edu/article/bharti-groups-sunil-bharti-mittal-on-lessons-of-entrepreneurship-and-leadership/

Moore, Michele-Lee, Darcy Riddell, and Dana Vocisano. 2015, June. 'Scaling Out, Scaling Up, Scaling Deep: Strategies of Non-profits in Advancing Systemic Social Innovation.' *The Journal of Corporate Citizenship* 2015 (58): 67–84.

Mueller, S. L., and A. S. Thomas. 2000. 'Culture and Entrepreneurial Potential: A Nine Country Study of Locus of Control and Innovativeness.' *Journal of Business Venturing* 16: 51–75.

Müller J., and C. Neuhäuser. 2011. 'Relative Poverty: On a Social Dimension of Dignity.' In *Humiliation, Degradation, Dehumanization. Library of Ethics and Applied Philosophy*, edited by P. Kaufmann, H. Kuch, C. Neuhaeuser, and E. Webster, vol. 24. Dordrecht: Springer.

Napoletano, Erika. 2012. 'Tips to Help the Next Generation of Entrepreneurs.' *Entrepreneur India*, February 10. Accessed October 1, 2019. https://www.entrepreneur.com/article/222576

Narayan, D., R. Chambers, M. K. Shah, and P. Petsch. 2000. *Voices of the Poor: Crying Out for Change.* New York, NY: Oxford University Press.

National Commission for Enterprises in the Unorganised Sector. 2007. *Report on Conditions of Work and Promotion of Livelihoods in the Unorganised Sector.* New Delhi: National Commission for Enterprises in the Unorganised Sector.

Omidyar, Pierre. 2002. 'From Self to Society: Citizenship to Community for a World of Change.' The Keynote Address at Tufts University's 2002 Commencement Ceremonies on Sunday, May 19. Accessed on October 1, 2019. https://web.archive.org/web/20020825024615/http://enews.tufts.edu/stories/052002Omidyar_Pierre_keynote.htm

Osberg, S. A., and R. L. Martin. 2015, May. 'Two Keys to Sustainable Social Enterprise.' *Harvard Business Review* 2015: 86–94.

Pal, Parthapratim, and Jayati Ghosh. 2007. 'Inequality in India: A Survey of Recent Trends.' Working Papers 45. United Nations, Department of Economics and Social Affairs.

Palmer, M. 1971. 'The Application of Psychological Testing to Entrepreneurial Potential.' *California Management Review* 13: 32–38.

Pandey, Soumitra, Rohit Menezes, and Swati Ganeti. 2017, Spring. 'Why Indian Nonprofits Are Experts at Scaling Up.' *Stanford Social Innovation Review,* 17–21.

Powell, J. A., C. C. Heller, and F. Bundalli. 2011. 'Systems Thinking and Race: Summary & Exercises' [PDF document]. Accessed on October 1, 2019. http://www.racialequitytools.org/resourcefiles/Powell_Systems_Thinking_Structural_Race_Overview.pdf

Prabhu, G. 1999. 'Social Entrepreneurial Leadership.' *Career Development International* 4 (3): 140–145.

Prabhu, M. J. 2013. 'Creating a Transparent Market for Cotton Growers.' *The Hindu*, December 5. Accessed on October 30, 2019. https://www.thehindu.com/sci-tech/agriculture/creating-a-transparent-market-for-cotton-growers/article5422115.ece

Prahalad, C. K. 2004. *The Fortune at the Bottom of the Pyramid.* Philadelphia PA: Wharton School Publishing.

Priem, R. L., A. A. Rasheed, and A. G. Kotulic. 1995. 'Rationality in Strategic Decision Processes, Environmental Dynamism, and Firm Performance.' *Journal of Management* 21 (5): 913–929.

Pune Mirror. 2017. 'Pune Hero: Pradeep Lokande.' *Pune Mirror*, August 11. Accessed on October 30, 2019. https://punemirror.indiatimes.com/pune-talking-/hero-of-the-day/pune-heroes-pradeep-lokande/articleshow/60009873.cms

Rabi, Abdi Rahman Jama. 2016. 'How Social Enterprises Manage Mission Drift.' Master Thesis submitted to School of Business, Örebro University. Accessed on October 1, 2019. https://www.diva-portal.org/smash/get/diva2:1076297/FULLTEXT01.pdf

Ramachandran, J., Anirvan Pant, and Saroj Kumar Pani. 2012. 'Building the BoP Producer Ecosystem: The Evolving Engagement of Fabindia with Indian Handloom Artisans.' *The Journal of Product Innovation Management* 29 (1): 33–51. Accessed on October 1, 2019. https://doi.org/10.1111/j.1540-5885.2011.00877.x

Rao, M. 2016. 'Swachh Suvidha.' *Outlook Business*, September 9. Accessed on October 1, 2019. https://www.outlookbusiness.com/specials/good-businesses_2016/swachh-suvidha-3011

Rauch, Andreas, and Frese, Michael. 2007. 'Let's Put the Personback into Entrepreneurship Research: A Meta-analysis on the Relationship Between Business Owners' Personality Traits, Business Creation, and Success.' *European Journal of Work and Organizational Psychology* 16 (4): 353–385. Accessed on October 1, 2019. https://doi.org/10.1080/13594320701595438

Ray, S., and R. N. Cardozo. 1996. *Sensitivity and Creativity in Entrepreneurial Opportunity Recognition: A Framework for Empirical Investigation.* London, UK: Global Entrepreneurship Research Conference.

Rediff.com. 2006. 'How Prof Yunus Conquered Poverty.' Rediff.com, October 14. Accessed on April 10, 2016. http://m.rediff.com/money/2006/oct/14yunus.htm

Reeler, Doug. 2007. 'A Three-fold Theory of Social Change.' Community Development Resource Association. Accessed on October 1, 2019. https://www.cdra.org.za/threefold-theory-of-social-change.html

Ronstadt, Robert. 1988. 'The Corridor Principle.' *Journal of Business Venturing* 3 (1): 31–40.

Rorty, Richard. 1986, May. 'The Contingency of Selfhood.' *London Review of Books* 8 (8): 11–15. Accessed on October 30, 2019. https://www.lrb.co.uk/v08/n08/richard-rorty/the-contingency-of-selfhood

Rosen, Amy. 2015. 'Why Collaboration Is Essential to Entrepreneurship.' *Entrepreneur India*, May 7. Accessed on October 1, 2019. https://www.entrepreneur.com/article/245599

Rosenberg, H. 2010. 'Lessons from Evaluators' Experiences with Scale.' *The Evaluation Exchange* 15 (1): 10–11.

Roy, Aruna. 2018. *The RTI Story*. New Delhi: Roli Books.

Roy, Aruna, Nikhil Dey, and Shanker Singh. 2001. 'Demanding Accountability.' *Seminar*, April 2001. Accessed on October 30, 2019. http://www.india-seminar.com/2001/500/500%20aruna%20roy%20et%20al.htm

Rutherford, S. 2002. *The Economics of Poverty: How Poor People Manage Their Money*. Dhaka: SafeSave.

Sahlman, W. A., and H. H. Stevenson. 1991. 'Introduction.' In *The Entrepreneurial Venture*, edited by W. A. Sahlman and H. H. Stevenson. Boston, MA: McGraw Hill.

Santos, F., A. C. Pache, and C. Birkholz. 2015. 'Making Hybrids Work: Aligning Business Models and Organizational Design for Social Enterprises.' *California Management Review* 57 (3): 36–58.

Sarasvathy, Saras D. 2001. *What Makes Entrepreneurs Entrepreneurial?* Accessed on October 1, 2019. https://prawfsblawg.blogs.com/prawfsblawg/files/Sarasvathy-Entrepreneurial.pdf

Sarasvathy, Saras D. 2008a. *Effectuation: Elements of Entrepreneurial Expertise*. Cheltenham, UK: Edward Elgar Publishing Limited.

Sarasvathy, Saras D. 2008b, October. 'The Bird-in-Hand Principle: Who I Am, What I Know, and Who I Know.' Accessed on October 1, 2019. https://www.researchgate.net/publication/228145520_The_Bird-in-Hand_Principle_Who_I_Am_What_I_Know_and_Who_I_Know

Schirone, B., A. Salis, and F. Vessella. 2011, January. 'Effectiveness of the Miyawaki Method in Mediterranean Forest Restoration Programs.' *Landscape and Ecological Engineering* 7 (1): 81–92. Accessed on October 1, 2019. https://doi.org/10.1007/s11355-010-0117-0

Schumpeter, Joseph A. 1934. 'Economic Development and Entrepreneurship.' http://www.panarchy.org/schumpeter/development.html

Schumpeter, Joseph A. 1942. *Capitalism, Socialism and Democracy*, vol. 36, 132–145. New York, NY: Harper & Row.

Scott, Ryan. 2015. 'Why Collaboration Is the Only Path to Social Progress.' *Forbes*, November 16. Accessed on October 30, 2019. https://www.forbes.com/sites/causeintegration/2015/11/16/why-collaboration-is-the-only-path-to-social-progress/#2642f94c398a

Seelos, C., and Johanna Mair. 2005. 'Social Entrepreneurship: Creating New Business Models to Serve the Poor.' *Business Horizons* 48 (3): 241—246.

Segran, Grace. 2009. 'Social Entrepreneurship in India: Going Beyond the Symptoms.' *INSEAD Knowledge*. Accessed on October 1, 2019. https://knowledge.insead.edu/responsibility/social-entrepreneurship-in-india-going-beyond-the-symptoms-1732

Sethi, S. 2010. 'The FabIndia Story,' SPAN, 2010 July/August. Accessed on October 1, 2019. https://span.state.gov/business/fabindia-story/20100701

Sexton, D. L., and N. B. Bowman-Upton. 1984. 'Personality Inventory for Potential Entrepreneurs: Evaluation of a Modified JPI/PRF-E test Instrument,' In Frontiers of Entrepreneurship Research, edited by J. A. Hornaday, F. Tarpley, J. A. Timmons, and K. H. Vesper, 513–528. Wellesey, MA: Babson College, Centre for Entrepreneurial Studies, Babson College.

Shainesh, G., and S. Kulkarni. 2016. *Aravind Eye Care's Vision Centers— Reaching Out to the Poor*. Bangalore: Indian Institute of Management.

Shane, S. 2000. 'Prior Knowledge and the Discovery of Entrepreneurship Opportunities.' *Organization Science* 11: 448–469.

Shane, S., and S. Venkataraman. 2000. 'The Promise of Entrepreneurship as a Field of Research.' *Academy of Management Review* 25 (1): 217–226.

Sharma, P. 2014. *Democracy and Transparency in the Indian State: The Making of the Right to Information Act*. London: Routledge/Edinburgh South Asian Studies Series.

Sheehy-Skeffington, J., and J. Rea. 2017. *How Poverty Affects People's Decision-making Processes*. York, UK: Joseph Rowntree Foundation.

Shockley, Gordon E., and Peter M. Frank. 2011. 'Schumpeter, Kirzner, and the Field of Social Entrepreneurship.' *Journal of Social Entrepreneurship* 2 (1): 6–26. Accessed on October 1, 2019. http://dx.doi.org/10.1080/19420676.2010.544924

Shukla, Madhukar. 2010. 'Landscape of Social Entrepreneurship in India.' Paper presented in 3rd Research Colloquium on Social Entrepreneurship, June 27–29. Skoll Center for Social Entrepreneurship, Said Business School, University of Oxford.

Shukla, Madhukar, Gerard Farias, and Tata L. Raghuram. 2012. 'The Growing Social Entrepreneurship Ecosystem in India: Innovation in Action.' Paper presented in 2012 Research Colloquium on Social Entrepreneurship, July 16–19. Skoll Center for Social Entrepreneurship, University of Oxford.

Shumate, M., Y. Atouba, K. R. Cooper, and A. Pilny. 2014. 'Two Paths Diverged: Examining the Antecedents to Social Entrepreneurship.' *Management Communication Quarterly* 28 (3): 404–421.

Singh, N. 2016. 'This Man Is Helping Farmers Fight Both Dry Spells and Water Logging with a Unique RWH Technology.' *The Better India*, July 27. Accessed on October 30, 2019. https://www.thebetterindia. com/62677/water-management-gujarat-bhungroo/

Singh, Charan, and Kishinchand Poornima Wasdani. 2016, July. 'Finance for Micro, Small, and Medium-Sized Enterprises in India: Sources and Challenges.' ADBI Working Paper Series No. 581. Asian Development Bank Institute. Accessed on October 1, 2019. https://www.adb.org/ sites/default/files/publication/188868/adbi-wp581.pdf

Srinath, Ingrid. 2018. 'Questioning Scale as We Know it.' *India Development Review*, December 06. Accessed on October 1, 2019. https://idronline. org/questioning-scale-as-we-know-it/

Srinivasan, R. 2004. *Case Studies in Marketing: The Indian Context*. New Delhi: PHI Learning.

Stevenson Howard, H. 1983. 'A Perspective on Entrepreneurship.' Harvard Business School Working Paper No. 9-384-131.

Stevenson, Howard H., and J. Carlos Jarillo. 1990, Summer. 'A Paradigm of Entrepreneurship: Entrepreneurial Management.' *Strategic Management Journal* 11: 17–27. [Special Issue: Corporate Entrepreneurship]

Taplin, Dana, H. and Heléne Clark. 2012. 'Theory of Change Basics: A Primer on Theory of Change'. New York: ActKnowledge. Accessed October 10, 2015. https://www.theoryofchange.org/wp-content/uploads/ toco_library/pdf/ToCBasics.pdf

The Hindu. 2007. 'Let There be a Stock Market for Social Business: Yunus,' *The Hindu*, February 4. Accessed on April 3, 2016. http://www. thehindu.com/todays-paper/tp-national/let-there-be-a-stock-market-for-social-business-yunus/article1791969.ece

Tukiainen, T., Lindell, M., and Burström, T. 2014. *Finnish Startups in Globally Evolving Ecosystems: Value for Finland*. Helsinki, Finland: Hanken—The School of Economics, Management and Organization.

Ubhaykar, R. 2014. 'A Reservoir of Hope.' *Outlook Business*, September 5. Accessed on October 1, 2019. https://www.outlookbusiness.com/ specials/good-businesses_2014/a-reservoir-of-hope-1528

REFERENCES

UK Essays. 2017. 'McDonald's Standardisation of Products'. Accessed May 7, 2017. https://www.ukessays.com/essays/marketing/standardization-of-products-and-marketing-communications-marketing-essay.php

Venkataraman, S. 1997. 'The Distinctive Domain of Entrepreneurship Research: An Editor's Perspective.' In Advances in Entrepreneurship, Firm Emergence, and Growth, edited by J. Katz and R. Brockhaus, Vol. 3, pp. 119–138. Greenwich, CT: IAI Press.

Vitta, S. 2017. 'How GoCoop is Building an Online Marketplace for a Million Weavers and Artisans in India.' YourStory, February 28. Accessed on October 1, 2019. https://yourstory.com/2017/02/gocoop-2/

Wangchuk, R. N. 2019. 'Bihar IIT Grad Left Cushy Job to Build One-Stop Shop That Helps 65,000+ Farmers!' *The Better India*, April 10. Accessed on October 30, 2019. https://www.thebetterindia.com/178742/bihar-farmer-iit-delhi-innovation-dehaat-startup-india/

Wee, J. 2015. *Fabindia: Branding India's Artisanal Craft for Mass Retail.* Accessed on October 1, 2019. https://amitavac.com/cms/cache/2015/03/6107-Fabindia-CS-EN-0-01-2015-w.compressed.pdf

Weinberg, R. S., and D. Gould. 1999. *Foundations of Sport and Exercise Psychology.* Champaign, IL: Human Kinetics.

Yunus, Muhammad. 2006. *Social Business Entrepreneurs Are the Solution.* Paper Presented at the Skoll World Forum on Social Entrepreneurship, Said Business School, Oxford University. Accessed on November 23, 2015. http://www.caledonia.org.uk/papers/Social-Business-Entrepreneurs-Are-the-Solution-Yunis.doc

Yunus, Muhammad. 2007. *Banker for the Poor.* New Delhi: Penguin Books India.

Yunus, Muhammad. 2010. 'Grameen Bank, Micro-Credit.' *The Wall Street Journal.* Accessed on October 30, 2019. https://www.grameen-info.org/wall-street-journal/

Zahra, Shaker A., Eric Gedajlovic, Donald O. Neubaum, and Joel M. Shulman. 2009. 'A Typology of Social Entrepreneurs: Motives, Search Processes and Ethical Challenges.' *Journal of Business Venturing* 24 (5), 519–532.

ABOUT THE AUTHOR

Dr Madhukar Shukla is Chairperson, Fr Arrupe Centre for Ecology and Sustainability and Professor (Strategic Management & OB) at XLRI Jamshedpur (India). He has a keen interest in theory and practice of social entrepreneurship. He also serves on the Board of School of Management & Labour Studies, TISS, and is a member of the Board of Governors of XLRI Jamshedpur.

He was the conference coordinator of National Conference on Social Entrepreneurship during 2009–2017. He has served as a jury for the oikos Case Competition on Social Entrepreneurship, and as an assessor for the Echoing Green Fellowship Competition —a global competition to identify social entrepreneurs. In 2011, he was conferred the award for his contribution to the field of social entrepreneurship by Villgro Innovation Foundation and Centre for Social Innovation and Entrepreneurship, IIT Madras.

Dr Shukla holds a Master's degree in Psychology from Lucknow University and is a PhD from IIT, Kanpur. Prior to Joining XLRI in 1990, he has worked with National Productivity Council and Administrative Staff College of India, Hyderabad. He was also a visiting faculty to ESADE, Barcelona, during 1993–1994.

INDEX

3S India, 150–152

Aakar Innovation, 210–211
Aavishkaar India Micro Venture
    Fund, 8
Abed, Fazel, 3n1, 115
Acumen Fund, 8, 10
Aditya, Vijay Pratap Singh, 150
afforest, 121
afforestation, 121
Aga Khan Development Network
    (AKDN), 195
Agarwal, Ankit, 149
Agastya International Foundation,
    118
aggregated market linkage,
    211–217
Ahuja, Sandeep, 144
Ahuja, Vikram, 200
Airtel, 72
Akshay Patra Foundation, 203
American automobile industry,
    36
Amte, Baba, 5
Amul, 6, 50, 212
Appachi Eco-Logic Cotton Pvt.
    Ltd, 215
Arogya Swaraj, 105
Arvind Eye Hospital, 194
Ashoka Global Academy of Social
    Entrepreneurs, 3n1
Ashoka: Innovators for the
    Public, 3

Ashoka's Youth Venture, 10
Association for India's
    Development (AID),
    65–69

BabaJob, 219
Bachpan Bachao Andolan, 112
Bang, Abhay, 105
Bang, Rani, 104
Bangladesh Rural Advancement
    Programme (BRAC), 3n1,
    115, 192
Barefoot College, 122, 156n2
barefoot paraprofessionals,
    122
Basil, Paul, 166
BASIX, 104
Batra, Shelly, 144
behavioural poverty trap, 183
Benz, Carl, 36
Beyond Profit magazine, 13
Bhandari, Shriyans, 143
Bharti Telecom, 161
Bhatt, Ela, 3, 7, 56–57, 62
Bhave, Vinoba, 5
Bhungroo, 47
Bissell, John, 42–43
Bissell, William, 43
bookmybai, 218
Boond (social enterprise), 57–59
bottom of the pyramid, 171n2,
    178
Bronson, Richard, 72

Carnegie, Dale, 71
casual labour, 174
causal reasoning, 54–55, 60–62
Cellular Operators Association of
    India (COAI), 162
Central Himalayan Rural Action
    Group (CHIRAG), 11
Centre for Innovation Incubation
    and Entrepreneurship (CIIE),
    10
Centre for Social Initiative and
    Management (CSIM), 8
Centre for Social Innovation and
    Entrepreneurship (CSIE), 13
Chari, Shweta, 144
Chavan, Madhav, 147
Child Rights and You (CRY), 62
ChildLine India, 87, 123
Chinmaya Organization for Rural
    Development (CORD),
    205
Chotukool, 202, 204, 209
commercial entrepreneurs, 15–17,
    29, 39, 77–78, 81–83, 106
commercial entrepreneurship
    created wealth, beneficiaries of,
        81–84
    intended wealth, nature of,
        80–81
    wealth creation, dynamics of,
        77–80
Communications Today magazine,
    161
Confederation of Indian Industries
    (CII), 162
constructive opportunists, 148–
    155, 164
cross-subsidization, 81, 194–195
cultural opportunity structure,
    101–102

Daily Dump, 44–45, 47, 112
Daimler, Gottlieb, 36
Dasra, 9
deep procurement, 213–214, 216
DeHaat, 214–215
Deshpande Foundation, 11
DesiCrew, 225–227
de Souza, Gloria, 130
    Environmental Studies (EVS),
        40–41
Deve Gowda, H. D., 158
Development Dialogue, 11
Dey, Nikhil, 156, 156n2
Dhami, Ramesh, 143
Digital Green, 111–112, 123
Drayton, Bill, 3n1, 5n2, 30, 99
Drishtee, 126–127

EasyFix, 218
eBay, 63–64
Ecocabs, 219
economic development, 34
ecosystem builders, 160–168
effectual reasoning/effectuation,
    53–59
    affordable loss principle, 68–70
    bird in hand principle, 65–68
    and causal reasoning,
        comparison between, 60–62
    crazy quilt principle, 70–71
    equator principles, 79–80
    lemonade principle, 71–74, 102
    pilot-in-the-plane principle,
        74–75
    principles of, 65–75
    working methodology, 62–65
Eigen, Peter, 3n1
EkGaon Technologies Pvt. Ltd, 150
Ekjut, 205
Elevar Equity, 11

emergent strategy, 59
EnAble India, 48–49
Ennovent Fund, 11
entrepreneurial
    ecosystem, 162–163
    innovation, 35
    personality, 31–33
    strategy(ies), 30, 97, 138
    thinking, 53–59
    venture, characteristics of,
        47–50, 146–148
entrepreneur(s) (*see also* social
        entrepreneurs; social
        entrepreneurship)
    create social and economic value
        in economy and society,
        36–41
    functions of, 34–35
    identity gaps in society and
        markets, 45–47
    origin of, 33
    shift resources from areas of low
        yield, 42–45
    taxonomy of, 137–138
entrepreneurship (*see also* social
        entrepreneurs; social
        entrepreneurship)
    as a concept is sector agnostic,
        50–51
    decoded, 33–35
    impacts society and community
        or segment by creating new
        wealth or value, 52
    opportunity identification,
        51–52
Equator Principles, 78–80
eVidyaloka, 103

FabIndia, 42–43, 103
Facebook, 62, 166

farm equipment rentals (Fazilka
        Model), 200–201
Federation of Indian Chamber of
        Commerce & Industry
        (FICCI), 162
Ford Motor Company, 37
Ford, Henry, 37, 48
Fredrick Ebert Stiftung, 133
Freedom of Information Act 2002,
        158
frontier markets, 209

Gandhi, Mahatma, 5
Gates, Bill, 56
Genesis, 12
Ghose, Susmita, 102–103
Ghosh, Amitava, 141
GiveIndia, 164–165
Global Reporting Initiative
        (or Triple Bottom Line
        reporting), 78–79
GoCoop Solutions Pvt. Ltd.,
        215
Goonj, 17–18, 62, 87, 146
Grajew, Oded, 3n1
Grameen Bank, 1–3, 39, 48, 62,
        82, 100
Grameen Bank Replicator Program
        (GBRP), 39
gram swaraj, Gandhi's concept of, 5
GreenSole, 143–144
Gupta, Anshu, 17–18, 62, 146
Gupta, Manisha, 165
Gyan Shala, 206–207
Gyan-Key Library, 145

Hande, Harish, 17, 19–20, 69
Hasiru Dala, 99, 110–111, 155
Help Us Green, 149
Helpage, 87

HFCL, 161
Hrudaya Post/Narayana Hospitals, 9, 210
husk power systems, 49
hybrid ventures, 86, 88–89

ICICI Fellowship programme, 12
iDiya, 12
Inclusive Wealth Index, 78
Industree, 88, 155
Industrial Revolution, 33
innovation(s), 14, 16, 22–28, 34–36, 45, 47, 52, 84, 103–106, 119, 121–122, 129–130, 147–148
   entrepreneurial, 38, 142
   hub, 118
   in production methods, 48
   social, 46, 123, 166
International Labour Organisation (ILO), 133, 174–175
ITC e-Choupal, 211–213

Jagriti Yatra, 11
Jaipur Rugs, 212–213
Jamkhed Project (Comprehensive Rural Health Project), 207
Jan Swasthya Sahyog (JSS), 140, 205
Janta Meals, 184, 202–204
JP Movement, 125

kaamwalibais, 218
Kalam, A. P. J. Abdul, 8
Kalamandir, 140–141
Kamath, K. V., 169–170
Kapoor, Ashmeet, 151
Kapoor, Sonal, 141
Kapur, Rippan, 62
Kasturi, Kiran Bir, 44

Kay, Alan, 74
Kedia, Anuradha, 165
Khemka Forum for Social Entrepreneurship, 12
Kher, Rajeev, 150
Kiva, 222
Knight, Phil, 62
Krishnan, Venkat N., 164
Kuchimanchi, Ravi, 65–66
Kurien, Verghese, 6, 50

Lemelson Recognition and Mentoring Programme (L-RAMP), 9
LifeSpring Hospitals, 203–204
Lijjat (or Shri Mahila Griha Udyog Lijjat Papad), 6
local changemakers, 138–140
Lok Capital, 9
Lokhande, Pradeep, 145–146

Mahajan, Vijay, 104
Maid in India, 218
Malhotra, Saloni, 225
Mann Deshi Foundation, 125
Mann Deshi Mahila Sahakari Bank, 125
Mann Deshi Udyogini programme, 126
Mann Vikas Samajik Sanstha, 125
Marico Innovation Foundation, 9
market, 172–174
   of the poor, 171–172, 186–189, 205, 209, 220
Marlin, Alice Tepper, 3n1
Mazdoor Kisan Shakti Sangathan (MKSS), 156, 156n2, 157
McDonald's, 120
Mehta, Kartik, 48
Menon, Sudesh, 46

micro-finance, 2–3, 95, 104, 152, 173
MicroGraam, 222
micro-investing/loaning, 88, 221–224
Microsoft, 56, 202
Milk Mantra, 117–118
Mishra, Satyan, 126
Misra, Srikumar, 117
mission
  drift, 152–155
  driven not-for-profits, 85–87, 90
  -driven social ventures, 85
Mittal, Sunil, 72
Modi, Telstra, 161
Mohan, Suhani, 48
Monitor Group, 12
Multidimensional Poverty Index (MPI), 176–178

Nand & Jeet Khemka Foundation, 9
Narain, Jai Prakash, 5
Narasimhan, T. T., 38
National Association of Street Vendors of India (NASVI), 131–134
National Campaign on People's Right to Information (NCPRI), 158
National Commission for Enterprises in the Unorganized Sector (NCEUS) report 20017, 133, 174
National Common Minimum Programme of UPA Government, 159
National Conference on Social Entrepreneurship, 12

National Telecom Policy 1994, 161
National Urban Livelihoods Mission (NULM), 134
Nidan, 17–19, 131
Nike, 62
no-frills offering, 201–204

Omidyar, Pierre, 63–64
Onergy, 210
Operation ASHA, 144–145
opportunity
  identification, 16, 45, 60–61, 73, 75
  structures, 100–103, 127
Otto, Nicolaus, 36
Outlook Business magazine, 13
Outlook magazine, 8

Pandey, Gyanesh, 49
para-skilling, 204–208
Parekh, Dhimant, 165
PARFI Gurukul, 197
Paul, Biplab Ketan, 47
pay-per-use model, 7, 199–201
Popat, Jaswantiben Jamnadas, 6
Prabhakar, Shekar, 99
Pratham, 87, 123, 147–148
product = product + finance model, 195–198
promoting replication, 121
Protsahan, 141–142
public goods providers, 142–148
pure-play commercial ventures, 86, 90–91
physical opportunity structure, 100–101
Piramal Foundation, 13
poor
  are consumers and producers, 178–180

challenges of serving market of, 186–189

lives managing around short-term cash flows, 180–181

market of opportunities and constraints, 189

poverty, 1–2, 65, 82, 104, 125, 133–134, 141, 169–171

dimensions of, 177–178

impairs decision-making ability 181–184

socio-emotional dimensions 184–186

Pravah, 10

Press Council of India, 158

producers' company, 94–95

profit-maximizing commercial, 86

pure-play commercial ventures, 90–91

Pathak, Bindeshwari, 6, 63

Patel, Tribhuvandas, 6, 50

paradigm, 22, 28

Raghavan, Shanti, 48

Ramakrishan, N. K., 222

Ram, Smita, 222

Rangasutra, 103

RangDe, 222–223

Rastogi, Karan, 149

Reliance, 161

Rent-a-Solar Battery Entrepreneur, 200

revenue

generating social ventures, 87–88

surplus social ventures, 85

Rickshaw Bank, 184, 197

Right to Information (RTI), 156–159

Roy, Aruna, 156–158

RUDI Multi Trading Company, 110–111

Rural Innovation Network (now Villgro), 8

Rural Technology Business Incubator (RTBI), 10

RuralShores, 226

salaried worker, 179

Sankalp Forum, 12

Saral Designs, 48

Sarmah, Pradip Kumar, 197

Sarukkai, Sekhar, 222

Sarvajal Water ATMs, 199–200

Satyarthi, Kailash, 112, 130

Sawant, P. B., 158

Say, Jean-Baptiste, 33–34

Say Organic, 151

scale/scaling, 116, 142, 148, 152

deep, 124–129

imperative to, 115–116

out, 120–124

for social impact, 112–114

through third-party administration, 201

up, 75, 117–120, 209

vertically, 129–135, 155

Schumpeter, Joseph, 34–35

Sebayan, 138–139

SELCO Solar, 19, 196

Self Employed Women's Association (SEWA), 3n1, 7, 39, 57, 62, 108–110

Sengupta, Rustam, 58

shared channels, 208–210, 214

Sharma, Shubhendu, 121

Shekar, Nalini, 99

Shenoy, Meera, 226

Shetty, Devi, 9

Shyam Telelink, 161

side-selling, 183, 217
Singer sewing machines, 50
Singer, Isaac, 50
Singh, Arbind, 17–19, 131
Singh, Shankar, 156, 156n2
Sinha, Chetna Gala, 125
Sinha, Manoj, 49
skilling for inclusion, 224–228
Skycell, 161
social
  bricoleur, 142
  enterprise/business, 86, 89–90
  entrepreneurship, 3n1, 4
  entrepreneurial ventures,
    organizational models for,
    84–86
  entrepreneurship ecosystem,
    8–13
  opportunity structure, 101
  transformers, 40, 155–160
social entrepreneurs, 5n2, 83,
    137–138
  agents of social change, 97
  are innovative, 103–106
  building for sustainability,
    109–112
  definition of, 97
  embedded in needs of served
    community, 106–109
  mission to create social change,
    98–99
  need to learn continuously,
    103–106
  scaling for social impact,
    112–114
social entrepreneurship, 229
  definitional challenge, 16–17
  definition of, 15–16, 90–91
  diversity of social entrepreneurial
    efforts, 17–20

ecosystem in India, growth of,
    8–13
embeddedness of the practice,
    20–21
emergence of sector, 5–15
infancy and diversity of
    discipline, 22
pre-paradigmatic stage, 22–29
umbrella perspective to define,
    29–30
social ventures in India, legal entity
    options for
  cooperative society, 94
  limited liability partnership
    (LLP), 95
  Non-Banking Financial
    Company (NBFC), 95
  producers' company, 94–95
  private or public limited
    company, 95–96
  public charitable trust, 91–92
  registered society, 92–93
  Section 8 Company, 93–94
socially responsible commercial
    ventures, 86, 90
Society for Education, Action and
    Research in Community
    Health (SEARCH), 104
Start Up!, 3n1, 10, 14, 42, 165,
    167
Sulabh/Sulabh Shauchalay, 6–7,
    63, 199, 201
Sunderraman, Gopalan, 202
Super Cassettes, 208
supply–demand matching,
    217–221
Sutariya, Dipesh, 48

Tata Institute of Social and UnLtd
    Foundation, 10

Tata Teleservices, 161
Telecom Regulatory Authority of
    India (TRAI), 161
TelecomLive magazine, 161
Textile Labour Association, 57
The Better India (BTI), 165–166
The Ethos Institute For Business
    Social Responsibility, 3n1
theory of change, 124
Think Change-India, 11
TiE Entrepreneurship Summit
    2008, 12
ToyBank, 144
Triple Bottom Line reporting,
    78–79
two Indias, parameters of
    development, 170–171

ultra-poor
    definition of, 191, 191n1
    graduation approach, 192–193
UN Global Compact, 78–79
United Nations Conference on
    Sustainable Development
    (Rio+20) 2012, 78
unorganized sector, 7, 57, 133,
    174, 178

Vaatsalya Hospitals (earlier
    Vaatsalya Healthcare
    Solutions), 89
Varadan, Rangan, 222
Vasudeva, H. D., 38

vertical
    scaling, 135
    scaling-up, 130
Villgro Innovation Foundation
    (formerly Rural Innovations
    Network), 7, 14, 166–167, 247
VisionSpring, 195
vocational skilling ventures,
    features of, 227–228
Voice&Data magazine, 161
v-shesh, 225
Vullaganti, Murali, 226

WaterLife Pvt. Ltd, 46–47
wealth creation, 38, 52, 171
    dynamics of, 77–78
    nature and purpose of, 82–83
Women in Informal Employment:
    Globalizing and Organizing
    (WIEGO), 133
World Bank, 39, 176
World Social Forum, 3n1
wPOWER/ Swayam Shikshan
    Prayog, 206–207

Yadav, Ratnesh, 49
Your Story, 12
Youth4Jobs, 226–227
Yunus, Muhammad, 1–4, 39, 62,
    82, 100

Ziqitza Health Care, 194
Zuckerberg, Mark, 62